Cool Cottages

235 Delightful Retreats
825 to 3,500 square feet

Design HPT210152, page 167

HOME PLANNERS, LLC
Wholly owned by Hanley-Wood, LLC

Cool Cottages

Published by Home Planners, LLC
Wholly owned by Hanley-Wood, LLC
3275 West Ina Road, Suite 110
Tucson, Arizona 85741

Distribution Center:
29333 Lorie Lane
Wixom, Michigan 48393

Jayne Fenton, *President*

Jennifer Pearce, *Vice President, Group Content*

Linda B. Bellamy, *Executive Editor*

Jan Prideaux, *Editor In Chief*

Marian E. Haggard, *Editor*

Jill M. Hall, *Plans Editor*

Paul Fitzgerald, *Graphic Designer*

Teralyn Morriss, *Graphic Production Artist*

Sara Lisa, *Senior Production Manager*

Brenda McClary, *Production Manager*

Photo Credits
Front Cover: Chris A. Little of Atlanta
Back Cover: ©1993 Donald A. Gardner Architects, Inc., photo courtesy of Donald A. Gardner Architects, Inc.

First Printing, October 2001
10 9 8 7 6 5 4 3 2

Library of Congress Catalog Card Number: 2001089601

ISBN softcover: 1-881955-91-5

On the front cover: Presenting a casual atmosphere, Plan HPT210001 by Chatham Home Planning, Inc., welcomes you to sit back, relax and enjoy life. See page 10 for more information.

On the back cover: A country cottage filled with comfortable amenities, Plan HPT210013 by ©1993 Donald A. Gardner Architects, Inc., can function as a weekend getaway or a year-round home. See page 28 for more information.

TABLE OF CONTENTS

Design HPT210010, page 25   ©1996 Donald A. Gardner Architects, Inc., photo courtesy of Donald A. Gardner Architects, Inc.

THE DOOR TO OUTDOOR LIVING

This spacious covered porch offers plenty of space for family and guests. Hanging plants highlight the beauty of nature. The picnic table is the perfect dinner table for this cottage.

Opposite top: This relaxing bench swing allows a beautiful view of wilderness while decorative porch details lend a more formal take on cottage life.

Opposite bottom: Wooden floors and dressers create a rustic, yet polished feeling in this bedroom.

Cottages are now entirely acceptable everywhere and can be located within the realm of remoteness and tranquility or in the midst of suburbia's hustle and bustle. They are no longer specifically destined to secluded wilderness areas or lakefront getaways. Nonetheless, the very essence of a cottage takes us closer to the outdoors. Despite constant attempts to replace the need for nature in our everyday lives as well as the inherent need to live off the land, there is still a prevailing drive to get back to the wilderness, and cottages are our comfortable tool for making that instinctual ideology a reality. Whether your cottage is used for everyday living or a vacation retreat, the furnishings and decorations you choose will transform your outdoor beauty into that of pure rustic nature or the eccentric castle you've always dreamed of. Embellish your cottage with that essence of personal choice and styling. It is, after all, an extension of your being.

Furnishings for cottages typically replicate the beauty and freshness of the very environment in which they are placed. Previously, when cabins and cottages were exclusively a way to escape the hub of the city, fanciness and beautifully classy furnishings were out of the question. These items were characterized as "citylike," and the wilderness was no place for sophistication. The best way to furnish a cabin was also by the knowledge and skill of homeowner. Once, the homeowner/builder would fetch all the extra lumber and scraps they could find and create every piece of furniture that was needed by hand. But the rules have since changed and the style and design of your cabin is strictly up to your liking. There is no longer a code of ethics to follow when building a cottage or cabin, nor is it thought as practical or feasible to tromp through the woods, find a perfect spot and proceed with cutting the lumber, nailing the frame and doing everything by hand. However, the previous construction of slab furniture and do-it-yourself wooden decor have lead to solidly built, well-finished furnishings. And of course, purpose and practicality must be taken into account for the type and style of the furniture. The more rustic the cabin, the more appropriate slab furniture is. Also, the more stylish the cabin, the more appropriate "citylike" furniture becomes.

For example, when staying in tune with the rustic appeal of the cottage or cabin, all you have to do is to stay true to the wooded theme. Wood floors and wood cabinetry in the kitchen will fit the home beautifully. The classic wooden rocker will be perfect for porches, living rooms and bedrooms. Log beds and rich oak armoires will lovelily and rustically adorn the master suite. For equally beautiful formal cabins or cottages, the decorations and furnishings can be simple to decide upon. Classic cast-iron decor fits into a stylish cabin or cottage impeccably, or consider the prestige offered by antique wooden furniture.

Accessories will also help to formalize or subdue certain areas of your cottage. Allow rugs, tapestries or mantelpieces to tell the story of the room.

Outdoor adornments are imperative to this style of home—where enjoying the outdoors is more of a lifestyle than an option. Grilling porches allow more living than the mere preparation of dinner. It's a conventional way to spend time with the entire family, not to mention a superb way to entertain guests. Swinging benches are another must have. These benches can be the place to fully enjoy warm summer evenings or brisk fall mornings. Picnic tables are an authentic replacement for lawn or patio furniture, too. Flowers, gardens and plenty of trees are also more than just necessary landscaping tools. We must not forget that we all ultimately live in nature and every bit of preservation counts. Plant new trees and protect the old. They will add timeless beauty to your cottage or cabin.

The overall mystery and enchantment of a cottage or cabin may lie specifically with one interior structure—the fireplace. It has the ability to envelop the entire family for hours at a time. Fireplaces have come a long way since they were the only source of heat for the home. With gas and electrical fireplaces now available, many new features have taken shape. The new styles of fireplaces are quite energy-efficient and inexpensive. With the innovative ventless options, the homeowner now has the choice of where to display the fireplace. Families can now achieve a peace of mind in the mesmerizing cinders as well as by their fuel-efficient hearth.

EX-SITE-MENT

Whether it is your family home or your get-away-from-home, your new cottage will not be perfect until you consider how you'll place it on the site. Think of your building site as a three-dimensional puzzle into which you have to fit the most essential piece—your home. If you don't take all of the puzzle's pieces into consideration, you could easily end up with the right house on the wrong lot, vice versa or even the right house on the right lot but in the wrong place!

One thing to do is to study the features of the land before you plan the site. Unavoidably, any construction will affect the environment and the landscape. The idea is to respect what nature has already established. Accept the terrain as a partner, rather than something to be conquered, and proceed accordingly, knowing you are making a lasting impact that can provide maximum comfort and economy for you with minimum harm to the area. The effort you invest in planning and locating your cottage will pay dividends in the form of enjoyable living and reduced energy demands. Privacy, views, wind directions, traffic convenience and sun travel in winter and summer are the primary considerations.

SOME FIRST CONSIDERATIONS

First and foremost in your planning should be the landscape itself. If you have a site already in mind (or in hand), you need to know that the physical contour of your site has a lot to do with the type of house best suited for it. Which direction, if any, does the land slope? Are there a number of trees already on the lot you'd like to keep? Would you like to add regionally native trees for specific shade, or would you prefer an open view? In coastal areas there may be persistent onshore winds, especially in the afternoons. These are often strong enough to be downright annoying, particularly when you have to fight them for several months every summer.

SUN AND SHADE

Another key consideration is the sun and shade patterns that pass over your intended site (Figure 1-1). Determining these patterns will help orient your home on the land to "customize" what exposures exist or can be created—capturing sunlight in areas that need or appreciate it, such as a breakfast nook or a porch, or supplementing with artificial light and heat sources. A limited amount of sun, for instance, may lessen the effectiveness of solar or photo-

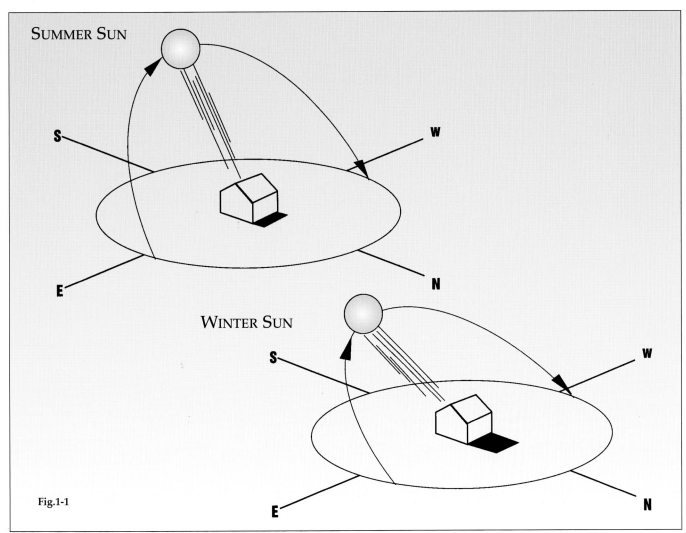

SUMMER SUN

WINTER SUN

Fig.1-1

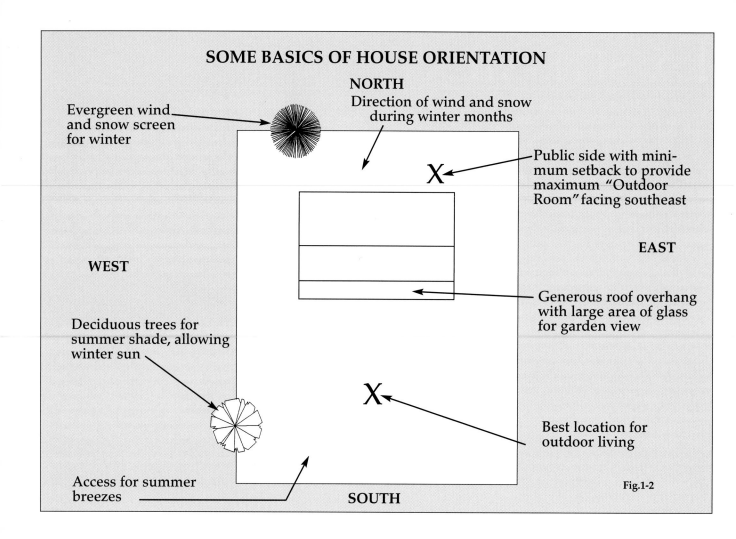

SOME BASICS OF HOUSE ORIENTATION

NORTH
Direction of wind and snow during winter months

Evergreen wind and snow screen for winter

Public side with minimum setback to provide maximum "Outdoor Room" facing southeast

EAST

WEST

Generous roof overhang with large area of glass for garden view

Deciduous trees for summer shade, allowing winter sun

Best location for outdoor living

Access for summer breezes

SOUTH

Fig.1-2

voltaic devices, while enough natural shade may allow you to reduce the size and cost of cooling equipment.

A true study of orientation is a detailed science, one that would require a daily inspection of the conditions of your site over a year's period. Yet there are basic considerations, as shown in Figure 1-2, and general rules apply even though they are most applicable in the belt between 35 and 45 degrees north latitude (Figure 1-3). This belt includes the majority of the country's most populated areas. When the house is below this belt, taking advantage of summer breezes and seeking protection from intense sun heat are major considerations. When building above the belt, designing for protection from cold winter winds and getting the most from the winter sun are prime objectives.

The summer sun is high overhead at midday and has an extended arc. In winter, there is a reduced arc and the midday sun is lower in the sky at the same time. The object is to protect your interior from baking in the overhead summer sun, but also to capture as much of the winter sun as possible (Figure 1-4). Having the kitchen and breakfast room face east is one thought—catching the morning sun as it breaks over the horizon and floods your early morning coffee time is an appealing notion. North-facing kitchens pose a different sort of problem than south- or west-facing ones—a lack of sunlight at all

times. The south- and west-facing rooms, on the other hand, are bombarded by the summer sun, not only increasing the heat in the rooms, but probably bleaching out your furniture too!

If your site has a lot of trees, the ability to cut them down or otherwise clear the land for construction may be limited, depending on your zoning laws. This will be fine if you wish to live under a canopy of trees and not get a lot of sun exposure. But there is also the potential hazard created during snowfall or heavy winds. Roof overhangs make the most sense for sun protection on the south side of the home. Tall plantings and outbuildings can protect the west sides from the hot afternoon sun, while tall evergreens can do much to screen the northwest direction— providing plenty of protection from cold winter winds. Another consideration for protection against the northern chill is the minimal use of windows on the north side of your cottage. Small, double-paned windows are best for keeping the cold out and letting the sun in.

YOU AND VIEWS

If you are looking to capture awe-inspiring views, this will also affect the placement and orientation of your home on its site. Certainly, a bank of windows and/or a long covered porch are an appropriate means to view an ocean, lake, well-kept golf course or peaceful wilderness setting.

But such exposures need to be protected with windows or other materials that maintain a comfortable climate inside the house as well as give you optimum viewing pleasure. They also should provide an adequate barrier to natural forces and maintain privacy from neighbors and passersby.

Before you build your dream cottage and install a wall of windows to capture a lush forest scene, check to make sure someone else isn't going to do the same thing—right in your sight line. And again, don't forget that while a panoramic view of the ocean is not only desirable as well as possible, it must be able to withstand potentially high winds, dramatic climate changes and the corrosive nature of sea air and moisture.

STREET INFLUENCE

If your cottage is near a street, be sure to check the orientation of the house relative to the both the sun as well as the street. The street usually dictates how a house will sit on a lot. Sometimes having to reverse the plan to fit the street orientation causes too many compromises. Faced with this, you may decide that the lot and the house you want just aren't compatible, thus making it time to search for a better location.

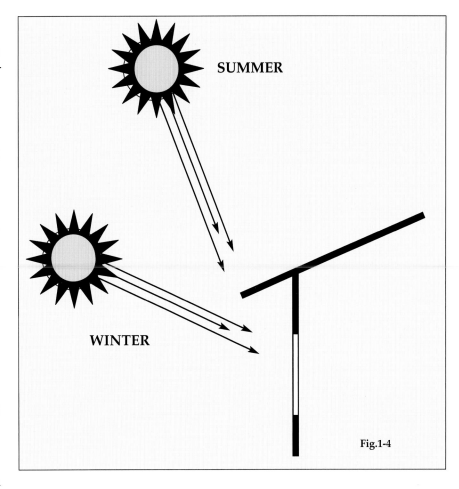

Fig.1-4

DOWN ON THE FARM

Building out in the country sounds both romantic as well as wonderfully healthy, but remember, if your prospective lot is close to farmland, you need to take a drive around just to see what kinds of farms there may be. Dairy farms, sheep farms and even small "general" farms produce odors that even gentle breezes can waft for a mile or so, making that wonderful covered porch MUCH less appealing, and causing you to spend more time indoors than you originally had planned.

PRIVACY ISSUE

Privacy wouldn't be difficult to achieve if you ignored all other factors and just put up solid walls and spent all your home time indoors. But today's lifestyles call for outdoor as well as indoor areas to relax, to eat and to enjoy friends and fun. Often, providing for privacy also affords a good measure of protection from noise—noise from the outside or noise you make that might bother your neighbors.

Your privacy goals can be combined with the private outlook—taking advantage of desirable scenery and screening out unpleasant views. The view doesn't have to be a snow-covered mountain, a lake or a spacious golf course. It can be as simple as a low or high flower-bed wall, an attractive trellis, a garden waterfall, groups of trees or shrubs and so on. Remember that your screening can also conceal potential eyesores on your own property, such as work areas, trash cans or tool storage.

If your dream is to create a getaway or a family home, keep in mind that a lot of what you will enjoy depends on the site you've chosen and how you orient your new home. If you take all of the factors mentioned here into account and work WITH the lot's design, your new cottage will bring you years of comfort and contentment.

45°
40°
35°

Fig.1-3

PLAN HPT210001

First Floor: 731 sq. ft.
Second Floor: 935 sq. ft.
Third Floor: 138 sq. ft.
Total: 1,704 sq. ft.

Width: 34'-0"
Depth: 38'-0"

Perfect for a seaside abode, this pier-foundation home has an abundance of amenities to offer, not the least being the loft lookout. Here, with a 360-degree view, one can watch the storms come in over the water, or gaze with wonder on the colors of the sea. Inside the home, just off the screened porch, the living room is complete with a corner gas fireplace. The spacious kitchen features a cooktop island, an adjacent breakfast nook and easy access to the dining room. From this room, a set of French doors leads out to a small deck—perfect for dining alfresco. Upstairs, the sleeping zone consists of two family bedrooms sharing a full hall bath, and a deluxe master suite. Amenities here include two walk-in closets and a private bath.

Patterns and sunlight dress up the stairs leading to the front door.

French doors open from a covered porch to a room filled with charm and welcome.

Balmy summer breezes will play with the drape on this elegant wrought-iron four-poster bed, encouraging a relaxing atmosphere on lazy sun-filled days.

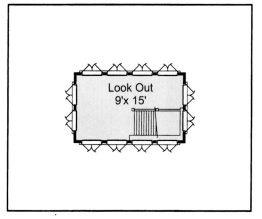

Look Out
9'x 15'

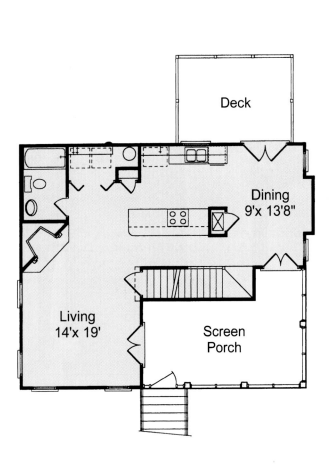

Deck

Dining
9'x 13'8"

Living
14'x 19'

Screen
Porch

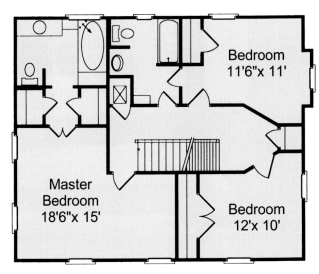

Bedroom
11'6"x 11'

Master
Bedroom
18'6"x 15'

Bedroom
12'x 10'

Bright and cheerful, the living room features hardwood floors, a ceiling fan and a comfy couch just begging to have you stretch out on it. This view from the kitchen seems to say that casual meals will easily spill out into easygoing camaraderie.

Photo by Andrew D. Lautman

This home, as shown in the photographs, may differ from the actual blueprints.
For more detailed information, please check the floor plans carefully.

PLAN HPT210002

First Floor: 1,111 sq. ft.
Second Floor: 886 sq. ft.
Total: 1,997 sq. ft.

Width: 34'-1"
Depth: 50'-0"

L

QUOTE ONE®

Cost to build? See page 246
to order complete cost estimate
to build this house in your area!

Imagine a hanging swing on the front porch or, as the home-owners featured here did, turn the screened porch into a tiled sun room for year-round enjoyment. From the foyer, the warmth of the central fireplace greets you as you enter the living room. Beyond this room sits the dining room with access to the screened porch. The sunny breakfast room and kitchen will quickly become a favorite place to gather. They feature open access to the rear terrace, lots of counter and cupboard space, a convenient pantry, separate writing desk, and nearby powder room. The upstairs bedroom area allows for privacy and continues the versatility of the home by providing for three bedrooms or two bedrooms and a study. Our featured home-owners provided their own special touch to this area by closing off the sloped ceiling of the downstairs kitchen and extending the bedroom above it. The spacious master suite offers luxury at its fullest with a large walk-in closet, separate dressing room, shower and a whirlpool tub. The other bedrooms share a full hall bathroom and lots of closet space.

A patchwork quilt dresses up a comfortable four-poster bed, while a rocking chair waits to ease you into complete relaxation.

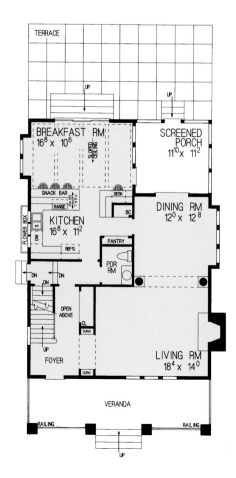

TERRACE

UP

UP

BREAKFAST RM
16⁸ x 10⁶

SLOPED CEILING

SCREENED PORCH
11¹⁰ x 11²

SNACK BAR

DESK

RANGE

PASS THRU

DINING RM
12⁰ x 12⁸

FLOWER BOX

S

DW

KITCHEN
16⁸ x 11²

BC

REF'G

PANTRY

PDR RM

DN

DN

DN

OPEN ABOVE

CL

CURIO

UP

FOYER

CURIO

LIVING RM
18⁴ x 14⁰

VERANDA

RAILING

RAILING

UP

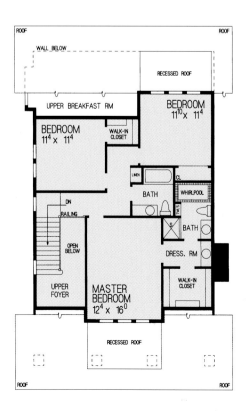

ROOF

ROOF

WALL BELOW

RECESSED ROOF

UPPER BREAKFAST RM

BEDROOM
11¹⁰ x 11⁴

BEDROOM
11⁴ x 11⁴

WALK-IN CLOSET

LINEN

CL

BATH

WHIRLPOOL

WHS

DN

RAILING

BATH

S

OPEN BELOW

DRESS. RM

UPPER FOYER

MASTER BEDROOM
12⁴ x 16⁰

WALK-IN CLOSET

RECESSED ROOF

ROOF

ROOF

Photo by Andrew D. Lautman

This home, as shown in the photograph, may differ from the actual blueprints.
For more detailed information, please check the floor plans carefully.

PLAN HPT210003

First Floor: 1,356 sq. ft.
Second Floor: 490 sq. ft.
Total: 1,846 sq. ft.

Width: 50'-7"
Depth: 38'-0"

L D

QUOTE ONE®

Cost to build? See page 246
to order complete cost estimate
to build this house in your area!

Around April, just after the snow melts, the grass in the upper hills of central Michigan begins to turn green again, transforming the pristine acreage surrounding this quaint cabin into prime real estate. The real treasure, though, lies within the walls of this log-studded retreat.

Knotty pine interior walls flavor the house with the rich patina of wood, enlivened with colorful, heirloom patchwork quilts and artful crafts. A hefty, native stone fireplace dominates the living room, where chilly evenings are made cozy by the hospitable aura of a crackling fire. Casual, rumply fabrics imbue each room with a romantic charm, and give personality to mellow furnishings.

From its welcoming front porch to its trim rear deck, the open-plan layout is well suited to its users. Incorporating the kitchen and the dining room with the general living area is a particularly good arrangement for a vacation home, where people come and go, and there's no rigid routine for meals.

Quarter-log siding gives the home the appearance of a log cabin, inside and out, with knotty pine hardwood used throughout the interior. Here in the living room, a native stone chimney is framed by clerestory windows, while an elegant patchwork quilt adds charm and color to its surroundings.

An easygoing atmosphere presides in rooms designed for lingering. The sociable nature of the house combines the feel of the outdoors with the shelter of the indoors, and embraces casual activities with a spirit of fun.

Another patchwork quilt graces the bed of this warmly inviting room.

17

Imagine sipping lemonade and enjoying pleasant summer breezes on this long covered porch.

SEAT

BATH

STORAGE

WH

DESK

DN

SLOPED CEILING

RAILING

LOFT
23^2 x14^{10}

LIVING ROOM BELOW

DINING

DW

KITCHEN

RANGE

REFG

LT

W

D

LAUNDRY

LINEN

BATH

SEAT

LINEN

VANITY

SHWR

MASTER BATH

LIVING RM
20^2 x18^2
VOL. CLG

RAILING

UP

BEDRM
10^{10} x11^8

MASTER BEDRM
12^0 x18^4

COVERED PORCH

RAILING

Photo by Laszlo Regos

This home, as shown in the photograph, may differ from the actual blueprints. For more detailed information, please check the floor plans carefully.

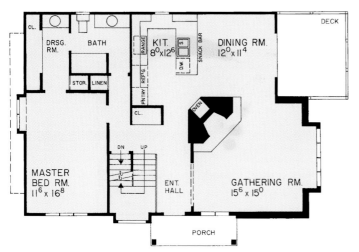

PLAN HPT210004

First Floor: 1,113 sq. ft.
Second Floor: 543 sq. ft.
Total: 1,656 sq. ft.

Width: 42'-0"
Depth: 28'-4"

D

QUOTE ONE®

Cost to build? See page 246 to order complete cost estimate to build this house in your area!

F or a lakeside retreat or as a retirement haven, this charming design offers the best in livability. The gathering room with a corner fireplace, a U-shaped kitchen with an attached dining room, and the lovely deck make a complete and comfortable living space. The first-floor master bedroom boasts His and Hers sinks, a large wall closet and extra storage space. Upstairs, two bedrooms with a full bath and a balcony lounge complete the design and provide sleeping accommodations for family and guests.

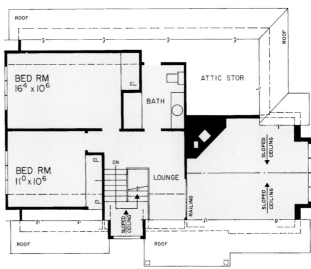

Photo by Pella® Corporation

This home, as shown in the photograph, may differ from the actual blueprints. For more detailed information, please check the floor plans carefully.

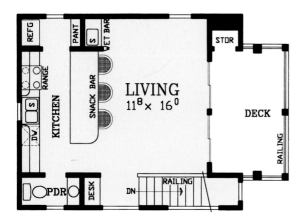

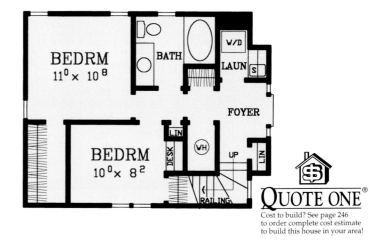

Cost to build? See page 246 to order complete cost estimate to build this house in your area!

 PLAN HPT210005

First Floor: 507 sq. ft.
Second Floor: 438 sq. ft.
Total: 945 sq. ft.

Width: 20'-0"
Depth: 26'-0"

Combine a shingled exterior and an upstairs deck, and you can recall the joy of seaside vacations. Let breezes ruffle your hair and ocean spray settle on your skin in this comfortable two-story home. Unique window treatments provide views from every room. The lifestyle is casual, including meals prepared in a kitchen separated from the living room by a snack-bar counter. A powder room and a wet bar complete the second floor. The first floor houses two bedrooms, a full bath and a laundry room. A walk-in closet enhances one of the bedrooms that could serve as the master suite. Built-ins make the most of compact space.

Photo by Oscar Thompson Photography

This home, as shown in the photograph, may differ from the actual blueprints.
For more detailed information, please check the floor plans carefully.

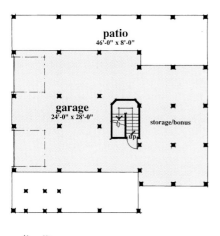

patio
46'-0" x 8'-0"

garage
24'-0" x 28'-0"

storage/bonus

up

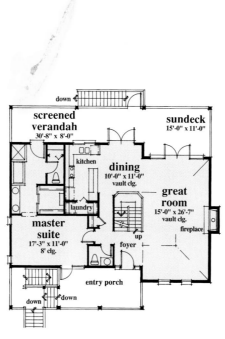

down

screened
verandah
30'-8" x 8'-0"

sundeck
15'-0" x 11'-0"

kitchen

dining
10'-0" x 11'-0"
vault clg.

great
room
15'-0" x 26'-7"
vault clg.

laundry

fireplace

master
suite
17'-3" x 11'-0"
8' clg.

up

foyer

entry porch

down   down

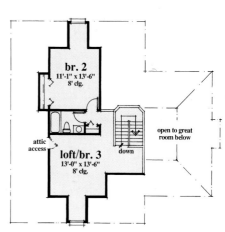

br. 2
11'-1" x 13'-6"
8' clg.

open to great
room below

attic
access

loft/br. 3
13'-0" x 13'-6"
8' clg.

down

PLAN HPT210006

First Floor: 1,189 sq. ft.
Second Floor: 575 sq. ft.
Total: 1,764 sq. ft.

Width: 46'-0"
Depth: 44'-6"

L

An abundance of porches and a deck encourage year-round indoor/outdoor relationships in this classic two-story home. The spacious great room, with its cozy fireplace, and the adjacent dining room both offer access to the screened porch/deck area through French doors. The private master suite accesses both front and rear porches and leads into a relaxing private bath complete with dual vanities and a walk-in closet. An additional family bedroom and a loft/bedroom are located upstairs.

Photo by Bob Greenspan

This home, as shown in the photograph, may differ from the actual blueprints. For more detailed information, please check the floor plans carefully.

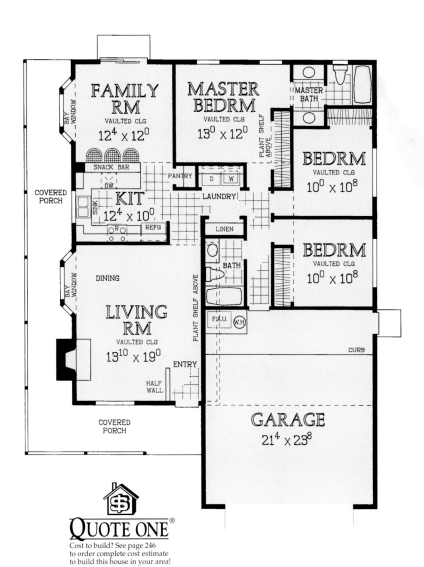

QUOTE ONE®

Cost to build? See page 246 to order complete cost estimate to build this house in your area!

PLAN HPT210007

Square Footage: 1,389

Width: 44'-8"
Depth: 54'-6"

L

Simple rooflines and an inviting L-shaped porch enhance this floor plan. A formal living room has a warming fireplace and a delightful bay window. The U-shaped kitchen shares a snack bar with the bayed family room. Note the sliding glass doors to the rear yard here. The vaulted master bedroom has its own private bath and ample closet space. Two family bedrooms are also complete with closet space and vaulted ceilings.

Photo by Exposures Unlimited, Ron & Donna Kolb

This home, as shown in the photograph, may differ from the actual blueprints.
For more detailed information, please check the floor plans carefully.

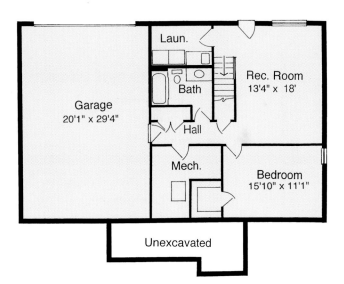

Laun.

Bath

Rec. Room
13'4" x 18'

Garage
20'1" x 29'4"

Hall

Mech.

Bedroom
15'10" x 11'1"

Unexcavated

PLAN HPT210008

Square Footage: 1,475
Basement: 722 sq. ft.

Width: 48'-8"
Depth: 30'-8"

Deck

walk-in closet

Bath

Kitchen
9'3" x 10'4"

Dining
10'7" x 12'1"

Bedroom
12'2" x 11'10"

Hall

Bath

Master Bedroom
13'1" x 15'4"

Great Room
20'2" x 17'

Foyer

Bedroom
11'1" x 11'9"

Porch

The mixture of shingles, stone and siding gives this home an eclectic facade. This pleasing cottage would be perfectly accented by trees and flowers. Cool summer evenings are happily spent on the front porch or rear deck. The great room is attached to the dining room for an open family floor plan. The L-shaped kitchen features a peninsula counter for extra space. The master bedroom contains a luxurious master bath. Two family bedrooms are located on the main floor. In the basement, there is space for another family bedroom along with a spacious recreation room. The laundry room and the garage complete this level.

Photo by Design Basics, Inc.

This home, as shown in the photograph, may differ from the actual blueprints. For more detailed information, please check the floor plans carefully.

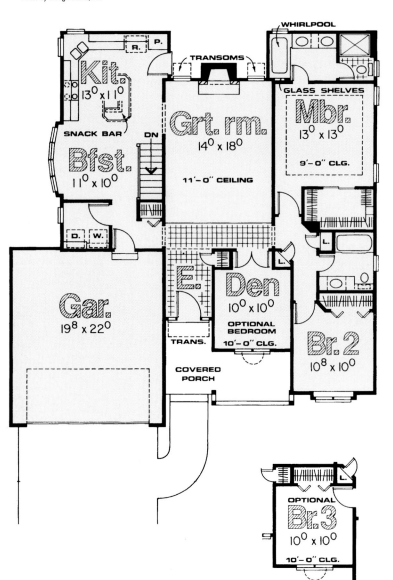

PLAN HPT210009

Square Footage: 1,479

Width: 48'-0"
Depth: 50'-0"

A covered porch and interesting window treatments add charisma to this cheerful ranch home. The entry opens to a sunny great room with a center fireplace framed with transom windows. Nearby, an efficient kitchen is highlighted by an island snack bar, a corner sink flanked with windows, and access to the backyard. The spacious master suite features a walk-in closet and a pampering bath with a whirlpool tub and compartmented toilet and shower area. Two secondary bedrooms—one an optional den designed with French doors—share a full hall bath.

24

©1996 Donald A. Gardner Architects, Inc., Photo courtesy of Donald A. Gardner Architects, Inc.

This home, as shown in the photograph, may differ from the actual blueprints.
For more detailed information, please check the floor plans carefully.

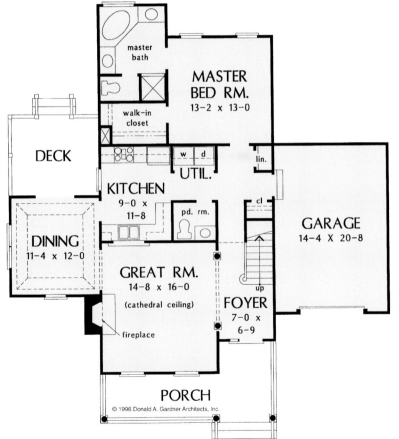

© 1996 Donald A. Gardner Architects, Inc.

PLAN HPT210010

First Floor: 1,116 sq. ft.
Second Floor: 442 sq. ft.
Total: 1,558 sq. ft.

Width: 49'-0"
Depth: 52'-0"

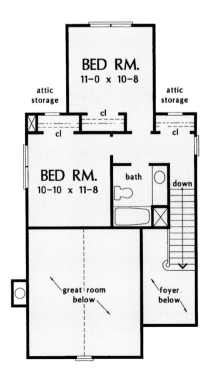

This two-story home is a great starter for a young family with plans to grow or for empty-nesters with a need for guest rooms. The two secondary bedrooms and shared bath on the second floor could also be used as office space. Additional attic storage is available as family needs expand. On the first floor, the front porch is perfect for relaxing. Inside, the foyer opens through a columned entrance to the large great room with its cathedral ceiling and fireplace. A tray-ceiling dining room offers access to both the deck and the central kitchen. The laundry room and a powder room are nearby. The master bedroom is located at the rear of the home for privacy and features a walk-in closet and a corner whirlpool tub.

25

Photo by Exposures Unlimited Ron & Donna Kolb

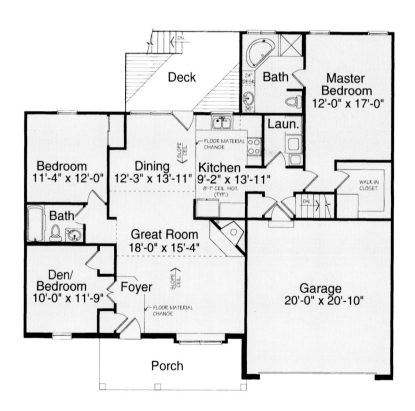

PLAN HPT210011

Square Footage: 1,488

Width: 51'-8"
Depth: 47'-0"

This one-level home with a front porch showcases an angled fireplace and sloped ceilings. The great room combines with the dining area, creating an open, spacious effect. A door leads to a raised deck for a favorable indoor/outdoor relationship. The master suite provides a large walk-in closet and deluxe bath with a unique half-moon tub and a separate shower. A bedroom accessed from the foyer creates an optional den. This house is drawn with a rear walkout basement, enabling the homeowner to increase the square footage.

Photo by Design Basics, Inc.

This home, as shown in the photograph, may differ from the actual blueprints. For more detailed information, please check the floor plans carefully.

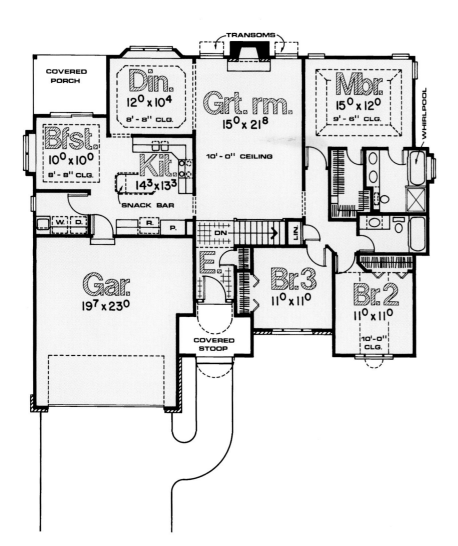

PLAN HPT210012

Square Footage: 1,666
Width: 55'-4"
Depth: 48'-0"

This delightfully updated European plan displays brick and stucco on the dramatic front elevation, showcased by sleek lines and decorative windows. An inviting entry has a view to the great room and is enhanced by an arched window. Sunny windows with transoms frame the great room's fireplace. The bayed dining room is nestled between the great room and the superb eat-in kitchen. The secluded master suite features a walk-in closet and a luxurious bath with dual lavatories and whirlpool tub. Two additional bedrooms share a hall bath.

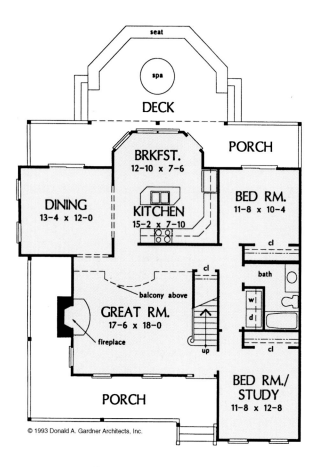

© 1993 Donald A. Gardner Architects, Inc.

PLAN HPT210013

First Floor: 1,271 sq. ft.
Second Floor: 665 sq. ft.
Total: 1,936 sq. ft.

Width: 41'-6"
Depth: 44'-8"

This gabled and dormered country home with an L-shaped wrapping porch fits unexpected luxury into this compact plan. A balcony adds drama to the vaulted great room, which offers a warming fireplace. The large island kitchen includes a bayed breakfast area that opens to the rear porch as does the dining room and a bedroom. The deck holds a spa area for great entertaining. A second bedroom on this floor can be easily converted to an office or study. Upstairs, the master bedroom features a bath with a double-sink vanity, compartmented toilet, walk-in closet, separate shower and skylit tub. An additional bedroom is found here with its own private bath.

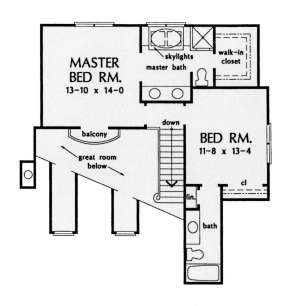

Photo by Stephen Fuller, Inc.

This home, as shown in the photograph, may differ from the actual blueprints.
For more detailed information, please check the floor plans carefully.

Cost to build? See page 246
to order complete cost estimate
to build this house in your area!

QUOTE ONE®

PORCH

BEDROOM/
OFFICE
10'-4" X 11'-0"

BREAKFAST
13'-4" X 9'-0"

BATH

LAUNDRY

KITCHEN
13'-4" X 10'-6"

DN.

GREAT ROOM
17'-0" X 17'-8"

MASTER
BATH

MASTER BEDROOM
16'-4" X 13'-6"

BEDROOM NO. 2
10'-4" X 12'-0"

BATH

TWO CAR GARAGE
20'-6" X 19'-6"

DINING ROOM
11'-4" X 12'-10"

FOYER
5'-4" X
12'-10"

BEDROOM/
STUDY
11'-2" X 12'-0"

PORCH

PLAN HPT210014

Square Footage: 2,090

Width: 61'-0"
Depth: 70'-6"

This traditional home features board-and-batten and cedar shingles in an attractively proportioned exterior. Finishing touches include a covered entrance, a porch with column detailing, an arched transom, flower boxes and shuttered windows. The foyer opens to both the dining room and the great room beyond, with French doors accessing the porch. To the right of the foyer is the combination bedroom/study. A short hallway leads to a full bath and a secondary bedroom with ample closet space. The master bedroom is spacious, with walk-in closets on both sides of the entrance to the full bath. This home is designed with a walk-out basement foundation.

Photo by Design Basics, Inc.

This home, as shown in the photograph, may differ from the actual blueprints.
For more detailed information, please check the floor plans carefully.

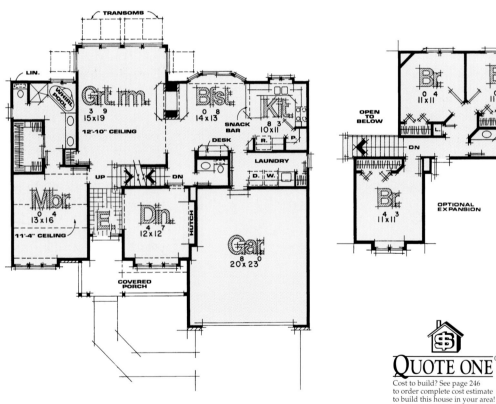

QUOTE ONE®

Cost to build? See page 246
to order complete cost estimate
to build this house in your area!

PLAN HPT210015

First Floor: 1,421 sq. ft.
Second Floor: 578 sq. ft.
Total: 1,999 sq. ft.

Width: 52'-0"
Depth: 47'-4"

Growing families will love this unique plan. Start with the living areas—a spacious great room with high ceilings, windows overlooking the back-yard, a see-through fireplace to the kitchen and access to the rear deck. The dining room with hutch space accommodates formal occasions. The hearth kitchen features a well-planned work space and a bayed breakfast area. The master suite with a whirlpool tub and walk-in closet is found downstairs, while three family bedrooms are upstairs. Please specify basement or slab foundation when ordering.

Photo by Design Basics, Inc.

This home, as shown in the photograph, may differ from the actual blueprints.
For more detailed information, please check the floor plans carefully.

S leek rooflines, classic window details and a covered front porch tastefully combine on the exterior of this three-bedroom home. A bright living room with an adjoining dining room is viewed from the volume entry. Meals will be enjoyed in the bayed breakfast area, which is served by a comfortable kitchen. A raised-hearth fireplace adds warmth to the family room. The second-level hall design provides separation between two secondary bedrooms and the luxurious master suite with a boxed ceiling. Two closets, a whirlpool bath with a plant sill, and double sinks are featured in the bath/dressing area. Please specify basement or block foundation when ordering.

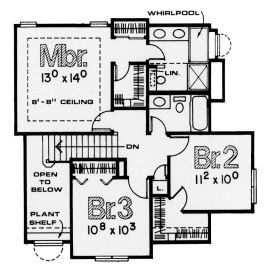

PLAN HPT210016

First Floor: 1,032 sq. ft.
Second Floor: 743 sq. ft.
Total: 1,775 sq. ft.

Width: 46'-0"
Depth: 42'-0"

This home, as shown in the photograph, may differ from the actual blueprints. For more detailed information, please check the floor plans carefully.

Porch
12'x 9'5"

Kitchen
8'8"x 18'

Dining
11'6"x 18'

Bedroom
13'x 10'11"

Living
16'6"x 14'5"

Bedroom
13'x 10'9"

Porch
20'6"x 5'

Deck
34'x 10'

Hours of enjoyment can be achieved listening to the sound of waves crashing from within the comfort of this two-story seaside home. The deck offers a great setting for relaxing or entertaining. The open floor plan provides an inviting atmosphere for family time. The focal-point fireplace in the living room becomes a wonderful retreat when the weather turns cold. The kitchen features an island and plenty of counter space. Two family bedrooms share a full bath on the first level. Another family bedroom and the master suite are located on the second level, completing the plan.

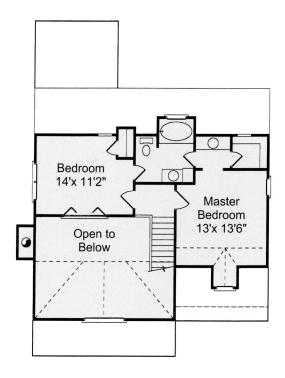

Bedroom
14'x 11'2"

Open to
Below

Master
Bedroom
13'x 13'6"

PLAN HPT210017

First Floor: 1,122 sq. ft.
Second Floor: 528 sq. ft.
Total: 1,650 sq. ft.

Width: 34'-0"
Depth: 52'-5"

Sitting on the wraparound porch sipping iced tea, the sound of children playing in the backyard and a simple, yet relaxing charm all combine to give you the flavor of country. Inside your cozy cottage, a fireplace awaits, in anticipation of cool fall evenings. Country cottages have been around for a long time. The desire to escape from city life has been a deep-felt necessity to survive the lengthy days of summer vacation. Identified by deep, covered porches and casual floor plans, country cottages convey warmth, charm and comfort. Ranging from 828 square feet to a little over 2,100 square feet, there are plenty here to choose from.

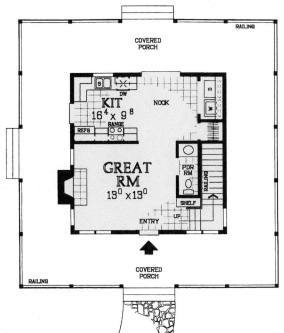

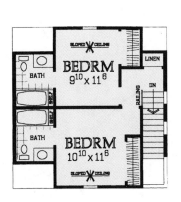

PLAN HPT210018

First Floor: 586 sq. ft.
Second Floor: 486 sq. ft.
Total: 1,072 sq. ft.

Width: 40'-0"
Depth: 40'-0"

Cost to build? See page 246 to order complete cost estimate to build this house in your area!

PLAN HPT210019

First Floor: 979 sq. ft.
Second Floor: 694 sq. ft.
Total: 1,673 sq. ft.

Width: 52'-0"
Depth: 63'-4"

This American classic features an elaborate wraparound porch. A Palladian dormer is perfectly situated between two gabled dormers. Two bayed windows portrude from the master bedroom and living room. Inside, the foyer leads to the living room where a fireplace becomes the focal point. The kitchen provides extra eating and cooking space with a snack bar. The breakfast room also has convenient access to the rear of the home. The master bedroom is located on the right side of the first level while two family bedrooms occupy the second level.

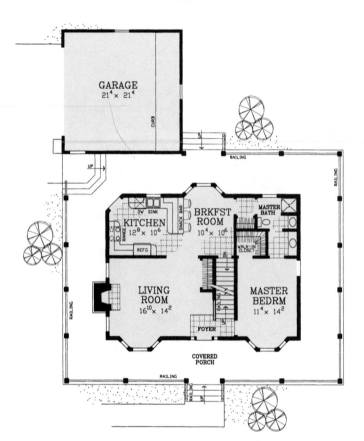

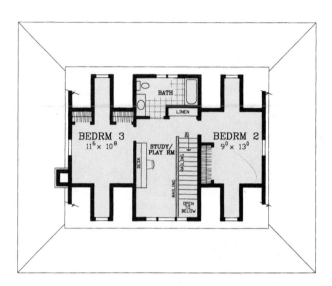

QUOTE ONE®

Cost to build? See page 246
to order complete cost estimate
to build this house in your area!

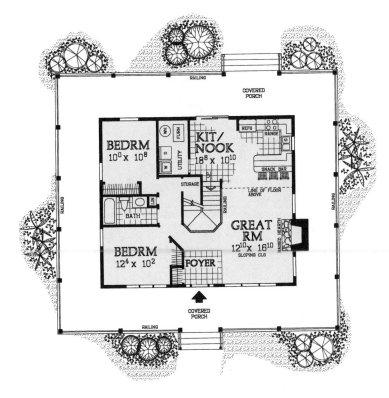

BEDRM 10⁰ x 10⁸

KIT/NOOK 18⁸ x 10¹⁰

WH

FURN

W

D

UTILITY

REFG

RANGE

STORAGE

SNACK BAR

LINE OF FLOOR ABOVE

RAILING

RAILING

COVERED PORCH

BATH

LIN

BEDRM 12⁴ x 10²

FOYER

GREAT RM 12¹⁰ x 16¹⁰ SLOPING CLG

RAISED HEARTH

RAILING

RAILING

RAILING

RAILING

COVERED PORCH

PLAN HPT210020

First Floor: 1,093 sq. ft.
Second Floor: 576 sq. ft.
Total: 1,669 sq. ft.

Width: 52'-0"
Depth: 46'-0"

L D

Here's a great country farmhouse with a lot of contemporary appeal. The generous use of windows—including two sets of triple muntin windows in the front—adds exciting visual elements to the exterior as well as plenty of natural light to the interior. An impressive tiled entry opens to a two-story great room with a raised hearth and views to the front and side grounds. The U-shaped kitchen conveniently combines with this area and offers a snack counter in addition to a casual dining nook with rear-porch access. The family bedrooms reside on the main level, while an expansive master suite with an adjacent study creates a resplendent retreat upstairs, complete with a private balcony, walk-in closet and bath.

QUOTE ONE®
Cost to build? See page 246
to order complete cost estimate
to build this house in your area!

SHWR

MASTER BATH

ATTIC ACCESS

WALK-IN CLOSET

RAILING

BALCONY

RAILING

MASTER BEDRM 14⁶ x 15⁰

LOFT/STUDY 11¹⁰ x 7²

RAILING

OPEN TO BELOW

LN

ATTIC ACCESS

SEAT

PLANT SHELF

Deck
14'-4" x 22'-4"

Garage
20'-0" x 20'-0"

Storage
14'-0" x 4'-0"

Kitchen
8'-0" x 14'-5"

Utility

Dining Rm.
10'-0" x 14'-5"

Pantry

Great Room
18'-0" x 16'-4"

Master
Bedroom
13'-5" x 16'-3"

Porch
36'-0" x 8'-0"

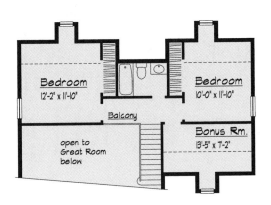

Bedroom
12'-2" x 11'-10"

Bedroom
10'-0" x 11'-10"

Balcony

open to
Great Room
below

Bonus Rm.
13'-5" x 7'-2"

Plan HPT210021

First Floor: 1,152 sq. ft.
Second Floor: 567 sq. ft.
Total: 1,719 sq. ft.
Bonus Room: 115 sq. ft.

Width: 36'-0"
Depth: 64'-0"

Simplicity is the best approach to this design. Twin chimneys serve as anchors to the home, while a deep front porch welcomes visitors. Inside, the cathedral ceiling and natural light from the dormers above enliven the great room. The dining room has convenient access to the kitchen. The kitchen features an island and plenty of counter space. The well-appointed master suite also enjoys a private fireplace. Two additional bedrooms are located on the second floor along with the bonus room, which will add 115 square feet if finished. Please specify basement or crawlspace foundation when ordering.

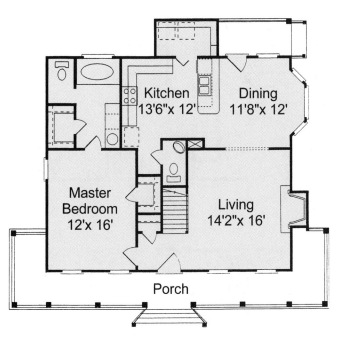

Kitchen
13'6" x 12'

Dining
11'8" x 12'

Master
Bedroom
12' x 16'

Living
14'2" x 16'

Porch

PLAN HPT210022

First Floor: 1,046 sq. ft.
Second Floor: 572 sq. ft.
Total: 1,618 sq. ft.

Width: 44'-0"
Depth: 39'-0"

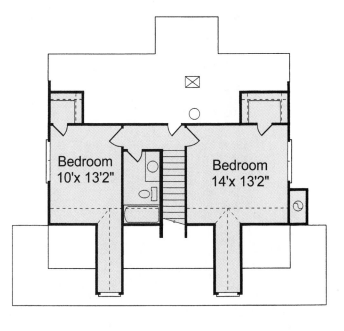

Bedroom
10' x 13'2"

Bedroom
14' x 13'2"

A deep wraparound porch trimmed with square pillars, a wood balustrade and traditional lattice adds character and interest to this Cape Cod design. Floor-to-ceiling double-hung windows and dormers complete the rustic look. The main level includes a fireplace in the living room, a bay window in the dining room and a master suite with a walk-in closet. The dining room and kitchen are divided by a peninsula with seating for informal dining. Upstairs, two bedrooms, each with a walk-in closet, share a bath. Please specify crawlspace or slab foundation when ordering.

PLAN HPT210023

First Floor: 836 sq. ft.
Second Floor: 581 sq. ft.
Total: 1,417 sq. ft.
Bonus Room: 228 sq. ft.

Width: 42'-0"
Depth: 33'-6"

Charming details add to the rustic appeal of this smaller farmhouse design. The covered porch shelters the entry that opens to a center hall with the living and dining rooms on one side and a cozy den on the other. The living/dining room is warmed by a fireplace. The den provides access to a full bath and doubles as a guest room. An L-shaped kitchen is both step-saving and convenient; just beyond is a laundry room and service entrance to the single-car garage.

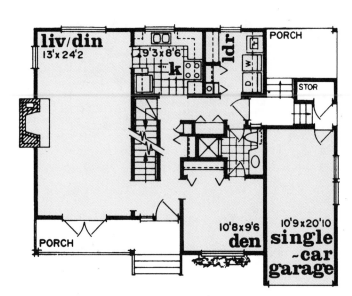

liv/din
13' x 24'2

9'3 x 8'6

k

ldr

PORCH

STOR

PORCH

10'8 x 9'6
den

10'9 x 20'10
single -car garage

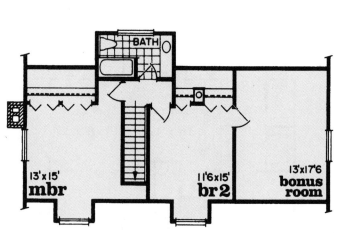

BATH

13' x 15'
mbr

11'6 x 15'
br 2

13 x 17'6
bonus room

COVERED PORCH

KITCHEN
13⁶ x 9⁰

W/D REFG. SINK D.W.

DINING
RM
10⁰ x 9⁰

SEAT

PDR

RANGE PASS THRU

BRM. CL.

W.H.

FURN

SLATE HEARTH

GARAGE
12⁸ x 22⁸

FOYER

UP

HALF WALL

LIVING ROOM
14⁶ X 13⁸

COVERED PORCH

BATH

SEAT

STORAGE

LINEN

DRESSING

STORAGE

BEDROOM
12⁴ x 12⁸

DOWN

OPEN BELOW

MASTER BEDROOM
19¹⁰ x 12⁸

SEAT

RAISED HEARTH

STOR.

STOR.

STOR.

PLAN HPT210024

First Floor: 663 sq. ft.
Second Floor: 624 sq. ft.
Total: 1,287 sq. ft.

Width: 40'-0"
Depth: 32'-0"

L

This home's covered front porch provides a warm welcome. Inside, a beam-ceilinged living room delights with a raised-hearth fireplace. The projecting bay window in the dining room offers a picturesque window seat. Upstairs, the master bedroom suite includes a raised-hearth fireplace, a walk-in dressing area and plenty of privacy. Additional livability can be developed over the garage as a den, guest room or hobby area.

QUOTE ONE®

Cost to build? See page 246
to order complete cost estimate
to build this house in your area!

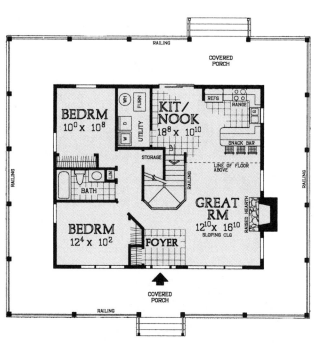

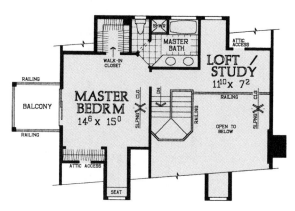

QUOTE ONE®

Cost to build? See page 246
to order complete cost estimate
to build this house in your area!

PLAN HPT210025

First Floor: 1,093 sq. ft.
Second Floor: 580 sq. ft.
Total: 1,673 sq. ft.

Width: 52'-0"
Depth: 52'-0"

L **D**

This fun country cottage sports two dormers and a second-story patio. A wraparound porch on the first level and a covered balcony above make indoor/outdoor living a reality in this three-bedroom-plus-study, 1½-story cottage. The great room offers the comforts of a built-in fireplace. The open kitchen and breakfast nook is flooded with sunlight and cooking delight. The entire second level is devoted to the master suite with a secluded loft and private balcony. Secondary bedrooms on the first level share a full bath.

© 1994 Donald A. Gardner Architects, Inc.

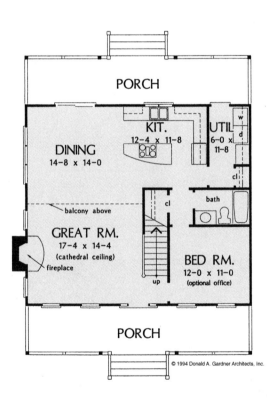

PORCH

KIT.
12-4 x 11-8

UTIL
6-0 x
11-8

DINING
14-8 x 14-0

balcony above

bath

GREAT RM.
17-4 x 14-4
(cathedral ceiling)

fireplace

up

BED RM.
12-0 x 11-0
(optional office)

PORCH

© 1994 Donald A. Gardner Architects, Inc.

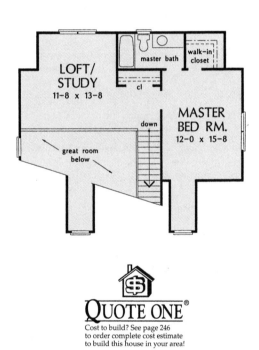

LOFT/
STUDY
11-8 x 13-8

master bath

walk-in
closet

cl

great room
below

down

MASTER
BED RM.
12-0 x 15-8

QUOTE ONE®

Cost to build? See page 246
to order complete cost estimate
to build this house in your area!

PLAN HPT210087

First Floor: 966 sq. ft.
Second Floor: 584 sq. ft.
Total: 1,550 sq. ft.

Width: 35'-9"
Depth: 43'-0"

A country farmhouse exterior combined with an open floor plan creates a comfortable home or vacation getaway. The great room, warmed by a fireplace and opened by a cathedral ceiling, combines well with the dining room and the kitchen. Flexibility is offered in a front bedroom with a full bath that easily doubles as a home office. The second floor contains the master bedroom with a walk-in closet and a private bath. The loft/study overlooks the great room below. Front and rear porches provide plenty of room for outdoor enjoyment.

PLAN HPT210027

First Floor: 1,093 sq. ft.
Second Floor: 580 sq. ft.
Total: 1,673 sq. ft.

Width: 36'-0"
Depth: 52'-0"

L D

Brackets and balustrades on front and rear covered porches spell old-fashioned country charm on this rustic retreat. Warm evenings will invite family and guests outdoors for watching sunsets and stars. In cooler weather, the raised-hearth fireplace will make the great room a cozy place to gather. The nearby kitchen serves both a snack bar and a breakfast nook. Two family bedrooms and a full bath complete the main level. Upstairs, a master suite with a sloped ceiling offers a window seat and a complete bath. The adjacent loft/study overlooks the great room.

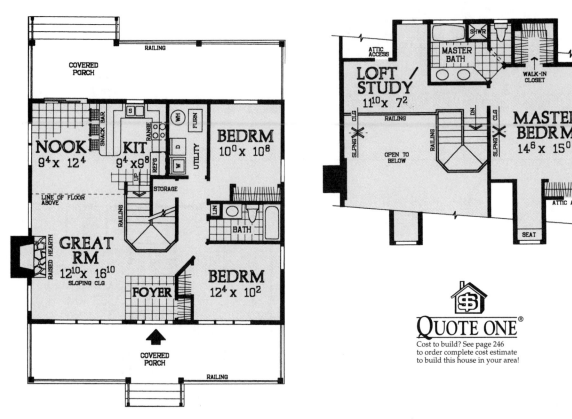

QUOTE ONE®

Cost to build? See page 246
to order complete cost estimate
to build this house in your area!

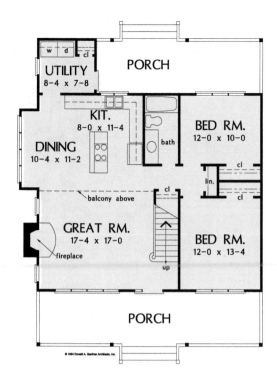

PLAN HPT210028

First Floor: 1,100 sq. ft.
Second Floor: 584 sq. ft.
Total: 1,684 sq. ft.

Width: 36'-8"
Depth: 45'-0"

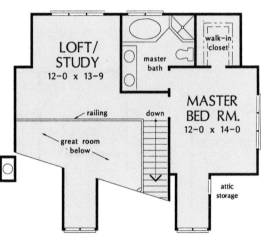

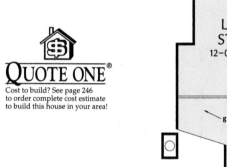

QUOTE ONE®

Cost to build? See page 246
to order complete cost estimate
to build this house in your area!

A relaxing country image projects from the front and rear covered porches of this rustic three-bedroom home. Open planning extends to the great room, the dining room and the efficient kitchen. A shared cathedral ceiling creates an impressive space. Completing the first floor are two family bedrooms, a full bath and a handy utility area. The second floor contains the master suite featuring a spacious walk-in closet and a private bath with a whirlpool tub and separate corner shower. A generous loft/study overlooks the great room below. ©1994 Donald A. Gardner Architects, Inc.

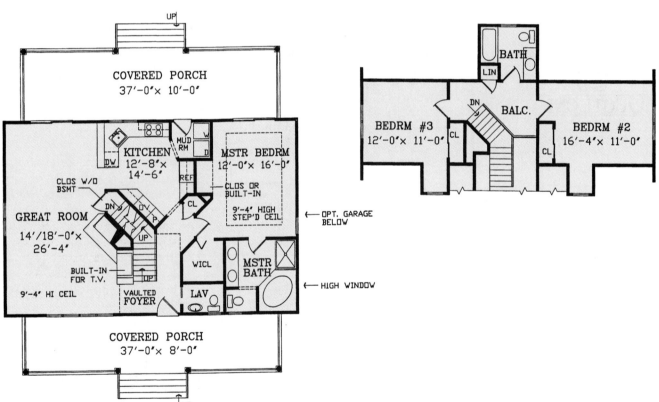

COVERED PORCH
37'-0" x 10'-0"

KITCHEN
12'-8" x 14'-6"

MUD RM

DW

REF

MSTR BEDRM
12'-0" x 16'-0"

CLOS OR BUILT-IN

9'-4" HIGH STEP'D CEIL

CLOS W/O BSMT

GREAT ROOM
14'/18'-0" x 26'-4"

DN

CL

UP

BUILT-IN FOR T.V.

9'-4" HI CEIL

VAULTED FOYER

WICL

MSTR BATH

LAV

← OPT. GARAGE BELOW

← HIGH WINDOW

COVERED PORCH
37'-0" x 8'-0"

UP

UP

BATH

LIN

DN

BALC.

BEDRM #3
12'-0" x 11'-0"

CL

CL

BEDRM #2
16'-4" x 11'-0"

PLAN HPT210029

First Floor: 1,134 sq. ft.
Second Floor: 545 sq. ft.
Total: 1,679 sq. ft.

Width: 42'-0"
Depth: 45'-0"

This country cottage offers an open, contemporary interior, suitable for year-round or vacation use. Entry from the large, covered front porch leads to a lovely vaulted foyer rising above a second-story balcony. The extremely accessible kitchen is open to the spacious great room, which includes a fireplace, a built-in entertainment center and glass doors to the rear porch. The beautiful, first-floor master bedroom suite includes a stepped ceiling, walk-in closet and private compartmented bath with a whirlpool tub. The second floor includes two additional bedrooms and a full bath. A garage is optional.

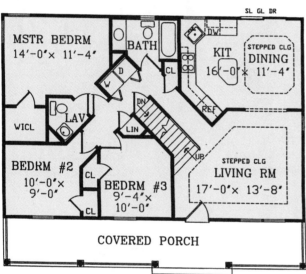

SL GL DR

MSTR BEDRM
14'-0" x 11'-4"

BATH

KIT
16'-0"

STEPPED CLG
DINING
x 11'-4"

CL

DW

REF

WICL

LAV

DN

LIN

UP

BEDRM #2
10'-0" x
9'-0"

CL

BEDRM #3
9'-4" x
10'-0"

STEPPED CLG
LIVING RM
17'-0" x 13'-8"

CL

COVERED PORCH

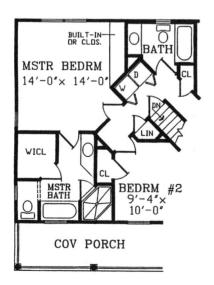

BUILT-IN
OR CLOS.

BATH

MSTR BEDRM
14'-0" x 14'-0"

D

CL

W

DN

LIN

WICL

CL

MSTR
BATH

BEDRM #2
9'-4" x
10'-0"

COV PORCH

Alternate Layout

PLAN HPT210030

Square Footage: 1,040
Bonus Space: 597 sq. ft.

Width: 40'-0"
Depth: 32'-0"

Two petite dormers accent the beauty and sophistication of this home. The covered porch provides the classic country feel. A stepped ceiling is featured in the angled living room. The spacious kitchen connects to the dining room. An island in the kitchen offers even more counter space. The master suite includes a private bath and a walk-in closet. This plan has the option to place two family bedrooms upstairs or leave them on the first level.

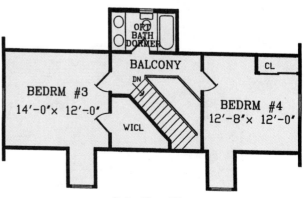

OPT
BATH
DORMER

BALCONY

CL

BEDRM #3
14'-0" x 12'-0"

DN

BEDRM #4
12'-8" x 12'-0"

WICL

Optional Second Floor

PLAN HPT210031

First Floor: 1,093 sq. ft.
Second Floor: 603 sq. ft.
Total: 1,696 sq. ft.

Width: 46'-0"
Depth: 52'-0"

L D

This two-story home's rustic design reflects thoughtful planning, including a porch that fully wraps the house in comfort and provides lots of room for rocking. A stone chimney and arched windows set in dormers further enhance this home's country appeal. Inside, the floor plan is designed for maximum efficiency. A great room with a sloped ceiling enjoys a raised-hearth fireplace whose warmth radiates into the kitchen/nook. The master suite is located on the first floor and includes plenty of closet space and a private bath filled with amenities. A utility room and a powder room complete this level. The second floor contains two secondary bedrooms, a full bath and a loft/study with a window seat.

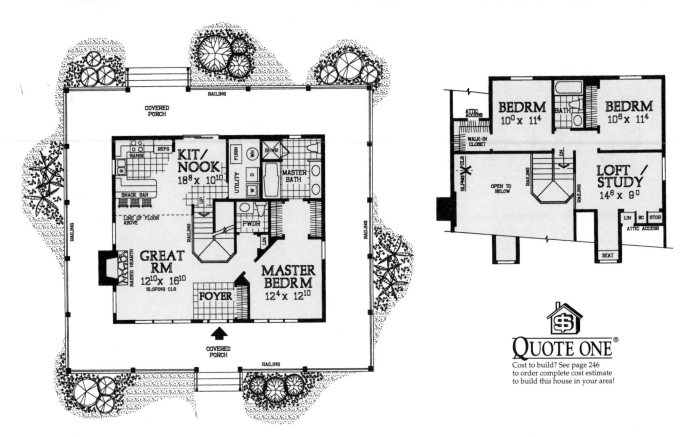

QUOTE ONE®

Cost to build? See page 246
to order complete cost estimate
to build this house in your area!

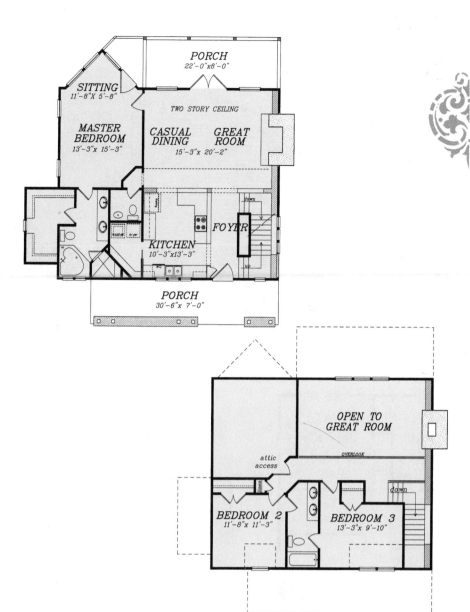

PORCH
22'-0"x8'-0"

SITTING
11'-8"X 5'-8"

TWO STORY CEILING

MASTER
BEDROOM
13'-3"x 15'-3"

CASUAL
DINING
15'-3"x 20'-2"

GREAT
ROOM

down

FOYER

KITCHEN
10'-3"x13'-3"

up

PORCH
30'-6" x 7'-0"

OPEN TO
GREAT ROOM

attic
access

OVERLOOK

down

BEDROOM 2
11'-8"x 11'-3"

BEDROOM 3
13'-3"x 9'-10"

PLAN HPT210032

First Floor: 1,180 sq. ft.
Second Floor: 528 sq. ft.
Total: 1,708 sq. ft.

Width: 41'-4"
Depth: 45'-0"

With a combination of shingles and flagstone detailing, this country home is perfect for a rustic setting. A spacious porch leads into the foyer, where a uniquely placed kitchen is at its right. The kitchen leads to a laundry area and a convenient powder room. The two-story casual dining area and great room are combined for a snug atmosphere and share a fireplace. The master bedroom boasts a sitting area, which opens to the rear porch, large walk-in closet, dual basins and a compartmented toilet. The second level is home to two family bedrooms which share a hall bath. Attic storage is available and a balcony overlook to the great room below is also provided.

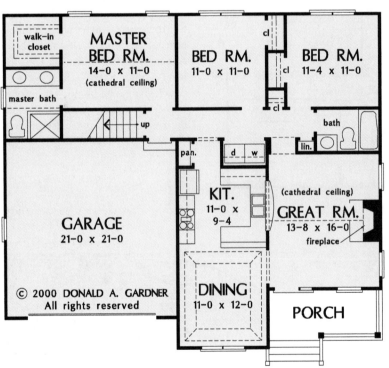

walk-in closet

MASTER BED RM.
14-0 x 11-0
(cathedral ceiling)

master bath

BED RM.
11-0 x 11-0

cl

cl

cl

BED RM.
11-4 x 11-0

bath

up

lin.

pan.

d   w

GARAGE
21-0 x 21-0

KIT.
11-0 x 9-4

(cathedral ceiling)

GREAT RM.
13-8 x 16-0
fireplace

DINING
11-0 x 12-0

PORCH

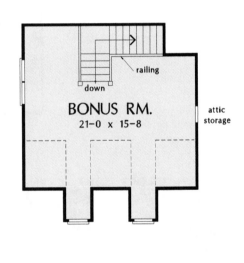

down

railing

BONUS RM.
21-0 x 15-8

attic storage

PLAN HPT210033

Square Footage: 1,264
Bonus Room: 397 sq. ft.

Width: 47'-0"
Depth: 40'-4"

Two dormers balanced with a double gable and arch-top windows impart poise and charm to this efficient three-bedroom home. Relax on the front porch, or go inside to warm up by the fireplace in the great room. A cathedral ceiling and windows on two walls lend a bright and fresh feel to the great room. Nearby, the kitchen benefits from a pantry and easy access to the dining room and great room. The dining room views the front yard through a beautiful picture window with an arch top. At the rear of the plan, two secondary bedrooms share a full bath. Protected from street noise by the garage, the master suite enjoys a view of the backyard, a private bath and a walk-in closet. This plan also allows for expansion into the second-floor bonus room.

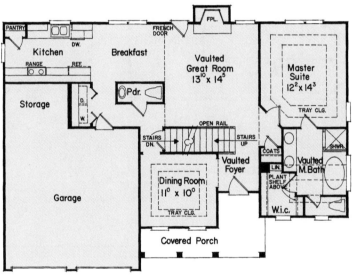

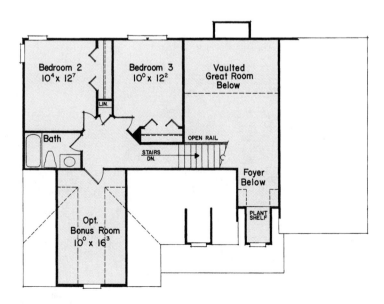

PLAN HPT210034

First Floor: 1,065 sq. ft.
Second Floor: 435 sq. ft.
Total: 1,500 sq. ft.
Bonus Room: 175 sq. ft.

Width: 50'-0"
Depth: 37'-4"

Although this home would work well on a narrow lot, it would fit just as comfortably on a lot surrounded by land available for a garden or for the kids to have plenty of running room. The front covered porch leads to a vaulted foyer and a formal dining room with a tray ceiling. A vaulted great room with a fireplace and rear-yard access will be ideal for family gatherings. The master suite is located on the first floor for privacy and features a vaulted bath with a walk-in closet, oversized tub and separate shower. Two bedrooms and a full bath are available upstairs, as well as an optional bonus room that can be developed later as needed. Please specify basement or crawlspace foundation when ordering.

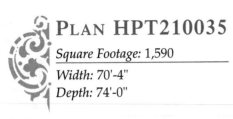

PLAN HPT210035

Square Footage: 1,590

Width: 70'-4"

Depth: 74'-0"

The open floor plan of this country farmhouse packs in all of today's amenities in only 1,590 square feet. Columns separate the foyer from the great room with its cathedral ceiling and fireplace. Serving meals has never been easier—the kitchen makes use of direct access to the dining room as well as a breakfast nook overlooking the deck and spa. A handy utility room even has space for a counter and cabinets. Three bedrooms make this an especially desirable design. The master bedroom, off of the great room, provides private access to the deck. This design is flexible enough to be accommodated by a narrow lot if the garage is relocated.

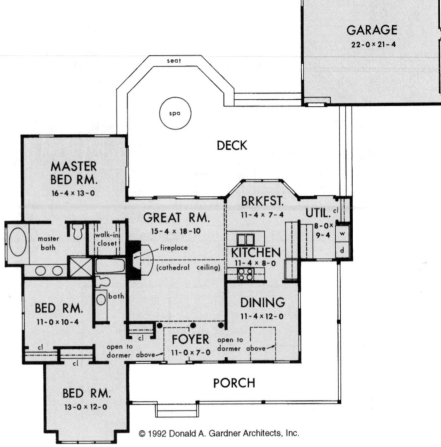

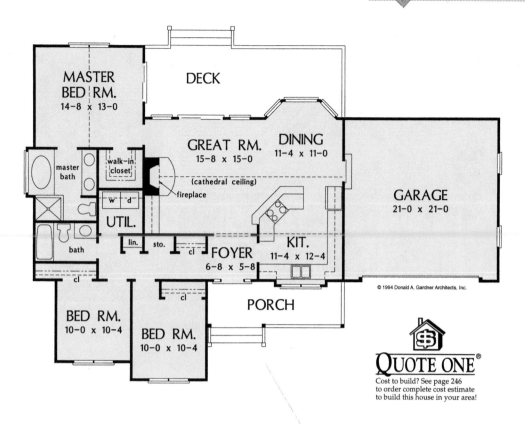

MASTER BED RM.
14-8 x 13-0

DECK

master bath

walk-in closet

GREAT RM.
15-8 x 15-0

(cathedral ceiling)

fireplace

DINING
11-4 x 11-0

GARAGE
21-0 x 21-0

w d

UTIL.

bath

lin. sto. cl

cl

FOYER
6-8 x 5-8

KIT.
11-4 x 12-4

© 1994 Donald A. Gardner Architects, Inc.

BED RM.
10-0 x 10-4

cl

BED RM.
10-0 x 10-4

PORCH

QUOTE ONE®
Cost to build? See page 246
to order complete cost estimate
to build this house in your area!

PLAN HPT210036

Square Footage: 1,346

Width: 65'-0"
Depth: 44'-2"

A great room that stretches into the dining room makes this design perfect for entertaining. A cozy fireplace, stylish built-ins, and a cathedral ceiling further this casual yet elegant atmosphere. A rear deck extends living possibilities. The ample kitchen features an abundance of counter and cabinet space and an angled cooktop and serving bar that overlooks the great room. Two bedrooms, a hall bath and a handy laundry room make up the family sleeping wing while the master suite is privately located at the rear of the plan.

© 1994 Donald A. Gardner Architects, Inc.

B. NATHAN

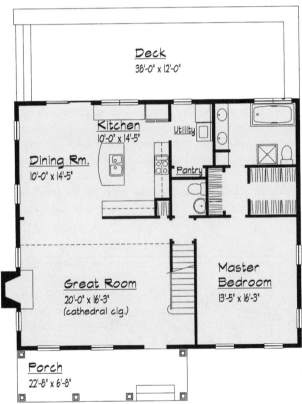

Deck
38'-0" x 12'-0"

Kitchen
10'-0" x 14'-5"

Utility

Dining Rm.
10'-0" x 14'-5"

Pantry

Great Room
20'-0" x 16'-3"
(cathedral clg.)

Master
Bedroom
13'-5" x 16'-3"

Porch
22'-8" x 6'-8"

Four pillars support a roof topped by an attractive gable—all covering the front porch of this fine three-bedroom home. Inside, the entrance opens directly to the great room, where a cathedral ceiling and a fireplace are enhancements. A gourmet kitchen offers a work island with a sink and serving counter for the nearby dining room. Located on the main level for privacy, the master bedroom is sure to please with two closets—one a walk-in—and a private bath with a separate tub and shower. Upstairs, two family bedrooms share a hall bath and access to a bonus room—perfect for a study or computer room. Please specify basement or crawlspace foundation when ordering.

PLAN HPT210037

First Floor: 1,216 sq. ft.
Second Floor: 478 sq. ft.
Total: 1,694 sq. ft.
Bonus Room: 115 sq. ft.

Width: 38'-0"
Depth: 38'-8"

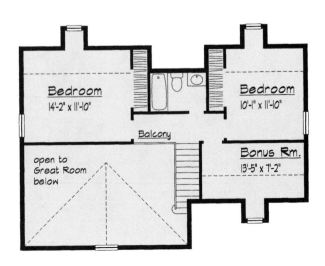

Bedroom
14'-2" x 11'-10"

Bedroom
10'-1" x 11'-10"

Balcony

open to
Great Room
below

Bonus Rm.
13'-5" x 7'-2"

© 1998 Donald A Gardner, Inc.

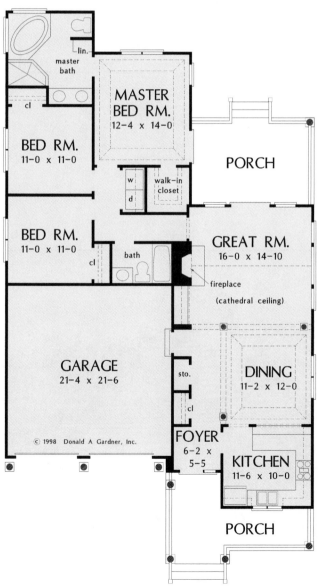

© 1998 Donald A Gardner, Inc.

PLAN HPT210038

Square Footage: 1,444

Width: 40'-4"
Depth: 70'-0"

Designed for longer lots, this home offers the ultimate in quiet living. Directly off the foyer, the U-shaped kitchen serves an elegant dining room, with a tray ceiling and pillars that separate it from the large great room. The great room offers a warming fireplace and a cathedral ceiling. The master bedroom features a coffered ceiling and a secluded master bath—complete with a whirlpool tub. Both the great room and the master suite provide access to the rear covered porch. Two secondary bedrooms share a hall bath.

PLAN HPT210039

Square Footage: 1,454
Bonus Room: 424 sq. ft.

Width: 41'-8"
Depth: 54'-6"

Country details reign supreme in this clever little design. Though small, it delivers great livability. The great room opens just beyond the covered front porch and has a fireplace and vaulted ceiling. A dining area is just to the left, connecting to a kitchen with deck access. Three bedrooms sit behind the two-car garage—a master suite and two family bedrooms. The master suite has a walk-in closet and a bath with double sinks and a separate tub and shower. Family bedrooms share a full bath that includes double sinks.

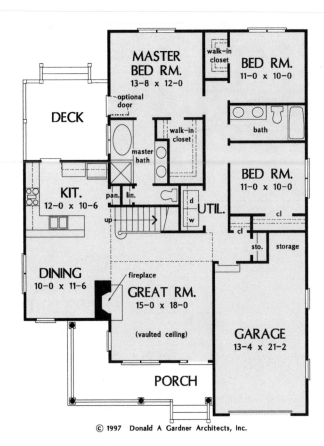

MASTER BED RM.
13-8 x 12-0

walk-in closet

BED RM.
11-0 x 10-0

DECK

optional door

walk-in closet

master bath

bath

KIT.
12-0 x 10-6

pan. lin.

BED RM.
11-0 x 10-0

up

d w

UTIL.

cl

cl

sto. storage

DINING
10-0 x 11-6

fireplace

GREAT RM.
15-0 x 18-0

(vaulted ceiling)

GARAGE
13-4 x 21-2

PORCH

© 1997 Donald A Gardner Architects, Inc.

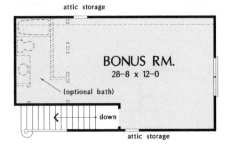

attic storage

BONUS RM.
28-8 x 12-0

(optional bath)

down

attic storage

B. NATHAN.

© 1997 Donald A. Gardner Architects, Inc.

This rustic Craftsman-style cottage provides an open interior with good outdoor flow. The front covered porch invites casual gatherings, while inside, the dining area is set for both everyday and planned occasions. Meal preparations are a breeze with a cooktop/snack-bar island in the kitchen. A centered fireplace in the great room shares its warmth with the dining room. A rear hall leads to the master bedroom and a secondary bedroom, while upstairs, a loft has space for computers.

PLAN HPT210040

Square Footage: 1,404
Bonus Room: 256 sq. ft.

Width: 54'-7"
Depth: 46'-6"

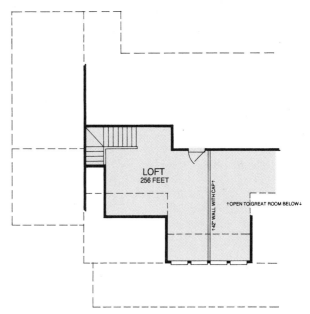

© 1997 Donald A Gardner Architects, Inc.

PLAN HPT210041

Square Footage: 1,246

Width: 60'-0"
Depth: 48'-0"

Open living spaces allow an easy flow in this gracious country cottage, and vaulted ceilings add volume. The front porch wraps slightly, giving the illusion of a larger home, while a cathedral ceiling maximizes space in the open great room and dining room. The kitchen features a center skylight, breakfast bar and screened-porch access. Two bedrooms share a bath near the entry, while the master suite enjoys a private location at the back of the plan. Luxuriate in the master bath with its separate shower, garden tub and twin-sink vanity.

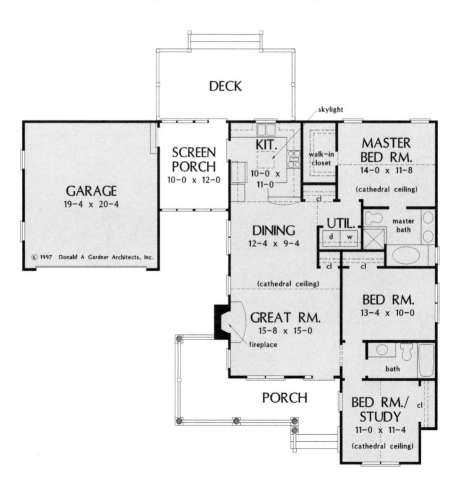

DECK

SCREEN PORCH
10-0 x 12-0

GARAGE
19-4 x 20-4

© 1997 Donald A Gardner Architects, Inc.

skylight

KIT.
10-0 x 11-0

walk-in closet

MASTER BED RM.
14-0 x 11-8
(cathedral ceiling)

UTIL.
d   w

master bath

DINING
12-4 x 9-4

(cathedral ceiling)

GREAT RM.
15-8 x 15-0

fireplace

BED RM.
13-4 x 10-0

bath

PORCH

BED RM./ STUDY
11-0 x 11-4

(cathedral ceiling)

© 1995 Donald A. Gardner Architects, Inc.

PLAN HPT210042

Square Footage: 1,246

Width: 60'-0"
Depth: 60'-0"

This one-story home offers tremendous curb appeal and many extras found only in much larger homes. A continuous cathedral ceiling in the great room, dining room and kitchen gives a spacious feel to an efficient plan. The kitchen, brightened by a skylight, features a pantry and a peninsula counter for easy preparation and service to the dining room and screened porch. The master suite opens up with a cathedral ceiling, walk-in and linen closets, and a private bath that includes a garden tub and a double-bowl vanity.

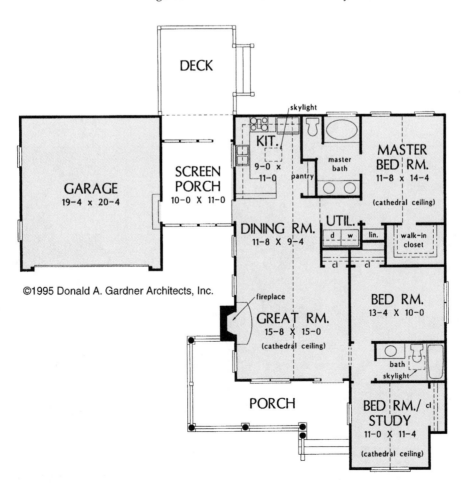

©1995 Donald A. Gardner Architects, Inc.

PLAN HPT210043

Square Footage: 1,655

Width: 81'-0"
Depth: 51'-0"

With its front porch and sloped roof, this house spells country! The expansive family room features a see-through fireplace which also faces the dining area and connecting L-shaped island kitchen. Your guests will gather on both sides of this appealing fireplace. All the bedrooms have roomy walk-in closets, providing ample storage space. Plus, there's a whole roomful of storage in the garage. And, with a covered walkway from the garage to the back door, there's no getting wet on those rainy days!

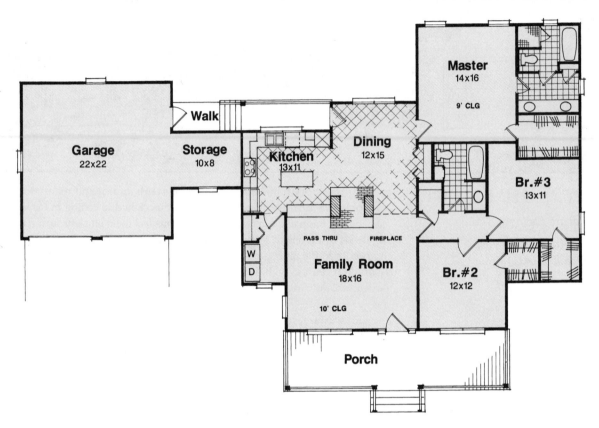

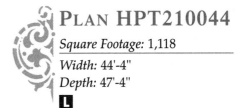

Floor plan labels:

- WALK-IN CLOSET
- SHOWER
- LIN
- MASTER BATH
- ULTRA TUB
- MASTER SUITE 15¹⁰ x 12⁸ SLOPED CLG
- COVERED PATIO
- LIVING RM 15⁰ x 14⁰ SLOPED CLG
- ARCHED OPENING
- BEDRM 9⁰ x 9⁸ SLOPED CLG
- LINEN
- BATH
- REFG
- RANGE
- ARCHED OPENING
- FOYER
- 3-SIDED FP
- SLVS
- CURIO
- HVAC · WH
- D · W
- KITCHEN 8⁰ x 14⁶
- P · DW · S
- CURB
- DINING RM 9¹⁰ x 9⁴ COFFERED CLG
- COVERED PORCH
- GARAGE 19⁴ x 22¹⁰
- RAILING · RAILING

PLAN HPT210044

Square Footage: 1,118

Width: 44'-4"
Depth: 47'-4"

L

Compact and perfect for starters or empty-nesters, this is a wonderful single-level home. The beautiful facade is supplemented by a stylish and practical covered porch. Just to the left of the entry is a roomy kitchen with bright windows and convenient storage. The octagonal dining room shares a three-sided fireplace with the living room. A covered patio to the rear enhances outdoor living. A fine master suite enjoys a grand bath and is complemented by a secondary bedroom and full bath.

QUOTE ONE®

Cost to build? See page 246 to order complete cost estimate to build this house in your area!

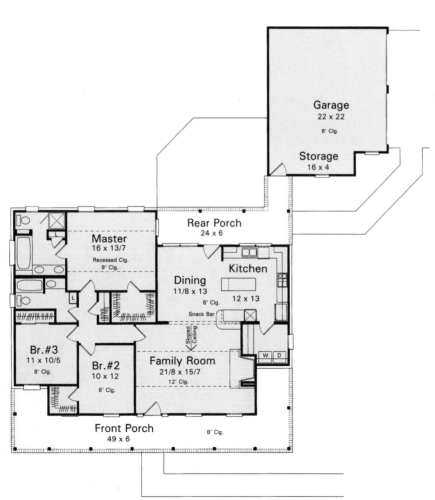

Garage
22 x 22
8' Clg.

Storage
16 x 4

Rear Porch
24 x 6

Master
16 x 13/7
Recessed Clg.
9' Clg.

Dining
11/8 x 13
8' Clg.

Kitchen
12 x 13

Snack Bar

Sloped Ceiling

Br. #3
11 x 10/5
8' Clg.

Br. #2
10 x 12
8' Clg.

Family Room
21/8 x 15/7
12' Clg.

W D

Front Porch
49 x 6
8' Clg.

PLAN HPT210045

Square Footage: 1,550

Width: 68'-3"
Depth: 73'-8"

A wide overhanging roof covers the welcoming front porch of this three-bedroom ranch home. The entrance opens directly to the family room where a sloped ceiling and a fireplace add charm to the feeling of spaciousness. A dining area is convenient to the L-shaped kitchen which offers a work island and a snack bar for casual times. The dining area also accesses the rear covered porch. A master bedroom suite features a walk-in closet, a dual-bowl vanity and a separate tub and shower. Two family bedrooms share a full hall bath and access to a hall linen closet. The two-car garage is reached via a covered walk.

KITCHEN & DINING
20'-0" x 8'-0"

D.W.

RANGE

SNK

REFRIG.

LAUNDRY ROOM

WASH

TUB

DRY

SHOWER BATH

CLOSET

CLOSET

CLOSET

STORAGE

W.H.

UP

RAILING

COATS

FIREPLACE

STONE

LIVING ROOM
20'-0" x 19'-0"

BEDROOM
11'-8" x 13'-0"

DN.

PORCH
36'-0" x 10'-0"

WOOD POSTS & RAILING

PLAN HPT210046

First Floor: 1,036 sq. ft.
Second Floor: 273 sq. ft.
Total: 1,309 sq. ft.

Width: 39'-0"
Depth: 38'-0"

D

This charming farmhouse design will be economical to build and a pleasure to occupy. Like most vacation homes, this design features an open plan. The large living area includes a living room, a dining room and a massive stone fireplace. A partition separates the kitchen from the living room. The first floor also holds a bedroom, a full bath and a laundry room. Upstairs, a spacious sleeping loft overlooks the living room. Don't miss the large front porch—this will be a favorite spot for relaxing.

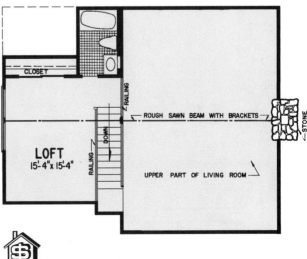

CLOSET

RAILING

DOWN

LOFT
15'-4" x 15'-4"

ROUGH SAWN BEAM WITH BRACKETS

STONE

UPPER PART OF LIVING ROOM

QUOTE ONE®
Cost to build? See page 246
to order complete cost estimate
to build this house in your area!

61

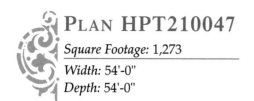

PLAN HPT210047

Square Footage: 1,273

Width: 54'-0"
Depth: 54'-0"

Enjoy the feel of country in this classic three-bedroom brick-and-siding home. A roomy front porch awaits summertime visitors or quiet contemplation of nature. Inside, the tiled entry introduces a faux-beamed living room. Curl up with a good book by the living-room fireplace or step out onto the side patio through the French door. Left of the living room, double doors open to the sleeping zone—two family bedrooms sharing a full hall bath and a master bedroom with a private bath. The kitchen opens to the dining room over a serving bar. Note the handy storage closet near the garage. Please specify crawlspace or slab foundation when ordering.

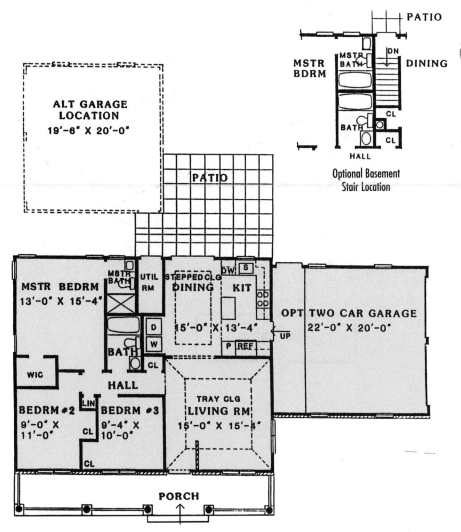

ALT GARAGE
LOCATION
19'-6" X 20'-0"

PATIO

MSTR BEDRM
13'-0" X 15'-4"

MSTR
BATH

UTIL
RM

STEPPED CLG
DINING

KIT

DW S

OPT TWO CAR GARAGE
22'-0" X 20'-0"

15'-0" X 13'-4"

D

W

BATH

CL

UP

P REF

WIC

HALL

BEDRM #2
9'-0" X
11'-0"

LIN

BEDRM #3
9'-4" X
10'-0"

CL

CL

TRAY CLG
LIVING RM
15'-0" X 15'-4"

PORCH

PATIO

MSTR
BDRM

MSTR
BATH

DN

DINING

CL

BATH

CL

HALL

Optional Basement
Stair Location

PLAN HPT210048

Square Footage: 1,097

Width: 59'-4"
Depth: 35'-8"

This charming home reflects Prairie-style influences in a compact and cozy floor plan. A large railed porch borders the entrance, which leads into an ample-sized living room, complete with a tray ceiling. Venture further and a dining room, with a stepped ceiling, easily accesses the kitchen for convenient dining and entertaining. A spacious patio lies directly outside the dining room. The sleeping quarters make up the left side of the plan, where two bedrooms share a full bath and a master bedroom is graced with a walk-in closet and a full bath of its own. Amenities include a utility room, shuttered windows and muntin windows.

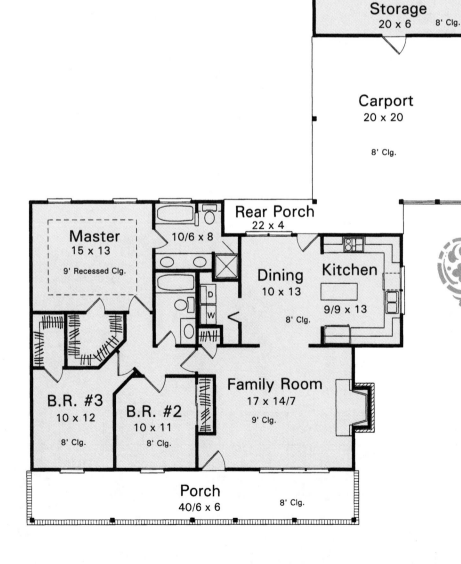

Storage
20 x 6   8' Clg.

Carport
20 x 20

8' Clg.

Master
15 x 13

9' Recessed Clg.

10/6 x 8

Rear Porch
22 x 4

Kitchen
9/9 x 13

Dining
10 x 13

8' Clg.

B.R. #3
10 x 12

8' Clg.

B.R. #2
10 x 11

8' Clg.

Family Room
17 x 14/7

9' Clg.

Porch
40/6 x 6   8' Clg.

PLAN HPT210049

Square Footage: 1,333

Width: 55'-6"
Depth: 64'-3"

The country home sports a cozy cottage look with its covered porch and chimney. The fireplace resides in the roomy family room and awaits guests. The open dining room and kitchen area provide plenty of casual dining space and access the rear porch. An island offers even more counter space. Two family bedrooms and a master bedroom are located on the left of the plan. The master bedroom enjoys a spacious private bath.

PLAN HPT210050

Square Footage: 1,406

Width: 76'-6"
Depth: 57'-1"

The covered porch provides shelter from the hot sun and breezy evenings, and leads to the family room where a warming fireplace awaits. The dining room is just left of the kitchen for serving convenience. The U-shaped kitchen also offers an island. A well designed walkway leads from the garage to the rear porch with access to the home through the dining area. Two family bedrooms enjoy closet space. The stepped-ceiling master bedroom features transoms and a private bath.

PLAN HPT210051

Square Footage: 1,120

Width: 52'-0"
Depth: 34'-0"

This low-sloped, side-gabled home offers a comfortable atmosphere with its covered front porch. Inside, the living room is open to both the dining room and the kitchen. The kitchen features a snack bar and the dining room accesses the rear patio. The master suite contains a walk-in closet and a private bath. Bedrooms 2 and 3 sport large windows to illuminate the interior. An attached garage is optional.

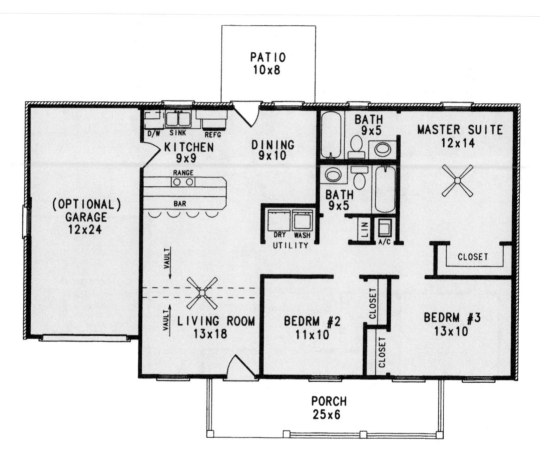

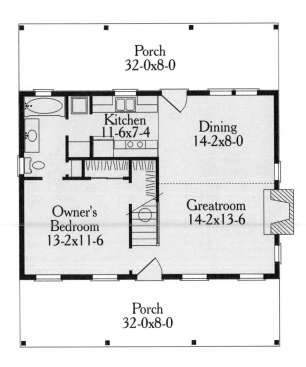

Porch
32-0x8-0

Kitchen
11-6x7-4

Dining
14-2x8-0

Owner's
Bedroom
13-2x11-6

Greatroom
14-2x13-6

Porch
32-0x8-0

The steeply pitched roof, shuttered windows and two full covered porches lend this two-bedroom plan great country charm. The covered front and rear porches are perfect places for quiet time or entertaining guests in the great outdoors. A warming fireplace, with windows on each side, is the focal point of the great room and the dining area. The master bedroom is located on the first floor and directly accesses the full bathroom. A galley kitchen leads directly to the dining room. One family bedroom is nested in the second floor. Please specify basement, crawlspace or slab foundation when ordering.

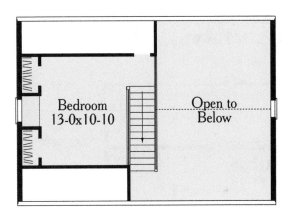

Bedroom
13-0x10-10

Open to
Below

PLAN HPT210052

First Floor: 720 sq. ft.
Second Floor: 203 sq. ft.
Total: 923 sq. ft.

Width: 32'-0"
Depth: 38'-6"

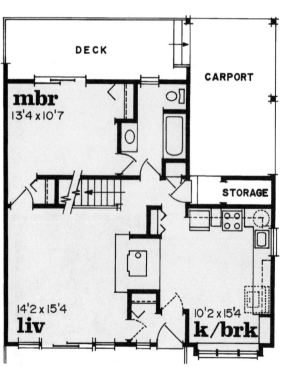

DECK

CARPORT

mbr
13'4 x 10'7

STORAGE

14'2 x 15'4
liv

10'2 x 15'4
k/brk

br2
9'5 x 9'

br3
9'4 x 12'6

BONUS RM.

PLAN HPT210053

First Floor: 843 sq. ft.
Second Floor: 340 sq. ft.
Total: 1,183 sq. ft.
Bonus Room: 217 sq. ft.

Width: 32'-4"
Depth: 44'-1"

This country-style vacation home is economical to build and offers additional space for future development. A bonus room of 217 square feet may be used as an extra bedroom, a playroom or a media center. The front veranda opens to a living room with a wood stove and vaulted ceiling. The master bedroom is on the first floor for privacy and has its own deck, accessed through sliding glass doors, and the use of a full hall bath. Note the storage room just beyond the carport. Family bedrooms are on the second floor, as is the bonus room.

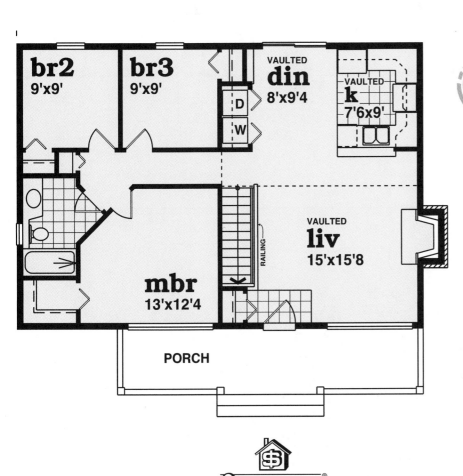

br2
9'x9'

br3
9'x9'

VAULTED
din
8'x9'4

VAULTED
k
7'6x9'

D

W

VAULTED
liv
15'x15'8

RAILING

mbr
13'x12'4

PORCH

PLAN HPT210054

Square Footage: 988

Width: 38'-0"
Depth: 32'-0"

This economical, compact home is the ultimate in efficient use of space. The central great room features a cozy fireplace and outdoor access to the front porch. A U-shaped kitchen serves both a dining area and a breakfast bar. Sliding glass doors lead from the kitchen/dining area to the rear. The front entry is sheltered by a casual country porch, which also protects the living-room windows. The master bedroom has a walk-in closet and shares a full bath with the secondary bedrooms. A single or double garage may be built to the side or to the rear of the home.

QUOTE ONE®
Cost to build? See page 246
to order complete cost estimate
to build this house in your area!

69

PLAN HPT210055

Square Footage: 1,541

Width: 87'-0"
Depth: 44'-0"

This popular design begins with a wraparound covered porch made even more charming with turned-wood spindles. The entry opens directly to the great room, which is warmed by a wood stove. The adjoining dining room offers access to a screened porch for outdoor after-dinner leisure. A country kitchen features a center island and a breakfast bay for casual meals. Family bedrooms share a full bath that features a soaking tub. The two-car garage connects to the plan via the screened porch.

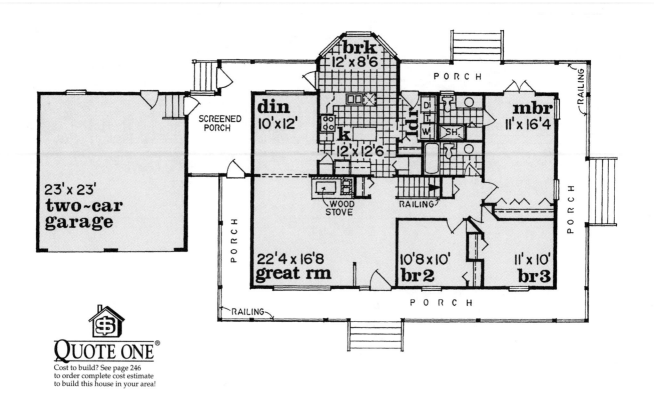

QUOTE ONE®

Cost to build? See page 246
to order complete cost estimate
to build this house in your area!

PLAN HPT210056

Square Footage: 1,668

Width: 70'-4"
Depth: 47'-4"

The wraparound porch and standing-seam roof design make this traditional style called "Cracker" a long-time favorite. The simplicity of the design is what gives it its charm and enduring quality. The living room is perfect for large family gatherings—as is the formal dining room with a view of the front porch. The split floor plan places the master suite to the left of the plan, with a walk-in closet, a private bath and a private entrance to the garage. Two family bedrooms—both with walk-in closets—share a roomy bath on the opposite end of the plan.

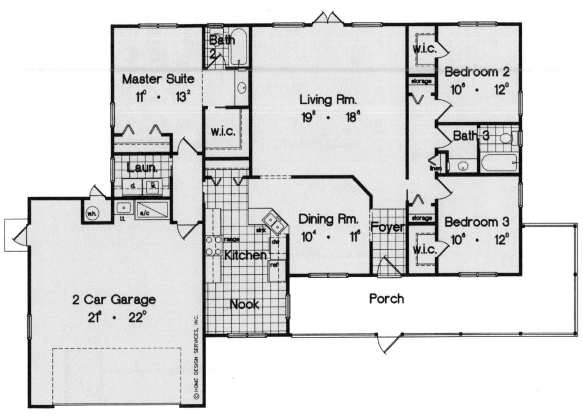

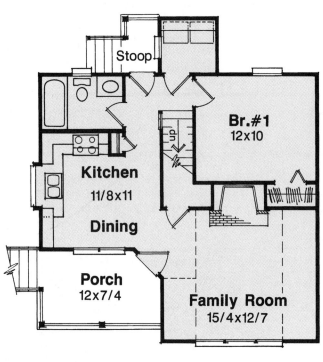

Stoop

Br.#1
12x10

up

Kitchen
11/8x11

Dining

Porch
12x7/4

Family Room
15/4x12/7

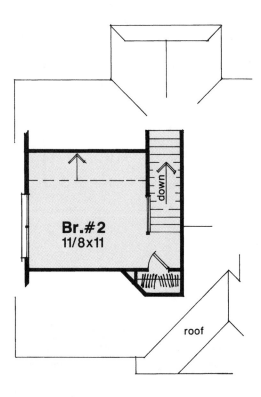

down

Br.#2
11/8x11

roof

PLAN HPT210057

Square Footage: 828

Width: 28'-0"

Depth: 32'-0"

This cozy two-bedroom plan makes the most of a narrow lot. Its exterior is distinguished by large expanses of windows, a hip-roof dormer and a side-access covered porch. The family room offers a brick fireplace, great views through huge windows and a sloped ceiling. The L-shaped kitchen is open to a casual dining area. Either of the bedrooms, which share a downstairs full bath, would serve well as an office or study. The backyard of this home offers a stoop area just off of the kitchen for those summer nights when sitting outside and enjoying the breeze is all that matters.

This adorable abode could serve as a vacation cottage, guest house, starter home or in-law quarters. The side-gabled design allows for a front porch with a "down-South" feel. Despite the small size, this home is packed with all the necessities. The first-floor master bedroom has a large bathroom—with a clawfoot tub!—and a walk-in closet and is ideal for older guests or family members. An open, functional floor plan includes a powder room, a kitchen/breakfast nook area and a family room with a corner fireplace. Upstairs, two additional bedrooms share a bath. One could be used as a home office.

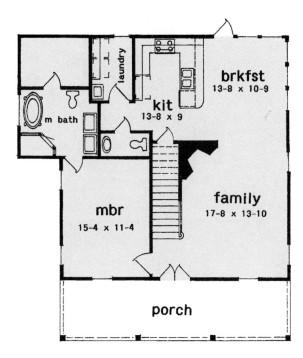

laundry

brkfst
13-8 x 10-9

kit
13-8 x 9

m bath

family
17-8 x 13-10

mbr
15-4 x 11-4

porch

PLAN HPT210058

First Floor: 1,050 sq. ft.
Second Floor: 458 sq. ft.
Total: 1,508 sq. ft.

Width: 35'-6"
Depth: 39'-9"

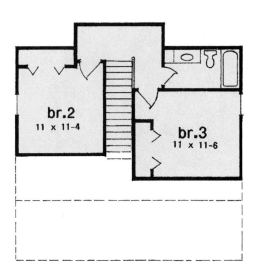

br.2
11 x 11-4

br.3
11 x 11-6

PLAN HPT210059

First Floor: 1,136 sq. ft.
Second Floor: 636 sq. ft.
Total: 1,772 sq. ft.

Width: 41'-9"
Depth: 45'-0"

L

This two-story home's pleasing exterior is complemented by its warm character and decorative "widow's walk." The covered entry—with its dramatic transom window—leads to a spacious great room highlighted by a warming fireplace. To the right, the dining room and kitchen combine to provide a delightful place for mealtimes, with access to a side sun deck through double doors. Two bedrooms and a full bath complete the first floor. The luxurious master suite on the second floor features an oversized walk-in closet and a separate dressing area. The pampering master bath enjoys a relaxing whirlpool tub, double-bowl vanity and compartmented toilet. Please specify slab or pier foundation when ordering.

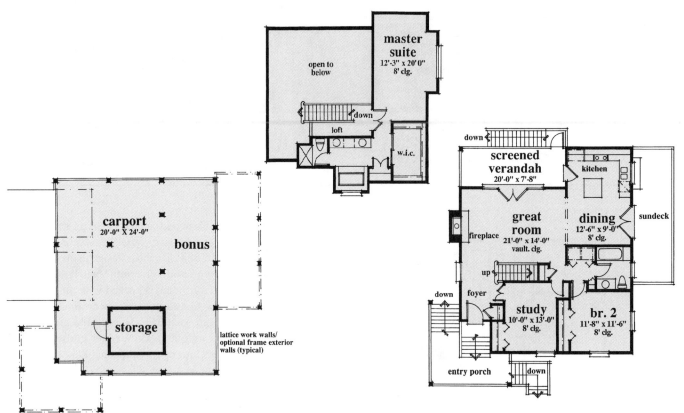

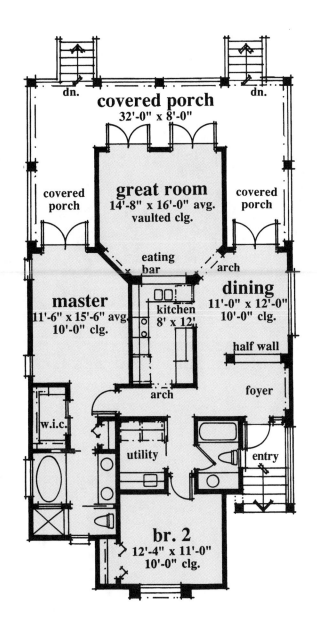

covered porch
32'-0" x 8'-0"

dn.　　　　　　　dn.

great room
14'-8" x 16'-0" avg.
vaulted clg.

covered
porch

covered
porch

eating
bar

arch

master
11'-6" x 15'-6" avg.
10'-0" clg.

dining
11'-0" x 12'-0"
10'-0" clg.

kitchen
8' x 12'

half wall

foyer

arch

w.i.c.

utility

entry

br. 2
12'-4" x 11'-0"
10'-0" clg.

PLAN HPT210060

Square Footage: 1,288

Width: 32'-4"
Depth: 60'-0"

Welcome home to casual, unstuffy living with this comfortable Tidewater design. Asymmetrical lines celebrate the turn of the new century, and blend a current Gulf Coast style with vintage panache brought forward from its regional past. The heart of this home is the great room, where a put-your-feet-up atmosphere prevails, and the dusky hues of sunset can mingle with the sounds of ocean breakers. French doors open the master suite to a private area of the covered porch, where sunlight and sea breezes mingle with a spirit of bon vivant.

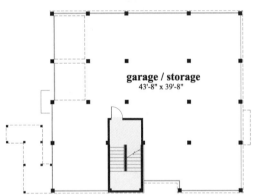

garage / storage
43'-8" x 39'-8"

open deck
17'-0" x 10'-6"

bedroom
13'-8" x 12'-0"
12' clg.

open

loft

bath

bedroom
10'-0" x 13'-2"
12' clg.

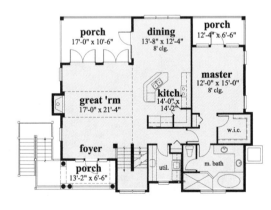

porch
17'-0" x 10'-6"

dining
13'-8" x 12'-4"
8' clg.

porch
12'-4" x 6'-6"

great 'rm
17'-0" x 21'-4"

kitch
14'-0" x
14'-2"

master
12'-0" x 15'-0"
8' clg.

w.i.c.

foyer

porch
13'-2" x 6'-6"

util.

m. bath

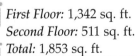

PLAN HPT210061

First Floor: 1,342 sq. ft.
Second Floor: 511 sq. ft.
Total: 1,853 sq. ft.

Width: 44'-0"
Depth: 40'-0"

Detailed fretwork complements a standing-seam roof on this tropical cottage. An arch-top transom provides an absolutely perfect highlight to the classic clapboard facade. An unrestrained floor plan offers cool digs for kicking back, and a sensational retreat for guests—whether the occasion is formal or casual. French doors open to a rear porch from the great room letting in fresh air and the sights and sounds of the great outdoors. Inside, the master bedroom leads to a dressing space with linen storage and a walk-in closet. The lavish bath includes a garden tub, oversized shower and a wraparound vanity with two lavatories. Two secondary bedrooms on the upper level share a spacious loft that overlooks the great room. One of the bedrooms opens to a private deck.

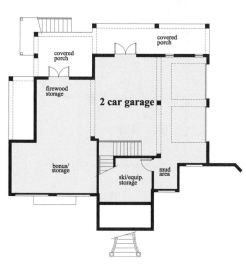

covered porch

covered porch

firewood storage

2 car garage

bonus/ storage

ski/equip. storage

mud area

deck

porch

covered porch

porch

fireplace

br. 3
11'-6" x 12'-0"
10'-0"h. clg.

great room
15'-0" x 19'-6"
vaulted clg.

dining
11'-0" x 12'-8"
11'-0" tray clg.

built ins

kitchen
11'-0" x 12'-0"

br. 2
12'-10" x 12'-0"
10'-0"h. clg.

up

stor.

util.

up
foyer

entry

porch

master suite
12'-8" x 17'-8"
10'-0" tray clg.

open to below

w.i.c.

overlook

dn

master bath

dn

porch

PLAN HPT210062

First Floor: 1,383 sq. ft.
Second Floor: 595 sq. ft.
Total: 1,978 sq. ft.

Width: 48'-0"
Depth: 48'-8"

The stone facade and woodwork detail give this home a Craftsman appeal. The foyer opens to a staircase up to the vaulted great room, which features a fireplace flanked by built-ins and French-door access to the rear covered porch. The open dining room with a tray ceiling offers convenience to the spacious kitchen. Two family bedrooms share a bath and enjoy private porches. An overlook to the great room below is a perfect introduction to the master suite. The second level spreads out master-suite luxury with a spacious walk-in closet, private porch and a glorious master bath with a garden tub, dual vanities and compartmented toilet.

Plan HPT210063

First Floor: 797 sq. ft.

Second Floor: 886 sq. ft.

Total: 1,683 sq. ft.

Width: 44'-0"

Depth: 34'-5"

The front of this home creates an inviting feel with its full front porch and gabled accents. The combination of brick and siding mixed with metal roof accents adds interest. The dramatic angled staircase in the two-story foyer increases the sense of space. A spacious living area that's open to the breakfast nook and kitchen opens up the entire rear of the house. Create an herb garden in the corner window of the kitchen sink. Upstairs, two secondary bedrooms share a vanity area which opens to a private commode and tub room. The master bath features a garden tub, His and Her vanities and a commode closet. Please specify basement, crawlspace or slab foundation when ordering.

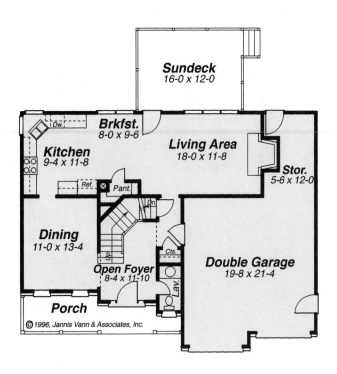

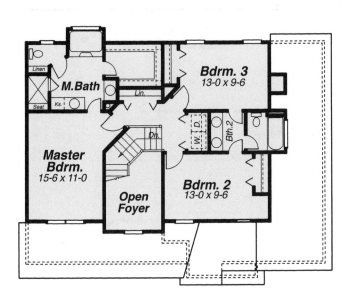

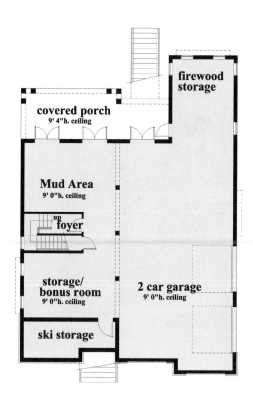
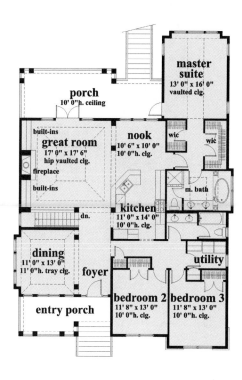

covered porch
9' 4" h. ceiling

firewood storage

Mud Area
9' 0" h. ceiling

up
foyer

storage/
bonus room
9' 0" ceiling

2 car garage
9' 0" h. ceiling

ski storage

porch
10' 0" h. ceiling

master suite
13' 0" x 16' 0"
vaulted clg.

built-ins

great room
17' 0" x 17' 6"
hip vaulted clg.

fireplace

built-ins

nook
10' 6" x 10' 0"
10' 0" h. clg.

wic

wic

m. bath

kitchen
11' 0" x 14' 0"
10' 0" h. clg.

dn.

dining
11' 0" x 13' 0"
11' 0" h. tray clg.

foyer

utility

bedroom 2
11' 8" x 13' 0"
10' 0" h. clg.

bedroom 3
11' 8" x 13' 0"
10' 0" h. clg.

entry porch

PLAN HPT210064

Square Footage: 2,137

Width: 44'-0"

Depth: 63'-0"

The horizontal lines and straightforward details of this rustic plan borrow freely from the Arts and Crafts style, remembered with a dash of traditional warmth. Gallery porches open the indoors to nature, and classy windows add plenty of wide views. Clustered sleeping quarters ramble across the opposite side of the main level, while the kitchen and nook at the heart of the home bring people together for easy meals and conversation. The master retreat is all decked out with a wall of glass, two walk-in closets and generous dressing space. The two-car garage leaves plenty of space for bicycles.

KITCHEN
15'-2" x 9'-0"

W
D

DINE

HVAC

PR

UP

LIVING ROOM
15'-2" x 11'- 3"

PORCH
16'-0" x 10'-0"

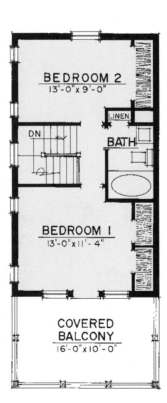

BEDROOM 2
13'-0" x 9'-0"

LINEN

DN

BATH

BEDROOM 1
13'-0" x 11'- 4"

COVERED
BALCONY
16'-0" x 10'-0"

PLAN HPT210065

First Floor: 448 sq. ft.
Second Floor: 448 sq. ft.
Total: 896 sq. ft.

Width: 16'-0"
Depth: 41'-6"

Perfect for a lakeside, vacation or starter home, this two-story design is sure to be a favorite. A large railed porch on the first floor and the covered balcony on the second floor are available for watching the sunrise. On the first floor, the spacious living room is convenient to the kitchen and dining area. A powder room finishes off this level. Upstairs, the sleeping zone consists of two bedrooms, each with roomy closets, and a full hall bath with a linen closet. The front bedroom accesses the balcony.

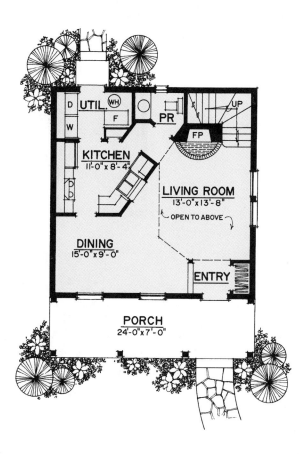

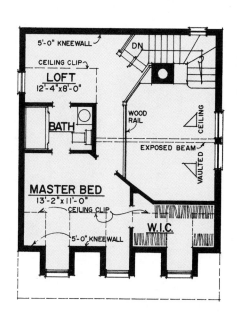

The steep rooflines on this home offer a sophisticated look that draws attention. Three dormers flood the home with light. The covered porch adds detailing to the posts. The entry leads to the two-story living room complete with a fireplace. The dining room is quite spacious and contains convenient access to the kitchen where a pantry room and plenty of country space make cooking a treat in this home. The stairs to the second floor wrap around the fireplace and take the homeowners to the master bedroom and loft area.

PLAN HPT210066

First Floor: 576 sq. ft.
Second Floor: 489 sq. ft.
Total: 1,065 sq. ft.

Width: 24'-0"
Depth: 31'-0"

PLAN HPT210067

First Floor: 820 sq. ft.
Second Floor: 350 sq. ft.
Total: 1,170 sq. ft.

Width: 37'-0"
Depth: 67'-0"

This home is distinguished by its two prominent dormers—one facing the front and the other on the left side. The dormer to the left boasts a sunburst window, which spills light into the family room. Enter through a large covered porch to a foyer that looks into the family room. Beyond, a vaulted kitchen/nook area is graced with an abundance of windows and rear-door access. The master bedroom is located at the front of the plan and is graced with a full bath. On the second floor are two additional bedrooms, each with ample closet space.

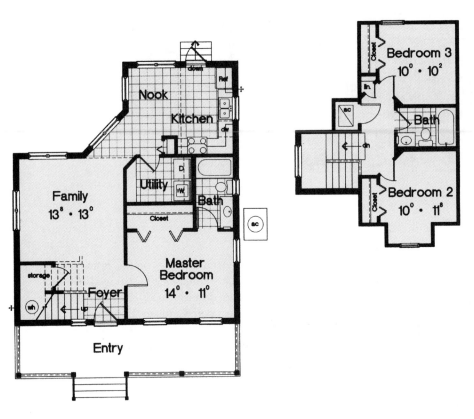

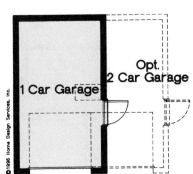

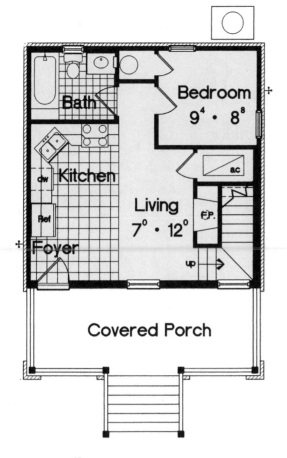

Covered Porch

PLAN HPT210068

Square Footage: 484 sq. ft.
Bonus Room: 220 sq. ft.

Width: 22'-0"
Depth: 30'-0"

A single dormer and a covered porch with rails invite you into an adorable home made for two. Immediately upon entry is a tiled L-shaped kitchen which opens to the cozy living room. In the living room, a fireplace awaits company or quiet evenings spent at home. The main bedroom is located in the left rear corner of the home; directly across is a full, tiled bath. Up the small staircase, near the fireplace, is a bonus room that's perfect for either an additional bedroom or extra storage space.

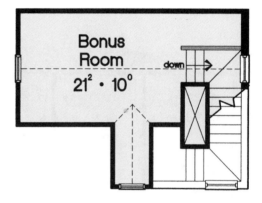

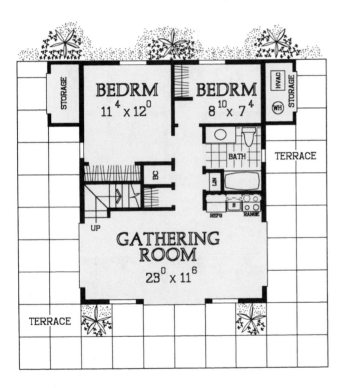

STORAGE

BEDRM
11⁴ x 12⁰

BEDRM
8¹⁰ x 7⁴

HVAC

STORAGE

WH

BATH

TERRACE

BC

LIN

S

REFG

RANGE

UP

GATHERING
ROOM
23⁰ x 11⁶

TERRACE

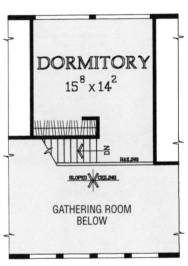

DORMITORY
15⁸ x 14²

DN

RAILING

SLOPED CEILING

GATHERING ROOM
BELOW

Quote One®

Cost to build? See page 246
to order complete cost estimate
to build this house in your area!

Plan HPT210069

First Floor: 784 sq. ft.
Second Floor: 275 sq. ft.
Total: 1,059 sq. ft.

Width: 32'-0"
Depth: 30'-0"

LD

This chalet-type vacation home, with its steep, overhanging roof, will catch the eye of even the most casual onlooker. It is designed to be completely livable whether it's the season for swimming or skiing. The dormitory on the upper level will sleep many vacationers, while the two bedrooms on the first floor provide the more convenient and conventional sleeping facilities. The upper level overlooks the beam-ceilinged living and dining area. With a wraparound terrace and plenty of storage space, this is a perfect design.

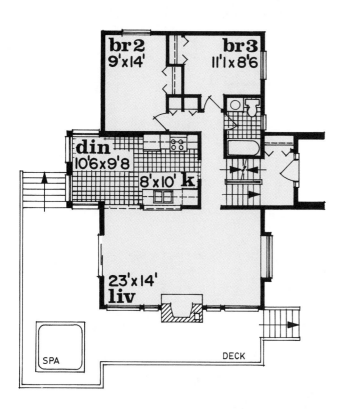

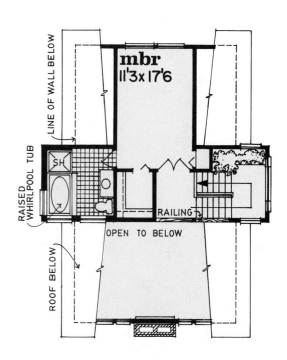

PLAN HPT210070

Main Level: 1070 sq. ft.
Upper Level: 552 sq. ft.
Total: 1,622 sq. ft.

Width: 38'-0"
Depth: 40'-0"

An expansive wall of glass, rising to the roof's peak, adds architectural interest and gives the living room of this home a spectacular view. The living room also boasts a vaulted ceiling, an oversized masonry fireplace and has access to a deck with a wonderful spa tub. The dining room is nearby, directly across from the galley-style kitchen. Two bedrooms sit to the rear of the plan and share a full bath. The second-level master suite caters to comfort with a walk-in closet, spa tub and separate shower. Note how the open-rail staircase winds to the gallery on the second floor and overlooks the living room below.

PLAN HPT210071

Main Level: 896 sq. ft.
Lower Level: 100 sq. ft.
Total: 996 sq. ft.

Width: 28'-0"
Depth: 32'-0"

This home is truly a study in symmetry and perfection. The facade is unique with its siding, octagon-shaped window and two symmetrical side porches on either end of the plan. The lower level is devoted to garage and storage space; steps lead upstairs to the main living quarters. Flanking the stairway on the left is a living room and on the right is an informal dining room and kitchen area, complete with plenty of counter space. Two bedrooms of equal size possess ample closet space, share a full bath and exit to their own private decks and outdoor access.

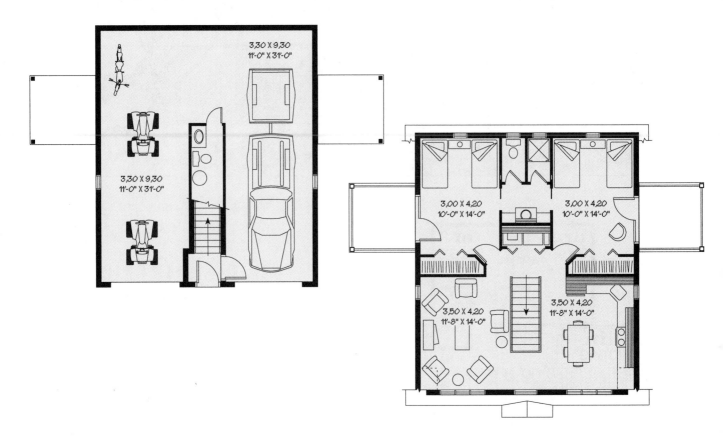

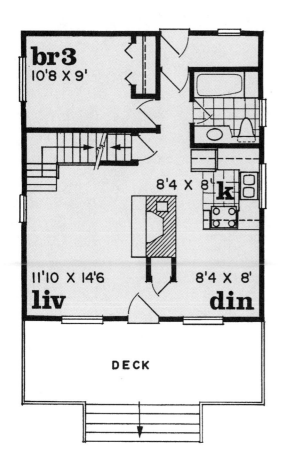

br3
10'8 X 9'

8'4 X 8' **k**

liv
11'10 X 14'6

din
8'4 X 8'

DECK

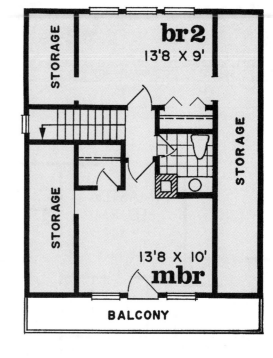

STORAGE

br2
13'8 X 9'

STORAGE

STORAGE

13'8 X 10'
mbr

BALCONY

This chalet plan is enhanced by a steep gable roof, scalloped fascia boards and fieldstone chimney detail. The front-facing deck and covered balcony add to outdoor living spaces. The fireplace is the main focus in the living room. The bedroom on the first floor has the use of a full hall bath. A storage/mudroom at the back is perfect for keeping skis and boots. Two additional bedrooms and a full bath occupy the second floor. The master bedroom contains a walk-in closet. Three storage areas are also found on the second floor.

PLAN HPT210072

First Floor: 672 sq. ft.
Second Floor: 401 sq. ft.
Total: 1,073 sq. ft.

Width: 24'-0"
Depth: 36'-0"

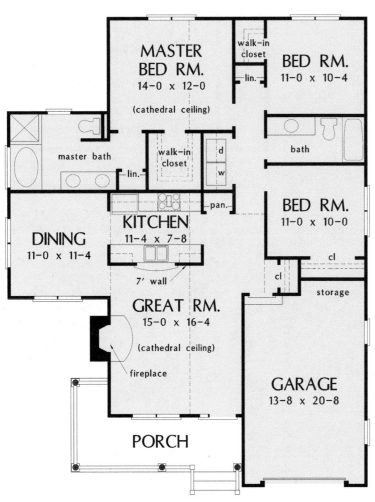

MASTER
BED RM.
14-0 x 12-0

(cathedral ceiling)

walk-in
closet

BED RM.
11-0 x 10-4

lin.

master bath

walk-in
closet

lin.

d

w

bath

pan.

KITCHEN
11-4 x 7-8

BED RM.
11-0 x 10-0

DINING
11-0 x 11-4

7' wall

cl

cl

storage

GREAT RM.
15-0 x 16-4

(cathedral ceiling)

fireplace

GARAGE
13-8 x 20-8

PORCH

PLAN HPT210073

Square Footage: 1,350

Width: 41'-0"
Depth: 51'-8"

A covered front porch welcomes both family and friends to this attractive three-bedroom home. Inside, the great room features a cathedral ceiling, warming fireplace and a pass-through to the kitchen. The kitchen easily serves the adjacent formal dining room, which provides plenty of space to enjoy company or a quiet family dinner. Two family bedrooms share a hall bath to the right of the plan. The master suite includes a private bath and a walk-in closet.

COVERED PORCH RETREAT

GREAT ROOM
17⁰ x 16⁴
SLOPED CEILING

MASTER SUITE
12⁸ x 14²
SLOPED CLG

KIT
10⁰ x 12²
9'-0" CLG

SNACK BAR

PANTRY

BATH

LOW WALL

PLANT SHELF ABOVE

LINEN

W D

LAUNDRY

WALK-IN CLOSET

DINING RM
10⁰ x 11⁰
COFFERED CLG

FOYER

BEDRM/ MEDIA
12⁸ x 11⁰
9'-0" CLG

MASTER BATH

GARDEN TUB

SHELF

SHWR

COVERED PORCH

RAILING

SLPNG CLG

STEP

SHELF

2-CAR GARAGE
19⁸ x 21⁰

QUOTE ONE®
Cost to build? See page 246
to order complete cost estimate
to build this house in your area!

PLAN HPT210074

Square Footage: 1,295

Width: 48'-0"
Depth: 59'-0"

L D

Equally gracious outside and inside, this one- or two-bedroom cottage has a post-and-rail covered porch hugging one wing, with convenient access through double doors or pass-through windows in the dining room and kitchen. The columned entry foyer has a sloped ceiling and leads past a second bedroom or media room into a great room with a sloped ceiling, fireplace and low wall along the staircase to the attic. The master suite fills the right wing and features a plant shelf in the bedroom and a garden tub in the master bath, plus a large walk-in closet and laundry facilities.

PLAN HPT210075

Square Footage: 1,273

Width: 40'-8"

Depth: 59'-0"

L D

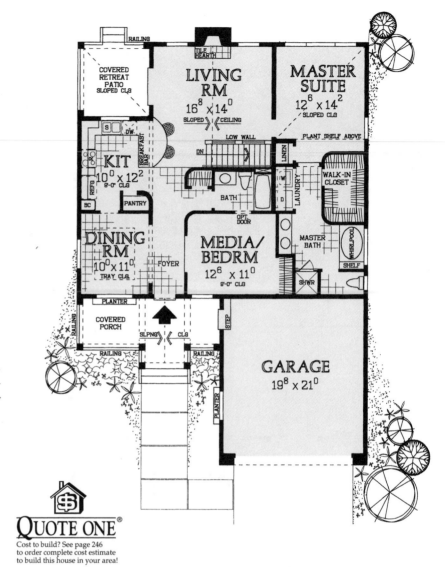

For those just starting out or for the empty-nester, this unique one-story plan is sure to delight. A covered porch introduces a dining room with views to the front and side properties. The kitchen just off this room is most efficient with a double sink and pantry. The living room gains attention with a volume ceiling, fireplace and access to a covered patio. The master bedroom also features a volume ceiling while enjoying the luxury of a walk-in closet, washer/dryer, double-bowl vanity, garden tub, separate shower and compartmented toilet. A second bedroom may easily convert to a media room or study—the choice is yours.

QUOTE ONE®

Cost to build? See page 246
to order complete cost estimate
to build this house in your area!

Romance, charm, exquisite details and the flavor of an era when life seemed more simple—Victorian-influenced cottages not only bring the past to life, they do it with a style all their own. With gingerbread trim, gazebo porches, fancy window finishes and varied rooflines, a Victorian-influenced cottage has plenty to offer, whether you build it in a mountain clearing, on an open prairie or deep in the heart of suburbia. What's presented here is a mixture of styles—Gothic, American Folk Victorian and fashionable Queen Anne—as well as a mixture of sizes—from under 900 square feet to just over 2,200 square feet.

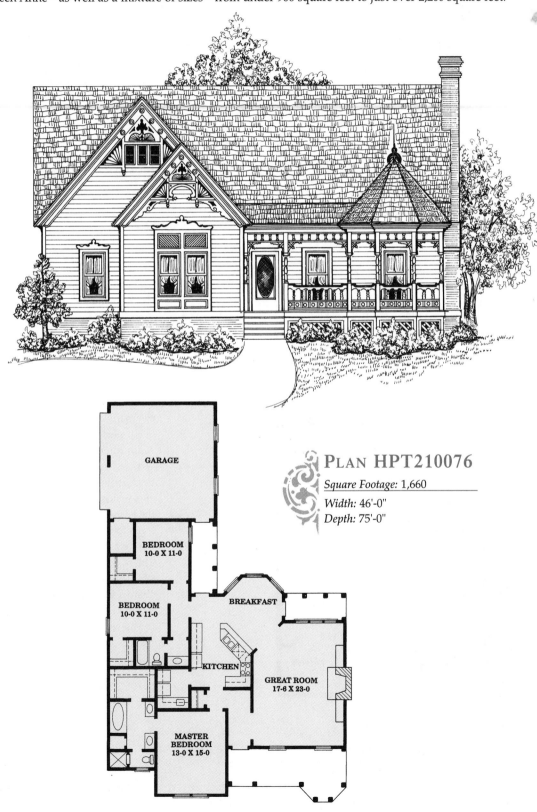

PLAN HPT210076

Square Footage: 1,660

Width: 46'-0"
Depth: 75'-0"

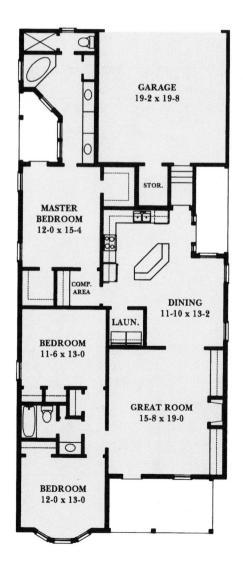

GARAGE
19-2 x 19-8

STOR.

MASTER
BEDROOM
12-0 x 15-4

COMP.
AREA

DINING
11-10 x 13-2

LAUN.

BEDROOM
11-6 x 13-0

GREAT ROOM
15-8 x 19-0

BEDROOM
12-0 x 13-0

PLAN HPT210077

Square Footage: 1,666

Width: 32'-0"
Depth: 75'-6"

This adorable Victorian is a perfect starter home. Enter directly into the great room with a fireplace and built-ins. Immediately following is the dining area which gracefully combines with the island kitchen. A computer area leads to the master bedroom featuring a walk-in closet and deluxe bath. The two family bedrooms are accessible through a secluded hall and share a full hall bath that includes a compartmented sink. The garage to the rear of the home provides an area for storage.

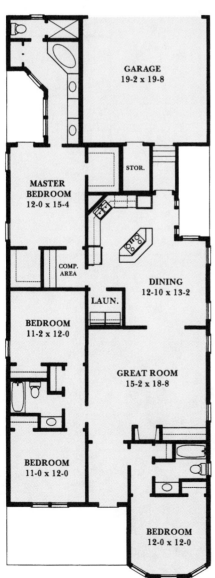

PLAN HPT210078

Square Footage: 1,949

Width: 32'-0"
Depth: 86'-0"

With a narrow width, this country cottage works well on almost any lot. The rooms inside are thoughtfully arranged and make a smaller space seem quite spacious. A bedroom lies just off the main entry and, as it features a private bath, would make a great guest suite. Family bedrooms and the master suite line the left side of the plan. Living areas include a great room with a fireplace, a dining area and a kitchen with an island cooktop. A laundry niche is found near the entry to the master suite—note the computer area here. Reach the garage via a service entry in the kitchen. A large storage space broadens the garage's usefulness.

PLAN HPT210079

First Floor: 593 sq. ft.
Second Floor: 383 sq. ft.
Total: 976 sq. ft.

Width: 22'-8"
Depth: 26'-8"

A stunning arch-top window sets off this charming European cottage. An angled entry and open planning allow a sense of spaciousness from the moment one enters the home. A voluminous bedroom on this floor adjoins a full bath. The staircase leads to a second-floor mezzanine, which overlooks the living area and may be used as a study area or an extra bedroom. This home is designed with a basement foundation.

2,80 X 3,10
9'-4" X 10'-4"

2,40 X 4,30
8'-0" X 14'-4"

3,90 X 3,60
13'-0" X 12'-0"

3,00 X 7,20
10'-0" X 24'-0"

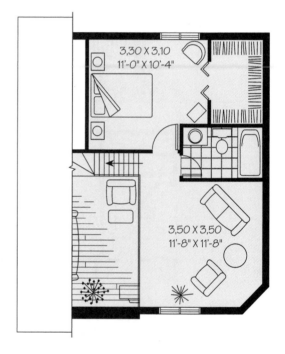

3,30 X 3,10
11'-0" X 10'-4"

3,50 X 3,50
11'-8" X 11'-8"

PLAN HPT210080

Square Footage: 958

Width: 30'-0"
Depth: 35'-4"

This sweet Folk Victorian cottage, decorated with a bit of gingerbread trim, features a unique bayed foyer with a generously sized coat closet. Additional windows—the elegant arched window in the front bedroom and four tall windows in the family room—fill this design with natural light. The family room adjoins a skylit kitchen, which provides a compact pantry, opens to a dining room and offers sliding glass doors to the backyard. Two bedrooms, both with long wall closets, share a bath that includes an angled vanity, corner shower and comfortable tub. This home is designed with a basement foundation.

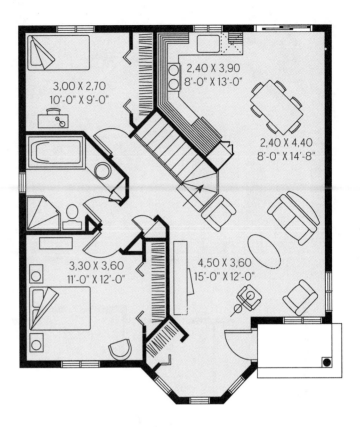

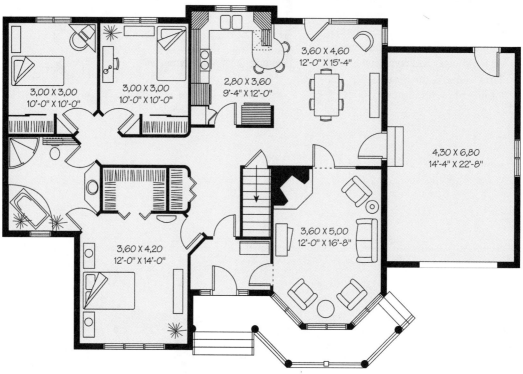

3,00 X 3,00
10'-0" X 10'-0"

3,00 X 3,00
10'-0" X 10'-0"

2,80 X 3,60
9'-4" X 12'-0"

3,60 X 4,60
12'-0" X 15'-4"

4,30 X 6,80
14'-4" X 22'-8"

3,60 X 4,20
12'-0" X 14'-0"

3,60 X 5,00
12'-0" X 16'-8"

PLAN HPT210081

Square Footage: 1,336

Width: 58'-0"
Depth: 36'-0"

The covered porch wraps around the turret, giving this home an inviting look. The bright Palladian window floods the master bedroom with natural light. The living room boasts a fireplace, making this room the perfect gathering area. The L-shaped kitchen is connected to the dining room and offers a rounded bar area. The dining room accesses the backyard. Each family bedroom holds ample closet space. The master bedroom privately accesses the family bath and features a spacious walk-in closet. This home is designed with a basement foundation.

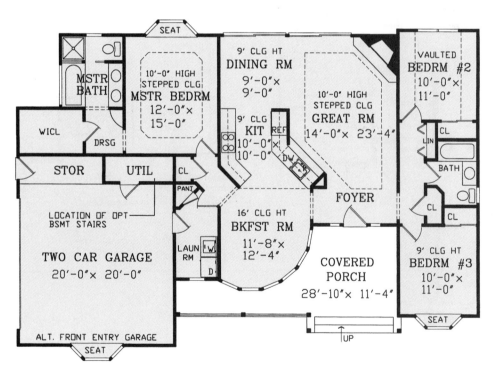

PLAN HPT210082

Square Footage: 1,466

Width: 60'-0"
Depth: 39'-10"

This absolutely charming Victorian-style ranch home is warm and inviting, yet the interior is decidedly up-to-date. An assemblage of beautiful windows surrounds the main entry, flooding the entrance foyer and adjoining great room with an abundance of shaded light. An elegant ten-foot stepped ceiling is featured in the great room, as is a corner fireplace and rear wall of French-style sliding doors. The beautiful multi-sided breakfast room features a sixteen-foot ceiling adorned with high clerestory windows, which become the exterior "turret." A private master suite includes a compartmented bath, dressing alcove, very large walk-in closet, ten-foot stepped ceiling and beautiful bay window overlooking the rear.

PLAN HPT210083

Square Footage: 2,277

Width: 87'-10"
Depth: 46'-10"

This Victorian farmhouse exterior features siding, brick and a long front porch to enjoy long summer evenings. The large brick entry leads into a huge living room with a fireplace and built-ins. A formal dining room or study has doors leading to the front porch. Doors off the breakfast room open to a covered patio to the rear of the plan. All bedrooms feature walk-in closets with the master suite enjoying His and Hers walk-in closets, plus a large bath with a garden tub and a stall shower.

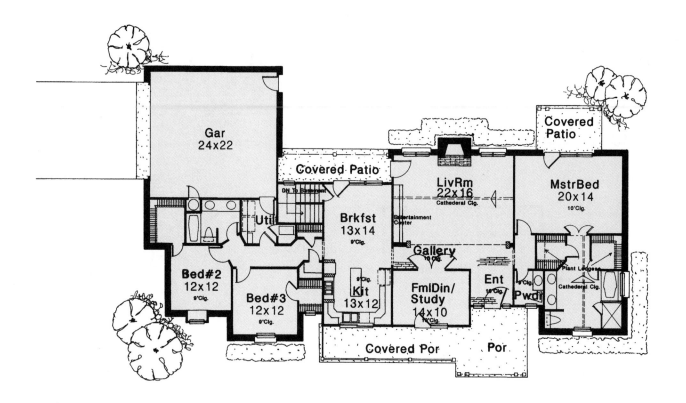

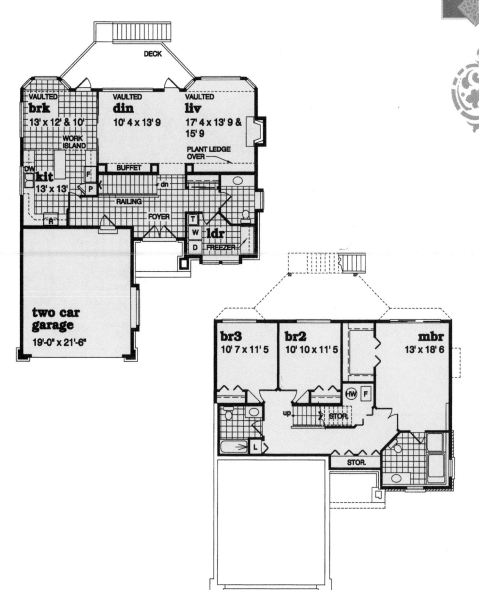

PLAN HPT210084

Main Level: 1,128 sq. ft.
Lower Level: 1,092 sq. ft.
Total: 2,220 sq. ft.

Width: 42'-0"
Depth: 46'-8"

Beautiful Craftsman accents are evident in this design, perfect for a sloping lot. A double-door entry opens off a covered porch to an impressive vaulted foyer. Living areas to the back manifest in vaulted living and dining rooms. The living room boasts a bay window and a fireplace. Access to the deck sits between the living and dining rooms. The L-shaped kitchen features an island work space and vaulted breakfast bay with deck access. The laundry area to the front of the house contains a half-bath. Stairs to the lower level are found in the foyer. Sleeping quarters are found below—two family bedrooms and a master suite. The master suite includes a walk-in closet and a bath with a separate tub and shower. Family bedrooms share a full bath.

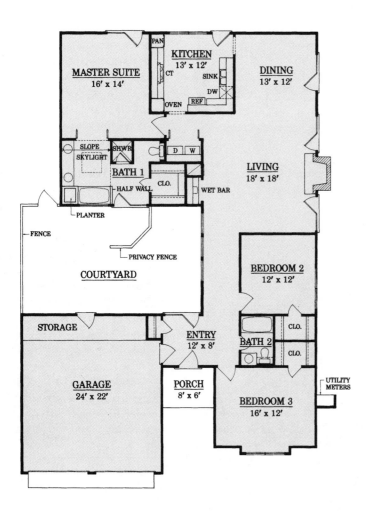

MASTER SUITE
16' x 14'

KITCHEN
13' x 12'

PAN

CT

SINK

DW

OVEN

REF

DINING
13' x 12'

SLOPE
SKYLIGHT

SHWR

BATH 1

CLO.

D

W

HALF WALL

WET BAR

LIVING
18' x 18'

PLANTER

FENCE

PRIVACY FENCE

COURTYARD

BEDROOM 2
12' x 12'

STORAGE

ENTRY
12' x 8'

BATH 2

CLO.

CLO.

GARAGE
24' x 22'

PORCH
8' x 6'

BEDROOM 3
16' x 12'

UTILITY
METERS

PLAN HPT210085

Square Footage: 1,732

Width: 46'-0"
Depth: 66'-0"

Simple Victorian detailing marks the exterior of this interesting plan. The interior surrounds a private court-yard. The entry leads to the two-car garage, the courtyard and two family bedrooms and their shared bath. Each bedroom is equipped with a walk-in closet. French doors accent the remainder of the home; they are found in the master bedroom, in the dining area and on each side of the living-room fireplace. A wet bar in the living room ensures successful entertaining. The master bath is a garden retreat with access to the courtyard and a planter inside next to the garden tub. A skylight brings in natural light to this incredible room. Please specify crawlspace or slab foundation when ordering.

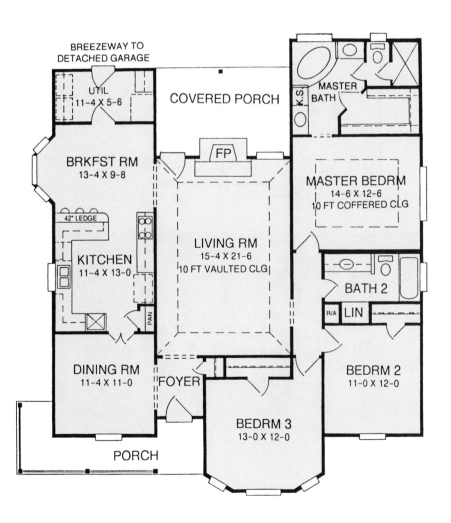

BREEZEWAY TO DETACHED GARAGE

UTIL
11-4 X 5-6

COVERED PORCH

MASTER BATH

K.S.

BRKFST RM
13-4 X 9-8

FP

MASTER BEDRM
14-6 X 12-6
10 FT COFFERED CLG

42" LEDGE

KITCHEN
11-4 X 13-0

LIVING RM
15-4 X 21-6
10 FT VAULTED CLG

PAN

BATH 2

R/A LIN

DINING RM
11-4 X 11-0

FOYER

BEDRM 2
11-0 X 12-0

BEDRM 3
13-0 X 12-0

PORCH

PLAN HPT210086

Square Footage: 1,772
Width: 45'-8"
Depth: 50'-2"

A Folk Victorian flair gives this home its curb appeal. Inside, a large living room boasts a centerpiece fireplace and a coffered ceiling. The kitchen has a 42-inch-high breakfast bar and a pantry. The master suite includes a ten-foot coffered ceiling and a luxury bath with a corner whirlpool tub, separate shower, His and Hers vanities and a roomy walk-in closet. Two additional bedrooms and a bath are nearby. A two-car garage plan is included with this design and can be connected to the home with a breezeway. Please specify crawlspace or slab foundation when ordering.

PLAN HPT210087

Square Footage: 1,029

Width: 34'-6"
Depth: 32'-6"

An overall sense of warmth is demonstrated in this traditional cottage. Large picture windows flood the great room and master suite with natural light. The open plan offers a spacious great room that is perfect for quality family time. The L-shaped kitchen offers a snack bar and access to the backyard. Bedrooms 2 and 3 include individual closets and window light to illuminate the interior. The master suite features a spacious walk-in closet and shares a compartmented bath with the family bedrooms. Please specify crawlspace or slab foundation when ordering.

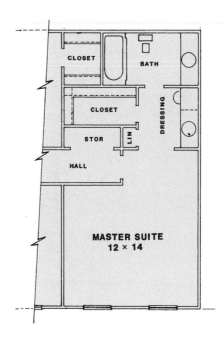

PLAN HPT210088

Square Footage: 947
Expansion Space: 392 sq. ft.

Width: 37'-0"
Depth: 33'-0"

Intricate detailing makes this petite cottage a treat. Symmetrical styling offers a sense of country warmth with the covered porch. The open living room is attached to the U-shaped kitchen and dining room. The dining room accesses the rear porch and its storage space. The rear porch will be a great way to relax in the great outdoors. The master bedroom and family bedroom share a bath and both rooms have their own closet space. The future expansion converts the master suite into a family bedroom and adds a master retreat with a spacious private bath, adding 392 square feet to the total.

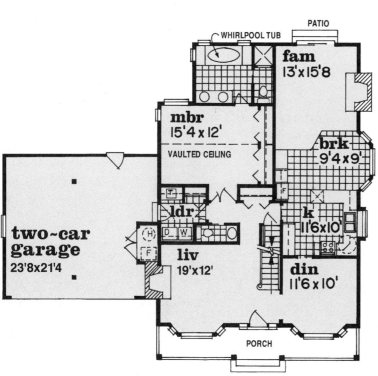

WHIRLPOOL TUB

PATIO

fam
13'x15'8

mbr
15'4 x 12'

VAULTED CEILING

brk
9'4 x 9'

two~car garage
23'8x21'4

ldr

liv
19'x12'

k
11'6x10'

din
11'6 x 10'

PORCH

Traditional accents and a covered porch lend charm to this Victorian home. The entry opens to a living room with a fireplace and a dining room. The U-shaped kitchen opens to an attached breakfast bay, which leads to the family room. A fireplace and sliding glass doors to the rear yard are highlights of the family room. The master bedroom is appointed with a vaulted ceiling and a private bath with a whirlpool tub. Three family bedrooms on the second floor share a full bath. Bonus space can be developed later into an additional bedroom, a media center or a game room.

PLAN HPT210089

First Floor: 1,360 sq. ft.
Second Floor: 734 sq. ft.
Total: 2,094 sq. ft.
Bonus Room: 378 sq. ft.

Width: 56'-0"
Depth: 48'-0"

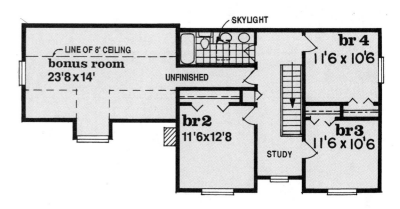

SKYLIGHT

LINE OF 8' CEILING

bonus room
23'8 x 14'

UNFINISHED

br 4
11'6 x 10'6

br 2
11'6 x12'8

STUDY

br3
11'6 x 10'6

PATIO

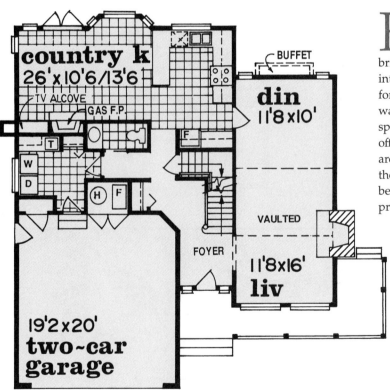

country k
26'x10'6/13'6

TV ALCOVE

GAS F.P

BUFFET

din
11'8x10'

VAULTED

FOYER

11'8x16'
liv

19'2x20'
two-car
garage

F

ish-scale siding and a covered porch with graceful arched woodwork provide stunning curb appeal for this three-bedroom home. The vaulted foyer is brightened by a distinctive second-story bay and spills into the living room and adjoining dining room. These formal areas are graced by a vaulted ceiling and share the warmth of the fireplace in the living room. Optional buffet space is available in the dining room. The country kitchen offers a U-shaped preparation area, a bay-windowed eating area, a gas fireplace, a TV alcove and a double door to the rear yard. Second-floor bedrooms include two family bedrooms with a shared bath and a master suite with a private bath.

PLAN HPT210090

First Floor: 963 sq. ft.
Second Floor: 753 sq. ft.
Total: 1,716 sq. ft.

Width: 45'-0"
Depth: 44'-0"

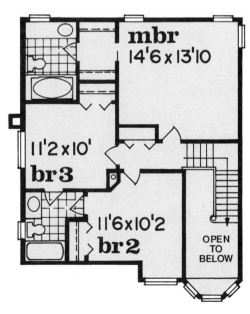

mbr
14'6 x 13'10

11'2 x 10'
br3

11'6 x 10'2
br2

OPEN
TO
BELOW

PLAN HPT210091

First Floor: 949 sq. ft.
Second Floor: 633 sq. ft.
Total: 1,582 sq. ft.

Width: 40'-3"
Depth: 40'-6"

Front and rear porches and bay windows lend this three-bedroom home Victorian flavor. Inside, the entry leads to the formal dining room with a bay window, and the living room. The kitchen adjoins both the formal and informal dining areas and is open to the living room via a snack bar. The informal eating area opens to the screened porch, expanding the living space to the outdoors. On the right of the first floor is a bedroom with a walk-in closet and full bath—perfect for a guest room or possibly an optional master suite. Upstairs, a family bedroom and a master bedroom share a full bath.

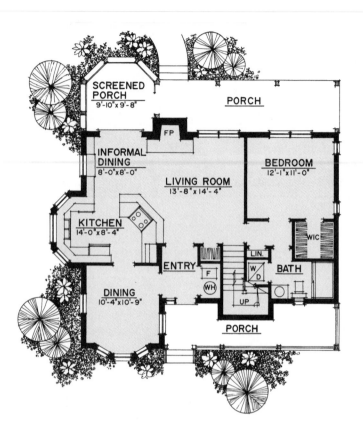

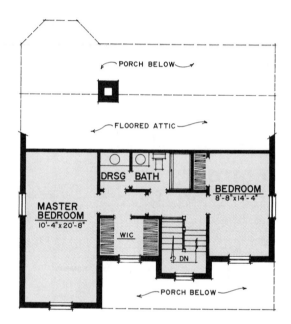

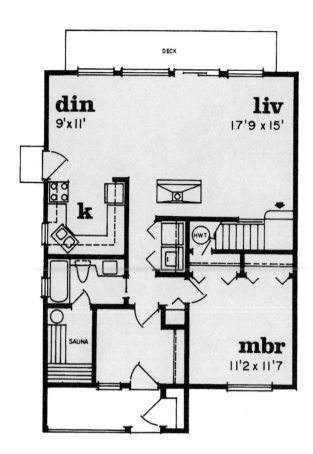

din
9'x11'

liv
17'9 x 15'

k

mbr
11'2 x 11'7

SAUNA

DECK

HWT

PLAN HPT210092

First Floor: 922 sq. ft.
Second Floor: 683 sq. ft.
Total: 1,605 sq. ft.

Width: 27'-7"
Depth: 39'-5"

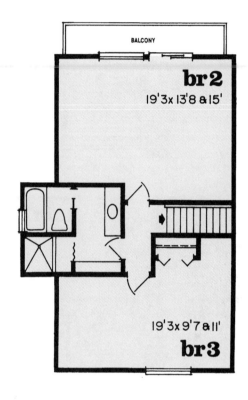

BALCONY

br2
19'3x 13'8 & 15'

19'3x9'7 a 11'

br3

This charming cottage is the perfect size and configuration for a leisure-time home. A weather-protected entry opens to a mudroom and serves as a storage space and air-lock. The gathering area is comprised of a living room and a dining room and is warmed by a wood-burning stove. An entire wall of glass with sliding doors opens to a rear deck. The master bedroom is on the first floor and features a main-floor bath with an attached sauna. Two bedrooms and a full bath are on the second floor. Bedroom 2 has a private balcony.

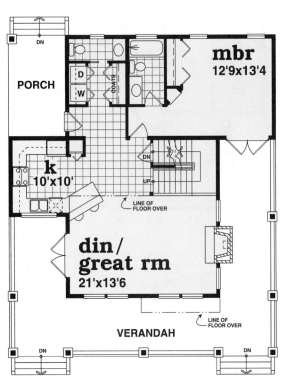

PORCH

DN

D
W

COATS

k
10'x10'

mbr
12'9x13'4

DN

UP

LINE OF
FLOOR OVER

**din/
great rm**
21'x13'6

LINE OF
FLOOR OVER

VERANDAH

DN

DN

br3
10'4x10'2

br2
10'4x11'2

DN

RAILING

**OPEN TO
GREAT ROOM
BELOW**

PLANT LEDGE

QUOTE ONE®
Cost to build? See page 246
to order complete cost estimate
to build this house in your area!

PLAN HPT210093

First Floor: 995 sq. ft.
Second Floor: 484 sq. ft.
Total: 1,479 sq. ft.

Width: 38'-0"
Depth: 44'-0"

What an appealing plan! Its rustic character is defined by cedar lattice, covered columned porches, exposed rafters and multi-pane, double-hung windows. The great room/dining room combination is reached through double doors off the veranda and features a fireplace towering two stories to the lofty ceiling. A U-shaped kitchen contains an angled snack counter that serves this area and loads of space for a breakfast table—or use the handy side porch for alfresco dining. To the rear resides the master bedroom with a full bath and double doors to the veranda. An additional half-bath sits just beyond the laundry room. Upstairs, two family bedrooms and a full bath finish the plan.

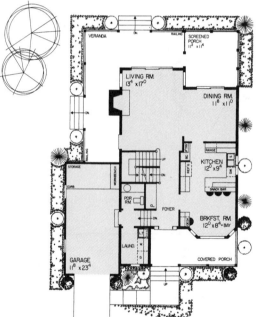

QUOTE ONE®

Cost to build? See page 246
to order complete cost estimate
to build this house in your area!

PLAN HPT210094

First Floor: 911 sq. ft.
Second Floor: 861 sq. ft.
Bonus Room: 884 sq. ft.
Total: 1,772 sq. ft.

Width: 38'-0"
Depth: 52'-0"

L

Victorian houses are well known for their orientation on narrow building sites. At only 38 feet wide, this home still offers generous style and comfort. Beautiful arched glass panels, skylights and large double-hung windows allow natural light to fill this home, giving a golden glow to oak and maple hardwood floors and trim. From the covered front porch, the foyer leads to the open living and dining rooms, with an extended-hearth fireplace and access to both the veranda and the screened porch. The U-shaped kitchen conveniently serves both the dining room and the bayed breakfast room. Sleeping quarters on the second floor include a master suite, plus two family bedrooms that share a full bath.

Plan HPT210095

First Floor: 880 sq. ft.
Second Floor: 880 sq. ft.
Total: 1,760 sq. ft.
Bonus Room: 256 sq. ft.

Width: 42'-0"
Depth: 40'-0"

This Country Victorian design comes loaded with charm and amenities. The entry leads to open living space, defined by a two-sided fireplace and a large bay window. An island counter with a snack bar highlights the L-shaped kitchen. A quiet sitting area opens to the outdoors. The master suite allows plenty of sunlight from the turret's bay window and boasts a step-up tub, dual vanities and separate shower. Bonus space above the garage offers 256 square feet for future expansion. This home is designed with a basement foundation.

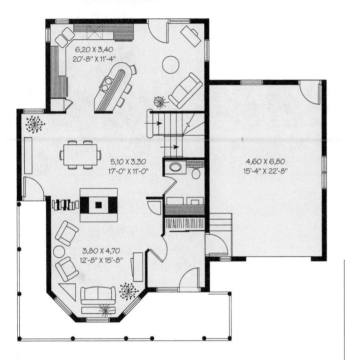

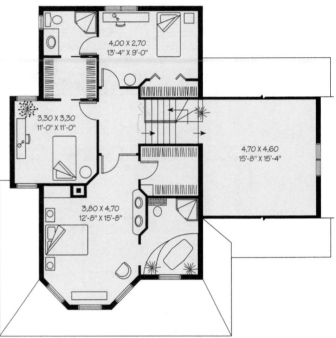

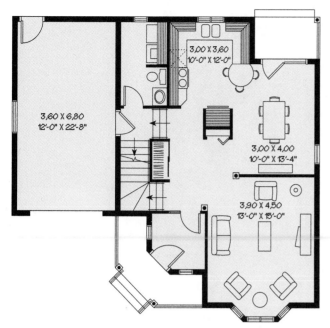

3,60 X 6,80
12'-0" X 22'-8"

3,00 X 3,60
10'-0" X 12'-0"

3,00 X 4,00
10'-0" X 13'-4"

3,90 X 4,50
13'-0" X 15'-0"

PLAN HPT210096

First Floor: 770 sq. ft.
Second Floor: 810 sq. ft.
Total: 1,580 sq. ft.
Bonus Room: 180 sq. ft.

Width: 38'-0"
Depth: 35'-0"

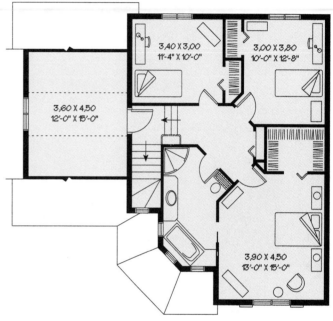

3,40 X 3,00
11'-4" X 10'-0"

3,00 X 3,80
10'-0" X 12'-8"

3,60 X 4,50
12'-0" X 15'-0"

3,90 X 4,50
13'-0" X 15'-0"

This lovely two-story home draws heavily on the Queen Anne period with the covered porch that encompasses the lower half of the nested tower. The living room contains plenty of space for quality family time. The spacious kitchen conveniently accesses the dining room. Two family bedrooms are located upstairs. The master bedroom accesses the second-floor bath with an efficient pocket door. This home is designed with a basement foundation.

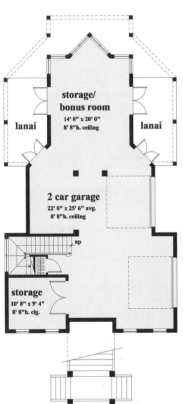

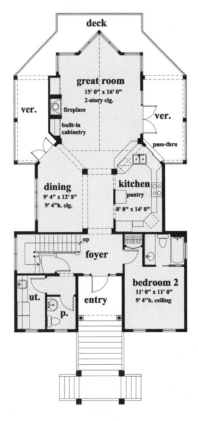

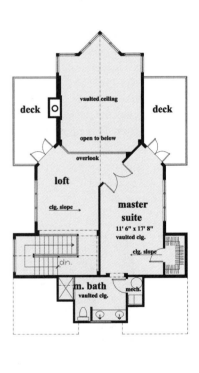

storage/
bonus room
14' 8" x 20' 0"
8' 8"h. ceiling

lanai

lanai

2 car garage
22' 0" x 25' 6" avg.
8' 8"h. ceiling

up

storage
10' 8" x 9' 4"
8' 8"h. clg.

deck

great room
15' 0" x 16' 0"
2-story clg.

ver.

ver.

fireplace

built-in
cabinetry

pass-thru

dining
9' 4" x 12' 8"
9' 4" clg.

kitchen

pantry

8' 8" x 14' 0"

up

foyer

bedroom 2
11' 0" x 11' 0"
9' 4"h. ceiling

ut.

p.

entry

deck

vaulted ceiling

deck

open to below

overlook

loft

master
suite
11' 6" x 17' 8"
vaulted clg.

clg. slope

clg. slope

dn.

m. bath
vaulted clg.

mech.

PLAN HPT210097

First Floor: 1,143 sq. ft.
Second Floor: 651 sq. ft.
Total: 1,794 sq. ft.

Width: 32'-0"
Depth: 57'-0"

This intriguing home is full of elegant Victorian detail and many amenities. Beyond the grand staircase and central foyer are the living areas; on the left is the dining room and on the right is the kitchen, which provides plenty of counter space and a pantry. The great room includes a fireplace and built-in cabinets. French doors in the great room and a second set in the dining room each lead to their own veranda and around to the rear deck. Towards the front of the first floor is a family bedroom with a private bath, a utility room and a powder room. The master suite (with a master bath) and a loft open to the great room below and dominate the second floor.

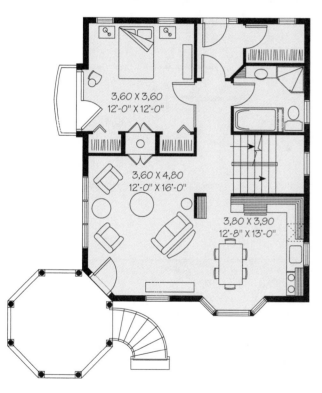

PLAN HPT210098

First Floor: 840 sq. ft.
Second Floor: 757 sq. ft.
Total: 1,597 sq. ft.

Width: 26'-0"
Depth: 32'-0"

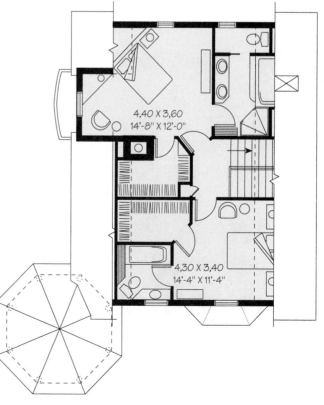

This amazing turret/gazebo porch has an authentic Victorian flavor. Exceptional details align this classic view. The bedroom on the first level offers a protruding balcony which adds appeal both inside and outside this beautiful home. The entrance leads to the living room, located just left to the dining area and L-shaped kitchen. The master suite features a walk-in closet and a private bath with dual sinks. Two more family bedrooms are located on the second level.

113

PLAN HPT210099

First Floor: 772 sq. ft.
Second Floor: 411 sq. ft.
Total: 1,183 sq. ft.

Width: 32'-0"
Depth: 28'-7"

This petite Gothic Revival cottage, with a steeply pitched roof, dormers and pointed-arch windows, would be perfect as a vacation or starter home. A large covered front porch is available for entertaining and relaxing, while the living room, warmed by a fireplace, offers access to a covered side porch. The U-shaped kitchen shares space with a cozy dining area. A boxed window allows natural light into the front bedroom, which is conveniently close to a bath. Upstairs, another bedroom, this one with a walk-in closet, accesses a full bath and overlooks the living room.

114

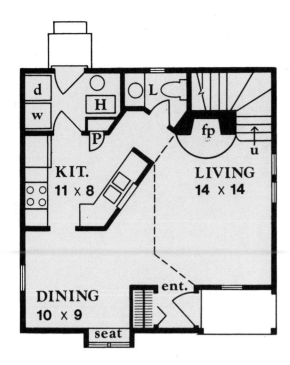

PLAN HPT210100

First Floor: 547 sq. ft.
Second Floor: 418 sq. ft.
Total: 965 sq. ft.

Width: 24'-0"
Depth: 25'-4"

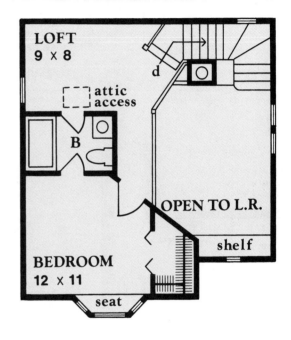

Graceful, curving gingerbread trim transforms this cozy cottage into a Carpenter Gothic-style confection. From the steep gable roof and appropriately detailed ornamentation on the outside, to the snug yet well-planned interior, this design is packed with vintage charm. A soaring two-story living room with a balcony overlook dominates the first floor. The fireplace and stair are combined into one unique architectural feature. The dining room has a cozy window seat; the kitchen offers a handy pass-through to the living area. Upstairs, the master bedroom enjoys an elaborate bay window and a walk-in closet. The sleeping loft, which can be enclosed for a second bedroom, shares a bathroom with the master bedroom.

PLAN HPT210101

First Floor: 448 sq. ft.
Second Floor: 448 sq. ft.
Total: 896 sq. ft.

Width: 16'-0"
Depth: 28'-0"

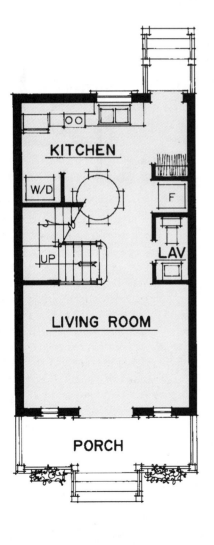

KITCHEN

W/D

F

UP

LAV

LIVING ROOM

PORCH

BEDROOM 2

LIN.

BATH

DN

BEDROOM 1

This petite Carpenter Gothic charmer would make an ideal vacation or starter home. The exterior boasts a heavy wood-shingled roof, board-and-batten siding and scroll-sawn detailing. A well-planned interior is simplicity itself: a double-door entry leads to an open living, dining and kitchen area. The kitchen is hidden from the living room by a stairway and a half-bath. Nine-foot ceilings highlight the second floor, which contains two bed-rooms—each with plenty of closet space—and a paneled bathroom.

PLAN HPT210102

First Floor: 836 sq. ft.
Second Floor: 481 sq. ft.
Total: 1,317 sq. ft.

Width: 38'-2"
Depth: 34'-0"

This sweet lakeside cottage is sure to please with its quaint charm and convenient floor plan. A covered porch greets family and friends and offers a place to sit and enjoy the summer breezes. Inside, the living room—with its warming fireplace—flows nicely into the kitchen/dining area. A snack bar, pantry and plenty of cabinet and counter space are just some of the features found here. The first-floor master suite includes a bay window, walk-in closet and private bath. Upstairs, two bedrooms share a bath and linen closet.

117

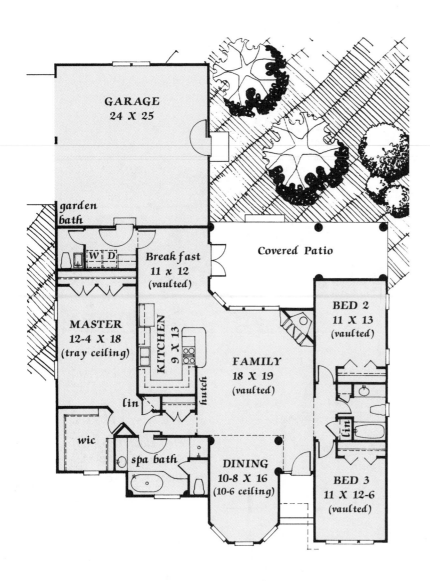

GARAGE
24 X 25

garden
bath

W D

Breakfast
11 x 12
(vaulted)

Covered Patio

MASTER
12-4 X 18
(tray ceiling)

KITCHEN
9 X 13

hutch

FAMILY
18 X 19
(vaulted)

BED 2
11 X 13
(vaulted)

lin

lin

wic

spa bath

DINING
10-8 X 16
(10-6 ceiling)

BED 3
11 X 12-6
(vaulted)

PLAN HPT210103

Square Footage: 1,897

Width: 53'-0"
Depth: 74'-0"

Elements of country charm adorn this lovely cottage, including shutters, keystone lintels, a dormer window, a spire and a bay window. Inside, the open floor plan allows for comfortable living and includes plenty of amenities, such as built-in cabinets, French doors and a main-floor master suite. Two vaulted family bedrooms share a full bath. A bayed dining room and a corner fireplace in the family room add the finishing touches to this petite home.

Classically modest, usually with a brick or siding facade, the traditional-style cottage features a sturdiness that encourages you to leave your worries at the door. Suitable for either the relaxed, laid-back attitude of the country or the more active urban setting, traditional cottages come in a large variety of flavors. Sharp and spiffy, with a combination of brick and siding on its facade, or more relaxed with simple horizontal siding, this collection of cottages is sure to meet your every need. Sizes range from 873 square feet to 2,208 square feet.

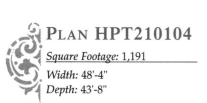

PLAN HPT210104

Square Footage: 1,191

Width: 48'-4"
Depth: 43'-8"

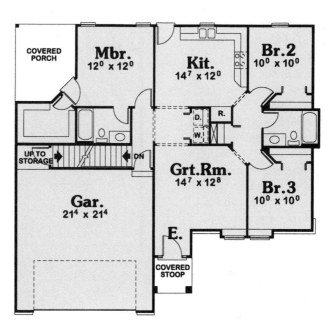

PLAN HPT210105

Square Footage: 1,392

Width: 42'-0"
Depth: 54'-0"

With an unusually narrow footprint, this one-story home will fit on most slender lots and still provide a great floor plan. The entry is graced with a handy coat closet and leads back to the spacious great room (note the ten-foot ceiling here) and to the right to two family bedrooms and a full bath. Stairs to the basement level are found just beyond the entry hall. The breakfast room and kitchen dominate the left side of the plan. Separating them is a snack-bar counter for quick meals. Pampered amenities in the secluded master bedroom include a walk-in closet, windowed corner whirlpool tub, dual sinks and a separate shower. A service entrance through the kitchen to the garage leads to a convenient laundry area and broom closet.

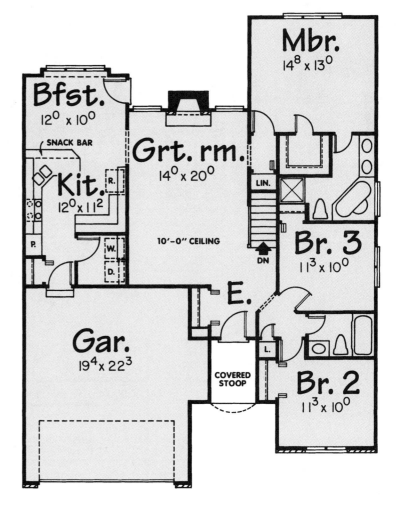

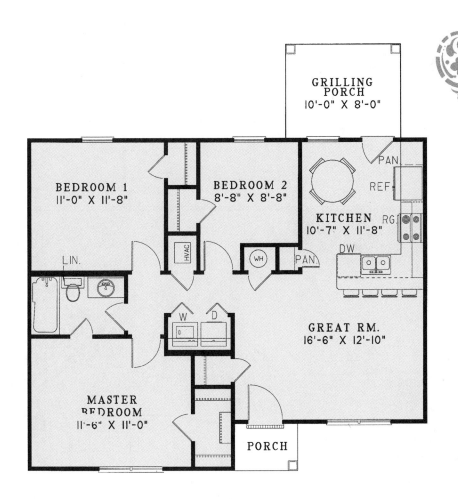

GRILLING PORCH
10'-0" X 8'-0"

BEDROOM 1
11'-0" X 11'-8"

BEDROOM 2
8'-8" X 8'-8"

KITCHEN
10'-7" X 11'-8"

PAN
REF
RG
DW

LIN.

HVAC

WH

PAN

W D

GREAT RM.
16'-6" X 12'-10"

MASTER BEDROOM
11'-6" X 11'-0"

PORCH

PLAN HPT210106

Square Footage: 930

Width: 35'-0"
Depth: 28'-6"

This petite cottage spends much of its time waiting for visitors, as it could be easily kept in your family's favorite vacation spot. The vacation time spent in it is well worth the wait. The large great room makes quality family time enjoyable. The L-shaped kitchen acts as a dining room after the food has been prepared. It opens to a grilling porch in the backyard. Two family bedrooms and a master suite comprise the sleeping area of the cottage. Please specify crawlspace or slab foundation when ordering.

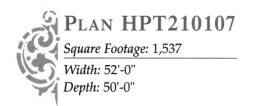

PLAN HPT210107

Square Footage: 1,537

Width: 52'-0"
Depth: 50'-0"

This ranch-style home possesses a dramatic open layout. Vaulted ceilings in the foyer and living room welcome you into this home. The living room features a fireplace surrounded by vast windows. This area flows smoothly into the dining area and then into the kitchen, which offers an eating bar and pantry. Just off the kitchen is a well-organized laundry room. Additionally, there are two spacious bedrooms and a master suite. Included in the master suite is a sensible master bath and a roomy walk-in closet. The large windows in the master bedroom allow radiant light into this room. Also offered in this home is another full bath and extra storage room.

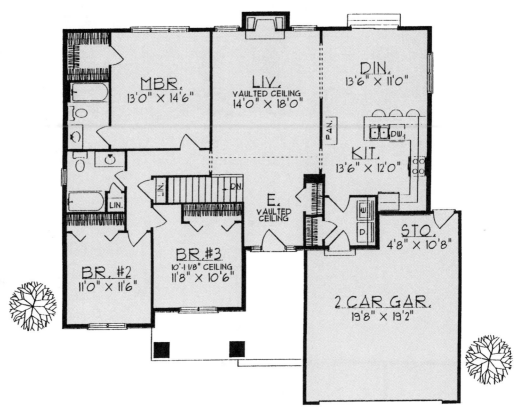

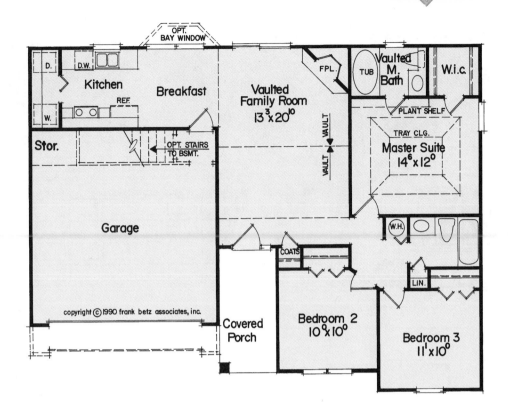

Floor plan labels:

- OPT. BAY WINDOW
- D.
- D.W.
- Kitchen
- Breakfast
- FPL
- TUB
- Vaulted M. Bath
- W.i.c.
- REF.
- W.
- Vaulted Family Room 13³ x 20¹⁰
- VAULT
- PLANT SHELF
- TRAY CLG.
- Stor.
- OPT. STAIRS TO BSMT.
- Master Suite 14⁶ x 12⁰
- Garage
- W.H.
- copyright © 1990 frank betz associates, inc.
- COATS
- LIN.
- Covered Porch
- Bedroom 2 10⁹ x 10⁰
- Bedroom 3 11' x 10⁰

PLAN HPT210108

Square Footage: 1,070

Width: 48'-0"
Depth: 36'-0"

This modest home takes a creative look at space to design an efficient floor plan that's comfortable yet compact. The vaulted family room has a lovely corner fireplace and sliding glass doors to the rear yard. A galley kitchen is designed for efficiency and includes a hidden laundry center and a window over the sink. The breakfast room offers an optional bay window. The master suite has a tray ceiling and a large walk-in closet. Two family bedrooms and a hall bath round out the plan. Please specify basement, crawlspace or slab foundation when ordering.

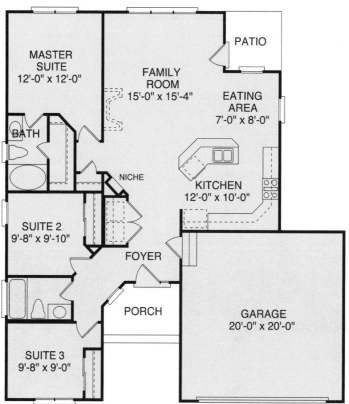

MASTER
SUITE
12'-0" x 12'-0"

FAMILY
ROOM
15'-0" x 15'-4"

PATIO

EATING
AREA
7'-0" x 8'-0"

BATH

NICHE

KITCHEN
12'-0" x 10'-0"

SUITE 2
9'-8" x 9'-10"

FOYER

SUITE 3
9'-8" x 9'-0"

PORCH

GARAGE
20'-0" x 20'-0"

PLAN HPT210109

Square Footage: 1,204

Width: 43'-1"

Depth: 47'-1"

This lovely three-bedroom, one-story home is a perfect choice for first-time homeowners. Two suites share a full bath, while the master suite provides a walk-in closet. The family room offers an optional fireplace along with a niche to display your treasures. The island kitchen serves both the eating area and the family room with ease, making entertaining a breeze. Laundry facilities are hidden out of view. A rear patio expands the living area to the outdoors. A two-car garage completes this home.

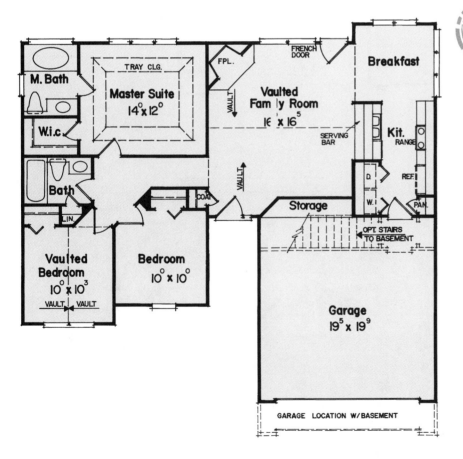

PLAN HPT210110

Square Footage: 1,104

Width: 46'-6"
Depth: 41'-0"

A simple yet classic facade, this plan is ideal for a family just starting out or for empty-nesters who want a little extra space. The entrance leads to a vaulted family room—complete with a fireplace and French door— which shares a serving bar with the kitchen. The kitchen leads to a cozy breakfast area that's provided with plenty of windows. The left side of the plan is devoted solely to sleeping quarters. The master suite is graced with a tray ceiling, while one of the other bedrooms boasts a vaulted ceiling, lending it a spacious air. Two full baths are shared amongst the three bedrooms. Please specify basement, crawlspace or slab foundation when ordering.

PLAN HPT210111

First Floor: 1,168 sq. ft.
Second Floor: 498 sq. ft.
Total: 1,666 sq. ft.

Width: 44'-0"
Depth: 44'-0"

This two-story home is just the right thing for starting a family. The foyer opens to the luxurious living room with a cozy fireplace surrounded by built-in cabinets. Sliding doors in the dining area are a perfect escape to the backyard. The kitchen, open to the dining area, offers a unique use of space with the appliances around the perimeter. A first-floor master bedroom is ideal for a getaway. Two additional bedrooms upstairs contain ample closet space and share a full bath. Upstairs or down, this two-story home is packed with features.

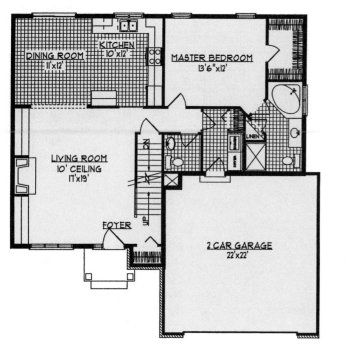

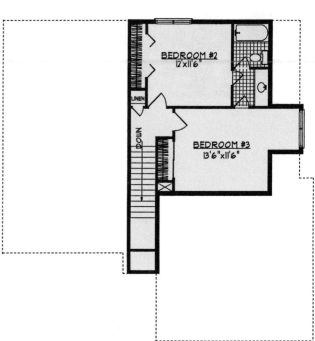

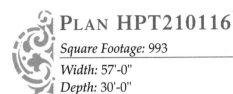

PLAN HPT210116

Square Footage: 993

Width: 57'-0"
Depth: 30'-0"

Cozy and refined, this home boasts a distinguished pediment, window shutters and lintels. Within, a vaulted family room—fireplace included—greets you and leads further into the kitchen and dining area. The kitchen is graced with a door that leads to storage space directly off the garage. The dining room has a vaulted ceiling and rear-door access. The master suite is unique with its tray ceiling and His and Hers walk-in closets. Bedrooms 2 and 3 share a full bath and sport front-facing windows. Please specify basement, crawlspace or slab foundation when ordering.

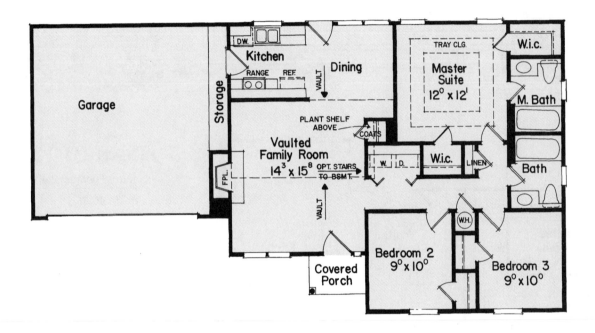

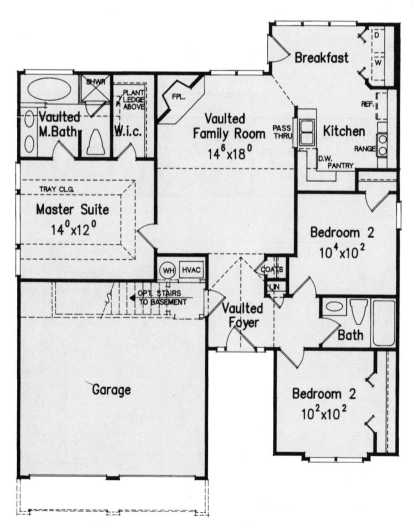

PLAN HPT210117

Square Footage: 2,479

Width: 40'-0"
Depth: 49'-6"

Though compact in size, this plan offers interesting details and well-chosen amenities. Both the family room and foyer feature vaulted ceilings, and the master bedroom has a lovely tray ceiling. A corner fireplace and pass-through counter to the kitchen further enhance the family room. Enjoy a cup of coffee in the well-lit breakfast room and relax while doing the laundry—washer/dryer space is conveniently located nearby. There are two family bedrooms, but you may choose to use one as a den or study. These bedrooms are separated by a full bath. The master suite has its own full bath with a vaulted ceiling, separate tub and shower, and compartmented toilet. Please specify basement, crawlspace or slab foundation when ordering.

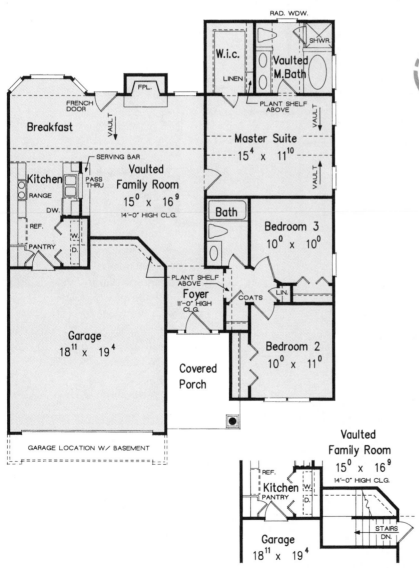

RAD. WDW.

W.i.c.

SHWR.

Vaulted M.Bath

LINEN

FPL.

FRENCH DOOR

Breakfast

VAULT

PLANT SHELF ABOVE

Master Suite
15⁴ x 11¹⁰

VAULT

SERVING BAR

Kitchen

RANGE

PASS THRU

Vaulted Family Room
15⁰ x 16⁹
14'-0" HIGH CLG.

DW.

Bath

REF.

W.
D.

Bedroom 3
10⁰ x 10⁰

PANTRY

PLANT SHELF ABOVE

Foyer
11'-0" HIGH CLG.

COATS

LIN.

Garage
18¹¹ x 19⁴

Bedroom 2
10⁰ x 11⁰

Covered Porch

GARAGE LOCATION W/ BASEMENT

Vaulted Family Room
15⁰ x 16⁹
14'-0" HIGH CLG.

REF.

Kitchen

W.
D.

PANTRY

STAIRS DN.

Garage
18¹¹ x 19⁴

Optional Basement Stair Location

PLAN HPT210118

Square Footage: 1,222

Width: 40'-0"

Depth: 49'-2"

This traditional one-story family house allows plant lovers to bring nature close to home. The facade features window boxes off of the bedroom and above the garage—perfect for geraniums! Inside, you'll find two plant shelves—one in the foyer and one in the master suite. The bayed breakfast nook lets the sun shine on morning meals. Vaulted ceilings in the family room and master bedroom lend spaciousness to the plan. Two family bedrooms are located near the front of the home, secluding the master suite at the rear. A large walk-in closet and luxurious bath with both a garden tub and shower will spoil any homeowner. Please specify basement or crawlspace foundation when ordering.

PLAN HPT210119

Square Footage: 1,772

Width: 57'-0"
Depth: 38'-0"

A beautiful Palladian window and the arched porch add an elegant style to this charming one-story home. Inside, the foyer opens directly to the formal dining room and living area. A fireplace, framed by a window and a door, is the focus of the living room. Nearby, the breakfast area joins the kitchen with a serving bar. The master bedroom features the Palladian window of the front exterior, and a well-appointed bath includes a large walk-in closet, oversized soaking tub, separate shower and twin vanity sinks. Two family bedrooms share a full bath and complete this simple design.

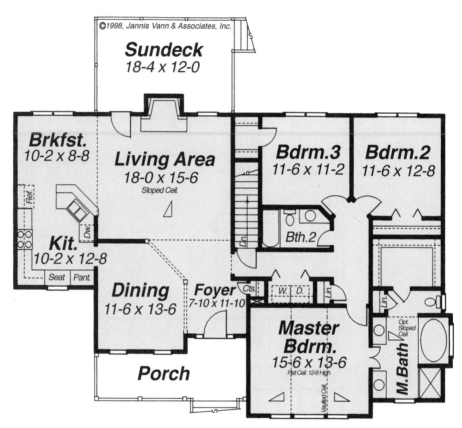

©1998, Jannis Vann & Associates, Inc.

Sundeck
18-4 x 12-0

Brkfst.
10-2 x 8-8

Living Area
18-0 x 15-6
Sloped Ceil.

Bdrm.3
11-6 x 11-2

Bdrm.2
11-6 x 12-8

Bth.2

Kit.
10-2 x 12-8

Ref.

Dw.

Seat | Pant.

Dining
11-6 x 13-6

Foyer
7-10 x 11-10

Cts.

W. D.

Lin.

Master
Bdrm.
15-6 x 13-6
Flat Ceil. 12-8 High

Vaulted Ceil.

M.Bath

Opt.
Sloped
Ceil.

Lin.

Porch

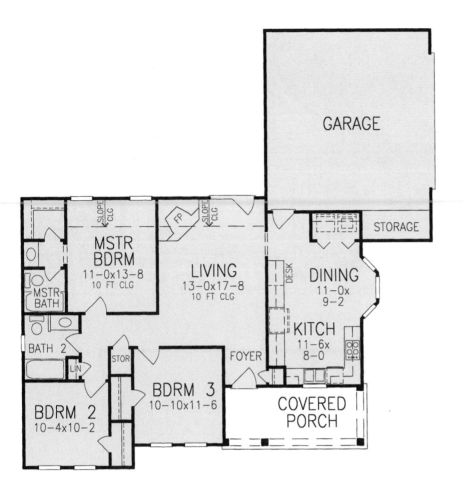

PLAN HPT210120

Square Footage: 1,170

Width: 51'-10"
Depth: 53'-6"

Timeless appeal is the hallmark of this charming traditional home with its sheltering porch that extends a gracious welcome. Inside, the foyer opens directly to the living room highlighted by a corner fireplace. To the right, enter the bayed dining room and enjoy the natural light that also fills the kitchen. A built-in desk simplifies meal planning and windows over the sink open up views of the covered porch and front property. The master suite will please with its large walk-in closet and a compartmented bath. Two family bedrooms have roomy closets. Please specify crawlspace or slab foundation when ordering.

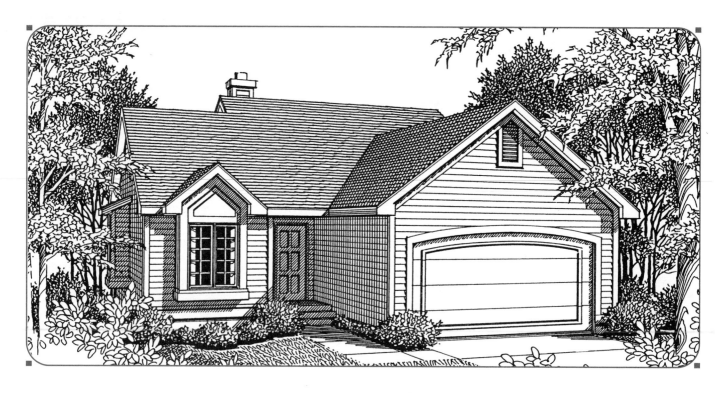

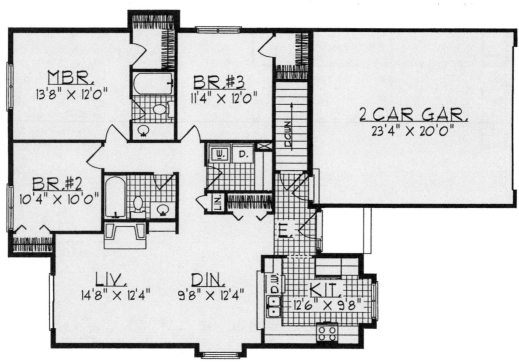

MBR.
13'8" X 12'0"

BR.#3
11'4" X 12'0"

2 CAR GAR.
23'4" X 20'0"

BR.#2
10'4" X 10'0"

LIN.

LIV.
14'8" X 12'4"

DIN.
9'8" X 12'4"

KIT.
12'6" X 9'8"

PLAN HPT210121

Square Footage: 1,342

Width: 37'-0"
Depth: 59'-4"

Build on a narrow lot with this plan—it's only thirty-seven feet wide. But that doesn't affect the classic floor plan at all. The recessed entry opens to a tiled hall with a stairway to the basement at one end and kitchen at the other. Straight ahead are the living and dining areas which combine to form one large, open space. A warm hearth is the focus at one end. Bedrooms are just down a short hallway. Bedroom 3 has a walk-in closet and shares a full bath with Bedroom 2. The master bedroom also contains a walk-in closet but has its own private bath. A laundry room with space for a washer and dryer and a utility closet sits close to the bedrooms for convenience. The two-car garage accesses the main house at the entry hall.

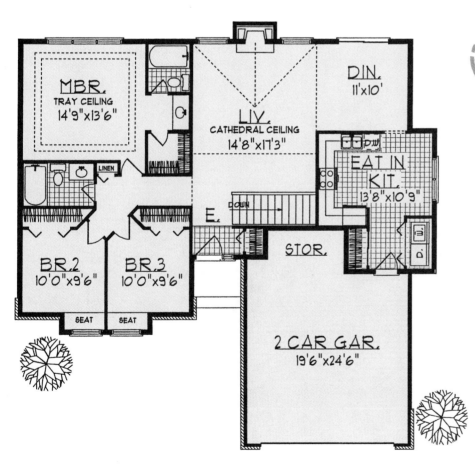

PLAN HPT210122

Square Footage: 1,387

Width: 50'-0"
Depth: 49'-0"

This cozy ranch is a perfect starter home. Two bedrooms with window seats and the master suite that features a tray ceiling and a master bathroom are just a few of this home's amenities. The roomy living room with its cathedral ceiling and fireplace make for an ideal gathering place for family and friends. Windows that surround the fireplace only add to the charm of this home. An eat-in kitchen is conveniently set up. Just off the kitchen you can serve more formal meals in the dining room, which offers a great view to the backyard.

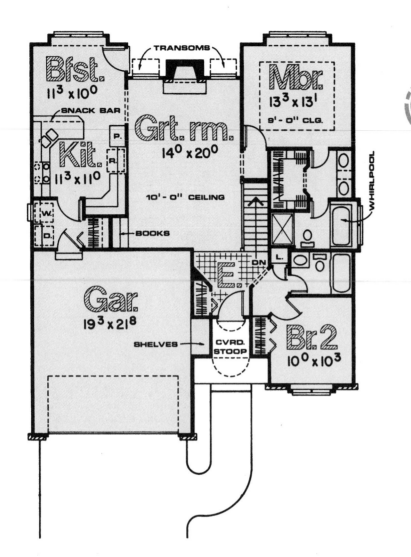

PLAN HPT210123

Square Footage: 1,205

Width: 40'-0"

Depth: 47'-8"

At only 1,205 square feet in size, this home feels considerably larger. The angled entry of this design features two plant shelves and a roomy closet. Straight ahead, the vaulted great room provides a window-flanked fireplace, a built-in bookcase and easy access to the kitchen and dinette. This area offers a snack bar, a wrapping counter and a pantry. The secondary bedroom extends privacy for guests or could easily serve as a den. The master bedroom is highlighted by a box ceiling and a bath with a whirlpool tub and dual sinks.

138

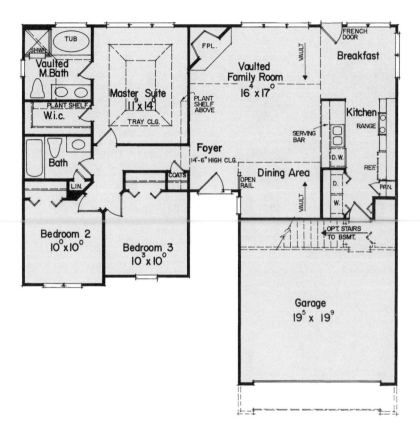

Floor plan labels:

- SHWR.
- TUB
- Vaulted M.Bath
- PLANT SHELF
- W.i.c.
- Bath
- LIN.
- Master Suite 11⁹ x 14⁰
- TRAY CLG.
- PLANT SHELF ABOVE
- FPL.
- Vaulted Family Room 16⁴ x 17⁰
- VAULT
- Breakfast
- FRENCH DOOR
- Kitchen
- RANGE
- SERVING BAR
- D.W.
- REF.
- D. W.
- PAN.
- Foyer 14'-6" HIGH CLG.
- COATS
- OPEN RAIL
- Dining Area
- VAULT
- Bedroom 2 10⁰ x 10⁰
- Bedroom 3 10³ x 10⁰
- OPT. STAIRS TO BSMT.
- Garage 19⁵ x 19⁹

PLAN HPT210124

Square Footage: 1,235

Width: 47'-0"
Depth: 43'-6"

Pedimented arches dress up this one-story traditional cottage. The foyer leads into the vaulted family room where a fireplace awaits the family. The dining area benefits from the kitchen's serving bar. The pantry treats the kitchen to much needed space. The breakfast room features a French door to the backyard. The left side of the plan consists of the sleeping quarters. The master suite enjoys a tray ceiling, walk-in closet and vaulted master bath. Please specify basement or crawlspace foundation when ordering.

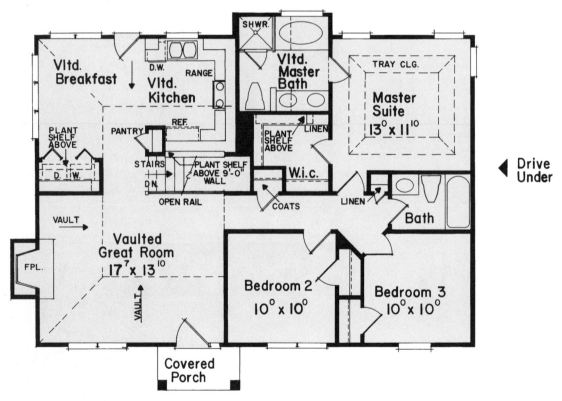

Vltd.
Breakfast

D.W. RANGE

Vltd.
Kitchen

SHWR.

Vltd.
Master
Bath

TRAY CLG.

Master
Suite
13⁰ x 11¹⁰

PLANT
SHELF
ABOVE

PANTRY

REF.

PLANT
SHELF
ABOVE

LINEN

D. W.

STAIRS

PLANT SHELF
ABOVE 9'-0"
WALL

W.i.c.

LINEN

DN

COATS

Bath

OPEN RAIL

VAULT

Vaulted
Great Room
17⁷ x 13¹⁰

FPL.

VAULT

Bedroom 2
10⁰ x 10⁰

Bedroom 3
10⁰ x 10⁰

▲ Drive
Under

Covered
Porch

PLAN HPT210125

Square Footage: 1,166

Width: 43'-4"

Depth: 34'-0"

A simple, one-story facade, this home features European elements such as hipped rooflines, front-facing pediments and shuttered windows. Enter through a covered porch into an expansive vaulted great room, complete with a fireplace. The kitchen and breakfast area also sport vaulted ceilings and include such luxuries as a pantry, plant shelf and door to the rear property. The master suite boasts a tray ceiling, vaulted full bath and walk-in closet. Bedrooms 2 and 3 share a full bath and have ample closet space.

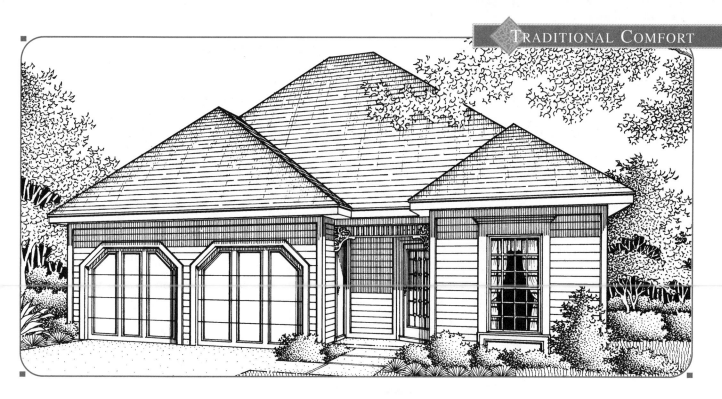

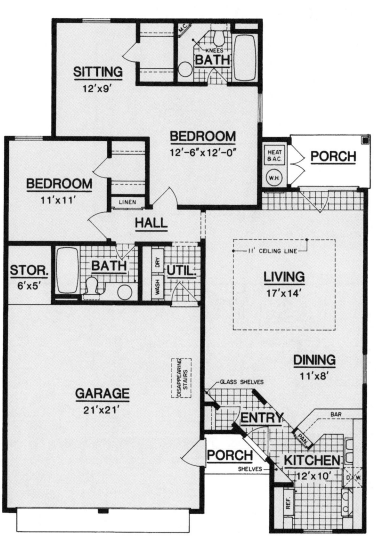

PLAN HPT210126

Square Footage: 1,150

Width: 38'-0"
Depth: 52'-0"

A hipped roof and interesting angles give this compact home its charm. Inside, the entry leads to a galley kitchen with a breakfast bar. A dining/living room creates a feeling of spaciousness. The living room has a raised ceiling and opens to the backyard. The master suite is complete with a private bath and a sitting room for quiet contemplation. The second bedroom also contains a complete bath. A two-car garage completes this simple design. Please specify crawlspace or slab foundation when ordering.

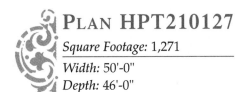

PLAN HPT210127

Square Footage: 1,271

Width: 50'-0"
Depth: 46'-0"

This charmingly snug three-bedroom home offers all the features you've been looking for in a family home. The great room has a lovely cathedral ceiling and a fireplace surrounded by windows. Nearby are the dining area and an efficient kitchen with a window box, planning desk, lazy Susan and snack-bar counter. Intriguing ceiling treatment dominates the master bedroom where you'll also find corner windows and a dressing area with a large vanity and a walk-in closet. Two family bedrooms share a full bath near the laundry room.

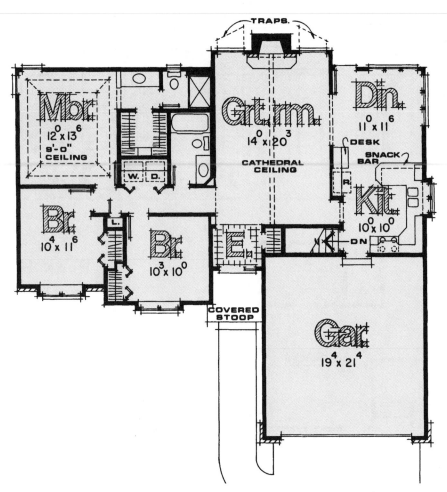

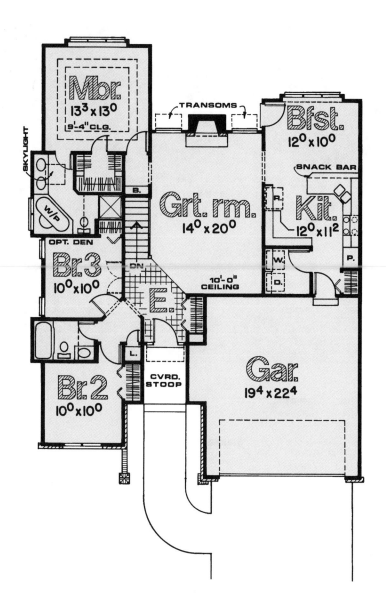

Mbr.
13³ x 13⁰
9'-4" CLG.

SKYLIGHT

W/P

OPT. DEN

Br.3
10⁰ x 10⁰

DN

E.

L.

Br.2
10⁰ x 10⁰

CVRD. STOOP

TRANSOMS

B.

Grt. rm.
14⁰ x 20⁰

10'-0" CEILING

Bfst.
12⁰ x 10⁰

SNACK BAR

R.

Kit.
12⁰ x 11²

W.

D.

P.

Gar.
19⁴ x 22⁴

PLAN HPT210128

Square Footage: 1,347

Width: 42'-0"
Depth: 54'-0"

From the ten-foot ceiling in the entry to the spacious great room with a fireplace, this plan expresses an open feeling. A snack bar and pantry in the kitchen complement the work area. Bright windows light up the breakfast room. To the left side of the plan are three bedrooms—two share a full bath. The master suite offers a box-bay window and tiered ceiling. The skylit dressing area features a double vanity, and there is a whirlpool spa in the bath. Reach the two-car garage through the service entrance, which has a laundry room. Extra storage space in the garage makes it even more handy.

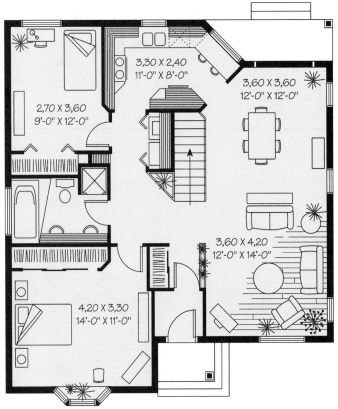

3,30 X 2,40
11'-0" X 8'-0"

3,60 X 3,60
12'-0" X 12'-0"

2,70 X 3,60
9'-0" X 12'-0"

3,60 X 4,20
12'-0" X 14'-0"

4,20 X 3,30
14'-0" X 11'-0"

PLAN HPT210129

Square Footage: 1,052

Width: 32'-5"
Depth: 36'-0"

This petite European-style cottage is perfect for the small family or retired couple. Inside, the formal living area is open to the dining room. The dining room provides a quaint atmosphere for a quiet meal or dinnertime with friends. The angled kitchen makes for convenient serving to the dining room and offers plenty of counter space. The master suite and guest bedroom share a full hall bath. A laundry closet is large enough for a washer and dryer. This home is designed with a basement foundation.

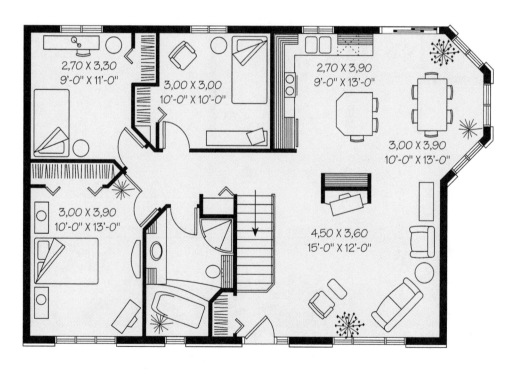

2,70 X 3,30
9'-0" X 11'-0"

3,00 X 3,00
10'-0" X 10'-0"

2,70 X 3,90
9'-0" X 13'-0"

3,00 X 3,90
10'-0" X 13'-0"

3,00 X 3,90
10'-0" X 13'-0"

4,50 X 3,60
15'-0" X 12'-0"

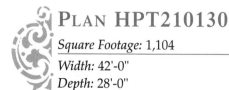

PLAN HPT210130

Square Footage: 1,104

Width: 42'-0"
Depth: 28'-0"

A covered front porch welcomes friends and family to this fine three-bedroom cottage. From the Palladian window in front to the rear sliding glass doors, the living/dining area is open under a cathedral ceiling. A large bay provides natural light to the dining room and the kitchen. Three bedrooms share a roomy bath that includes a garden tub and a separate shower. This home is designed with a basement foundation.

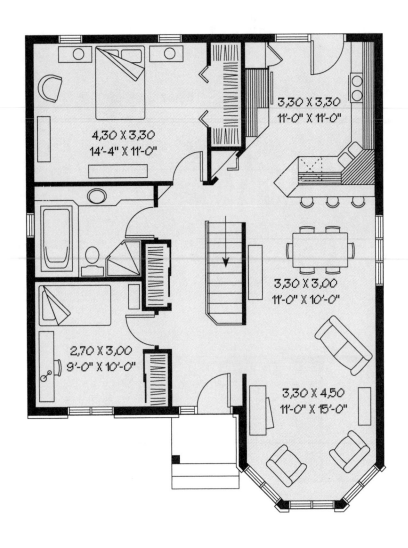

PLAN HPT210131

Square Footage: 994

Width: 30'-0"
Depth: 38'-0"

An alluring, quaint brick exterior creates a cozy ambiance inside this traditional family plan. Petite yet efficient, this plan is designed for the young family. Surrounded by brightly lit windows, the bayed sitting area is perfect for a living room setting. The dining area views the side yard, while the kitchen accesses the rear yard. The master bedroom features roomy closet space. An additional bedroom shares a full hall bath with the master bedroom. This home is designed with a basement foundation.

Floor plan dimensions:
- 4,30 X 3,30 — 14'-4" X 11'-0"
- 3,30 X 3,30 — 11'-0" X 11'-0"
- 3,30 X 3,00 — 11'-0" X 10'-0"
- 2,70 X 3,00 — 9'-0" X 10'-0"
- 3,30 X 4,50 — 11'-0" X 15'-0"

PLAN HPT212001

Square Footage: 1,268

Width: 38'-8"
Depth: 48'-4"

Charming accents over the sunburst window, garage door and at each gable peak add curb appeal to this three-bedroom home. A front porch welcomes guests and homeowners inside to the front entry. Two family bedrooms share a full bath to the left. An open plan links the kitchen, breakfast nook, dining and great rooms with a vaulted ceiling. The kitchen serving bar allows a wonderful view of the great room fireplace. Light will pour into the kitchen via the bay window in the breakfast nook. To the left of the great room resides the master bedroom, with its walk-in closet and roomy bath.

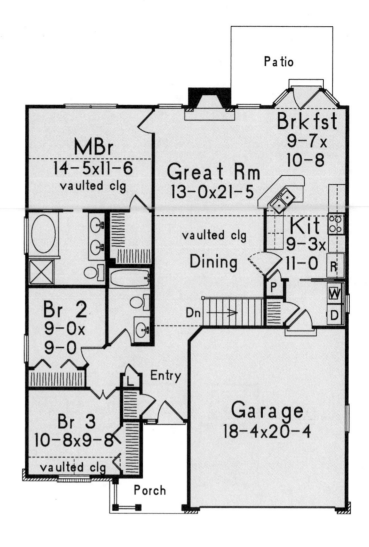

Patio

MBr
14-5x11-6
vaulted clg

Brk fst
9-7x
10-8

Great Rm
13-0x21-5

vaulted clg

Dining

Kit
9-3x
11-0

Br 2
9-0x
9-0

Dn

P

R

W
D

Entry

Br 3
10-8x9-8
vaulted clg

L

Garage
18-4x20-4

Porch

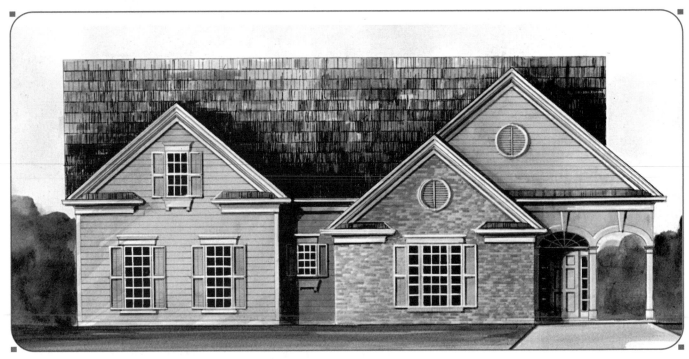

PLAN HPT210133

Square Footage: 1,670

Width: 50'-0"
Depth: 45'-0"

With an offset entrance, this home adds interest and charm to any neighborhood. Enter into a spacious family room, with a galley kitchen nearby that offers easy access to the sunny breakfast room. Bedrooms 2 and 3 each have walk-in closets and share a full hall bath. Bedroom 2, which opens off the family room, could also be used as a den. The formal dining room separates the master bedroom from the rest of the home, providing pleasant privacy. The master suite features many amenities, including a walk-in closet, a private bath and access to a private courtyard.

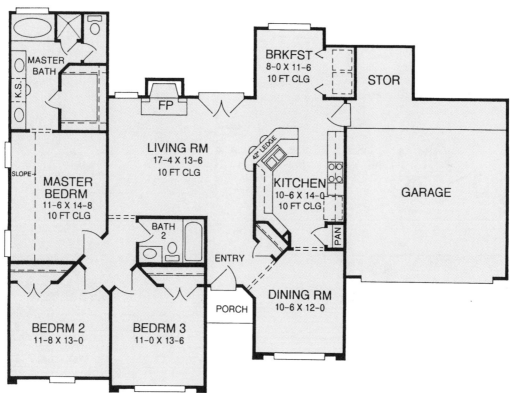

PLAN HPT210134

Square Footage: 1,553

Width: 61'-7"
Depth: 45'-4"

L

Two dominating brick gables give a unique look to this lovely starter home. Inside, the foyer opens to a great room with ten-foot ceilings. A dining room for formal entertaining is located to the right. Ten-foot ceilings continue throughout the kitchen and breakfast room and give the home an open, spacious feel. An angled kitchen sink and a snack bar open the kitchen to the great room and breakfast room, thus allowing the cook to be part of all family gatherings. As an added bonus, the angled design brings the fireplace into view from the kitchen. The master suite features a bath loaded with all the amenities, including double vanities, a whirlpool tub and a separate shower. Bedrooms 2 and 3 and the second bath are located close by. Please specify crawlspace or slab foundation when ordering.

PLAN HPT210135

Square Footage: 1,373

Width: 50'-4"
Depth: 45'-0"

A steep gabled roofline punctuated with dormer windows and a columned front porch give a traditional welcome to this family home. A vaulted ceiling tops the family and dining rooms, which are nicely accented with a fireplace and bright windows. An amenity-filled kitchen opens to the breakfast room. The master suite has a refined tray ceiling and a vaulted master bath. Two family bedrooms, a laundry center and a full bath—with private access from Bedroom 3—complete this stylish plan. Please specify basement or crawlspace foundation when ordering.

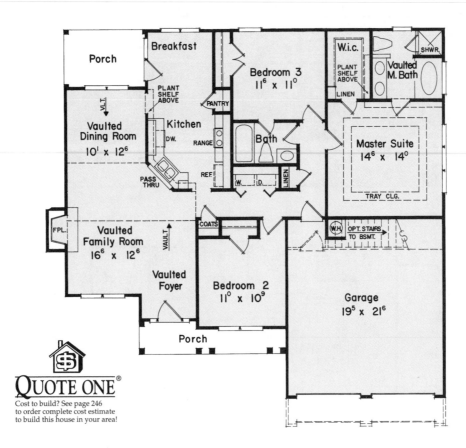

QUOTE ONE®
Cost to build? See page 246
to order complete cost estimate
to build this house in your area!

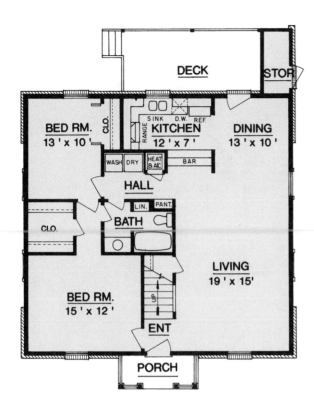

DECK | STOR

BED RM.
13' x 10'

CLO.

KITCHEN
12' x 7'

SINK   D.W.   REF.
RANGE

DINING
13' x 10'

WASH | DRY | HEAT & A/C | BAR

HALL

LIN. | PANT.

BATH

CLO.

LIVING
19' x 15'

BED RM.
15' x 12'

UP

ENT

PORCH

PLAN HPT210136

Square Footage: 1,088
Optional Second Floor: 580 sq. ft.

Width: 34'-0"
Depth: 44'-0"

Corner quoins, dormers and a combination of brick and wood siding define this charming country home. An open floor plan lends a spacious feel to the joined living and dining areas. An efficient U-shaped kitchen sports a breakfast bar and easy access to the dining room. The laundry facilities are located in a short hall that leads to the two bedrooms. The master bedroom, which shares a full bath with the second bedroom, has a large walk-in closet. Room for expansion is available on the second floor, where two additional bedrooms and a second full bath can be added. Please specify crawlspace or slab foundation when ordering.

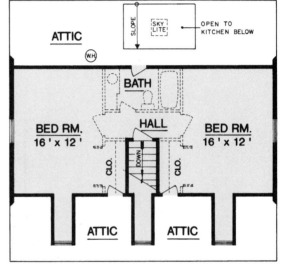

ATTIC

SLOPE | SKY LITE | OPEN TO KITCHEN BELOW

W.H.

BATH

BED RM.
16' x 12'

HALL

DOWN

CLO. | CLO.

BED RM.
16' x 12'

ATTIC | ATTIC

OPTIONAL SECOND FLOOR

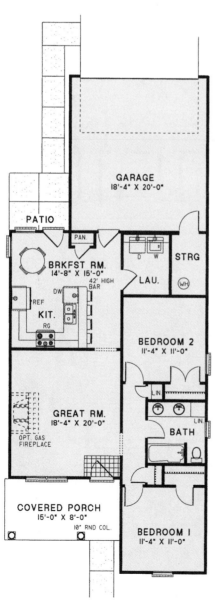

GARAGE
18'-4" X 20'-0"

PATIO

PAN.

D W

STRG

LAU.

WH

BRKFST RM.
14'-8" X 15'-0"

42" HIGH BAR

DW

REF

KIT.

RG

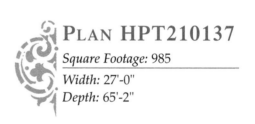

BEDROOM 2
11'-4" X 11'-0"

LIN.

GREAT RM.
18'-4" X 20'-0"

OPT. GAS FIREPLACE

LIN.

BATH

COVERED PORCH
15'-0" X 8'-0"

10" RND COL.

BEDROOM 1
11'-4" X 11'-0"

PLAN HPT210137

Square Footage: 985

Width: 27'-0"
Depth: 65'-2"

Round columns and muntin windows with shutters add curb appeal to this country cottage. This functional floor plan begins with the great room which offers space for an optional gas fireplace. The U-shaped kitchen is fully equipped with a pantry, breakfast room and high bar easily accessible to the rear patio. A full hall bath with dual vanities and two linen closets is available to both family bedrooms. Don't overlook the storage space available inside the garage and the utility room near the garage entrance. This comfortable, narrow floor plan is a perfect starter home. Please specify crawlspace or slab foundation when ordering.

Sundeck
10-0 x 10-0

M.Bath

Lin.

Bedroom 2

OPT. PLANT SHELF
OPEN TO BDRM.

W. D.

Bath 2

Kitchen
8-0 x 10-0

Dw.

Dining
10-4 x 10-0

Ref.

Master Bedroom
11-6 x 14-6

Cts.

Down

Family Room
18-4 x 13-0

Bedroom 3
11-0 x 10-0

Entry

©1998, Jannis Vann & Associates, Inc.

PLAN HPT210138

Square Footage: 1,208

Width: 48'-0"
Depth: 29'-0"

The details of the exterior of this small, attractive Colonial-style home include wood siding, shuttered windows, a gabled room and a stunning entry with sidelights. At the front of the house, the family room offers a fireplace to warm the cold night air. Beyond lies the dining room and U-shaped kitchen, which share a door to the sun deck. Two family bedrooms located at the middle of the home share a bathroom that contains a laundry. To the left of the house is the master bedroom with two closets, an optional plant shelf, and a bathroom with dual sinks and a linen closet.

PLAN HPT210139

Square Footage: 1,310

Width: 49'-10"
Depth: 40'-6"

This charming plan is perfect for families just starting out or for the empty-nester looking to pare down. Every room is designed for maximum livability, from the living room with a corner fireplace to the efficient kitchen with a snack bar and hidden washer and dryer. The master bedroom is fashioned with a dual-vanity bath and a walk-in closet equipped with shelves. Two additional bedrooms each have a walk-in closet and share a hall bath. Please specify crawlspace or slab foundation when ordering.

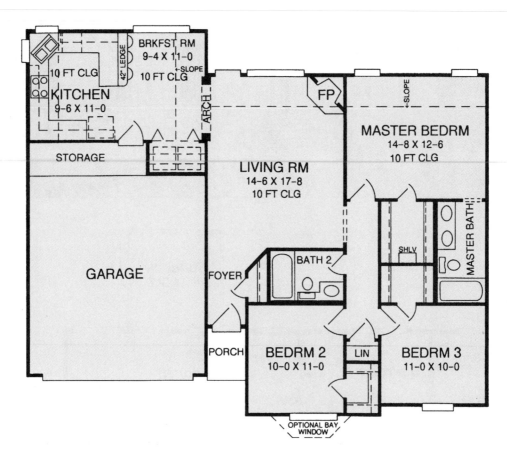

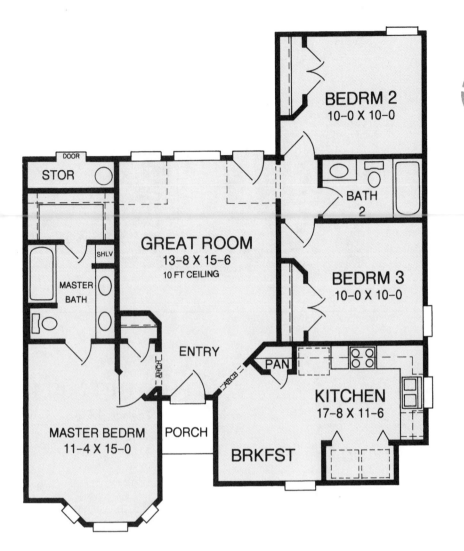

BEDRM 2
10-0 X 10-0

STOR

DOOR

GREAT ROOM
13-8 X 15-6
10 FT CEILING

BATH 2

SHLV

MASTER BATH

BEDRM 3
10-0 X 10-0

ENTRY

ARCH

PAN

ARCH

MASTER BEDRM
11-4 X 15-0

PORCH

KITCHEN
17-8 X 11-6

BRKFST

PLAN HPT210140

Square Footage: 1,087

Width: 35'-10"
Depth: 42'-2"

From the multi-pane windows to the corner quoins, this home's facade is enchanting. Inside, attractive arches flank the entryway; one arch leads to the breakfast room and an efficient kitchen, the other to the deluxe master suite. Directly ahead of the foyer is the large great room accessible to the rear yard and the two family bedrooms. In the master suite, a sumptuous bath offers a double-bowl vanity and a large walk-in closet. Two family bedrooms located on the opposite end of the home share a full hall bath. Please specify crawlspace or slab foundation when ordering.

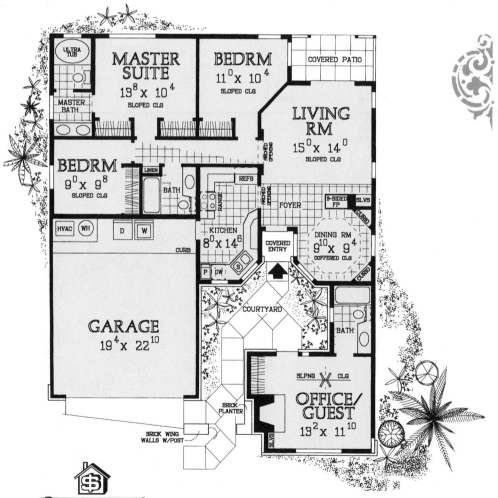

PLAN HPT210141

Square Footage: 1,418

Width: 44'-8"
Depth: 52'-4"

L

This cozy cottage offers the choice of a three- or four-bedroom plan. The design features a front-facing office/guest suite which provides privacy for the entry courtyard. With its separate entrance it offers the perfect haven for an in-home office or a separate suite for live-in parents. The remainder of the house is designed with the same level of efficiency. It contains a large living area with access to a covered patio and a three-sided fireplace that shares its warmth with a dining room featuring built-ins. A unique kitchen provides garage access. The bedrooms include a comfortable master suite with a whirlpool tub, a double-bowl vanity and twin closets.

QUOTE ONE®

Cost to build? See page 246
to order complete cost estimate
to build this house in your area!

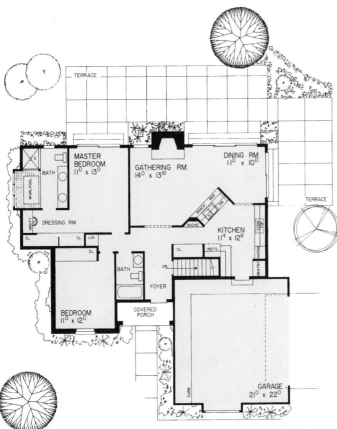

A low-budget home can be a showplace, too. Exquisite site proportion, fine detailing, projected wings and interesting rooflines help provide the appeal of this modest one-story. Each of the bedrooms has excellent wall space and wardrobe storage potential. The master bath features a vanity, twin lavatories, a stall shower and a whirlpool tub. Another full bath is strategically located to serve the second bedroom as well as other areas of the house. Open planning results in a spacious gathering/dining area with a fireplace and access to the outdoor terraces. Two kitchen layouts make the plan versatile.

PLAN HPT210142

Square Footage: 1,233

Width: 50'-0"
Depth: 47'-8"

OPTIONAL KITCHEN LAYOUT

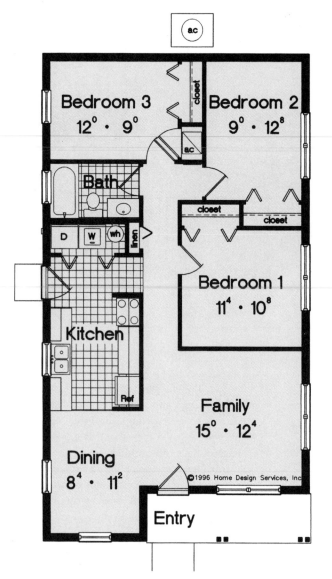

Bedroom 3
12⁰ · 9⁰

Bedroom 2
9⁰ · 12⁸

Bath

D W wh linen

Kitchen

closet closet

Bedroom 1
11⁴ · 10⁸

Family
15⁰ · 12⁴

Ref

Dining
8⁴ · 11²

©1996 Home Design Services, Inc

Entry

PLAN HPT210143

Square Footage: 996

Width: 25'-0"
Depth: 44'-4"

Simple, yet adequate, this plan is graced with plenty of windows, allowing for natural light to flood all the living areas in the home. A large family room is located to the right of the entry, while the dining room is situated at the left. A long, spacious kitchen, with dual basins and a washer and dryer closet, has side-door access. Three bedrooms share a full bath, and each room boasts folding doors to its closet space.

J.N.HANSEN S.D.G.

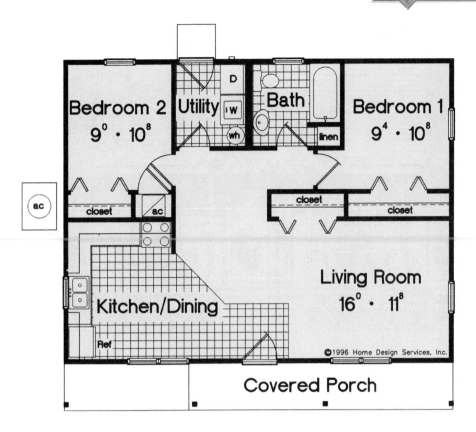

Bedroom 2
9⁰ · 10⁸

Utility

Bath

Bedroom 1
9⁴ · 10⁸

closet

closet

closet

Kitchen/Dining

Living Room
16⁰ · 11⁸

©1996 Home Design Services, Inc.

Covered Porch

PLAN HPT210144

Square Footage: 873

Width: 34'-0"
Depth: 29'-8"

A bungalow-style home, this plan boasts a large covered front porch. Enter directly into the kitchen/dining area where counter space abounds. A large living room is to the right and is enhanced with a spacious coat closet. Two bedrooms are positioned on either end of the plan, both with ample closet space, and share a full bath. A utility area has access to the rear property and could serve as an alternative entry and mudroom.

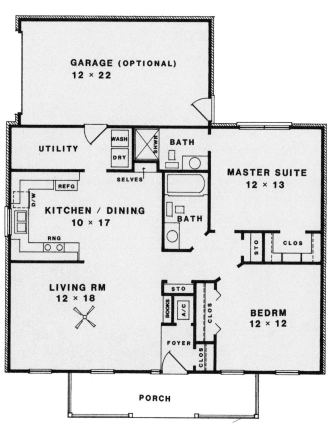

GARAGE (OPTIONAL)
12 × 22

UTILITY

WASH
DRY

SHWR

BATH

SELVES

REFG

D/W

KITCHEN / DINING
10 × 17

RNG

MASTER SUITE
12 × 13

BATH

STO

CLOS

LIVING RM
12 × 18

STO

BOOKS

A/C

CLOS

BEDRM
12 × 12

FOYER

CLOS

PORCH

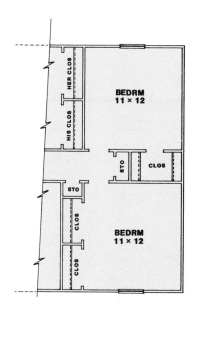

HER CLOS

BEDRM
11 × 12

HIS CLOS

STO

CLOS

STO

CLOS

CLOS

BEDRM
11 × 12

CLOS

PLAN HPT210145

Square Footage: 1,036

Width: 37'-0"
Depth: 45'-0"

This quaint Victorian cottage offers beautiful detailing and the possibility of later additions. Enter into the living room that is open to the dining area and U-shaped kitchen. A utility room is located just off the kitchen. On the right, a family or guest bedroom is steps away from a full bath. The master suite features a full bath and walk-in closet. The future expansion offers two more secondary bedrooms and provides the master bedroom with two closets instead of a walk-in for a total addition of 392 square feet. The garage is optional.

DECK
16'0" X 12'0"

MASTER
BEDROOM
12'0" X 13'0"

BATH

PANTRY

KITCHEN
15'4" X 13'8"

BATH

CL

LINEN

STAIRS TO FULL BASEMENT OPTION

DN

OPT. FIREPLACE

LINE OF OPTIONAL 1 CAR GARAGE

CURB

2 CAR
GARAGE
19'8" X 21'4"

BEDROOM
12'0" X 10'0"

BEDROOM
9'0" X 10'0"

CL

LIVING RM
15'2" X 13'4"

OPT. BAY WINDOW

PORCH
18' x 4'

QUOTE ONE®

Cost to build? See page 246
to order complete cost estimate
to build this house in your area!

PLAN HPT210146

Square Footage: 1,130

Width: 60'-0"
Depth: 28'-0"

Traditional charm is an apt description for this economical ranch home. The kitchen is designed to
serve as an eat-in kitchen. The master bedroom
offers a full bath plus ample closet space. A full-sized
bath adjoins the other two bedrooms. Options include a
one- or two-car garage, a front porch, a rear deck with
railing, a box-bay window and a fireplace. The blueprints for this house show how to build both the basic,
low-cost version and the enhanced, upgraded version.

TERRACE

DINING
8⁰ X 11⁰

GATHERING RM
15⁶ X 14⁴

STUDY/
BEDROOM
9⁰ X 11⁰

MASTER
BEDROOM
13⁸ X 11⁰

SLOPED
CEILING

SLOPED
CEILING

SLOPED
CEILING

BRKFST RM
9² X 8⁴

PANTRY

SNACK BAR

SHLVS

S

DW

KITCHEN
12⁰ X 9⁰

DESK

RANGE

REF'G

BC

D
W

LAUNDRY
DN

FOYER

CL

BATH

LINEN

CL

MASTER
BATH

VANITY

CL

SLOPED
CEILING

WHIRLPOOL

CURB

COVERED PORCH

BEDROOM
10⁰ X 10⁰

STORAGE

GARAGE
19⁴ X 21⁸

COURTYARD

$ QUOTE ONE®
Cost to build? See page 246
to order complete cost estimate
to build this house in your area!

PLAN HPT210147

Square Footage: 1,387

Width: 54'-0"
Depth: 52'-0"

L D

Though modest in size, this fetching one-story home offers a great deal of livability with three bedrooms (or two bedrooms and a study) and a spacious gathering room with a fireplace and a sloped ceiling. The galley kitchen, designed to save steps, provides a pass-through snack bar and has a planning desk and attached breakfast room. In addition to two secondary bedrooms with a full bath, there's a private master suite that enjoys views and access to the backyard. The private master bath features a large dressing area, a corner vanity and a raised whirlpool tub. Indoor/outdoor living relationships are strengthened by easy access from the dining room, study/bedroom and master suite to the rear terrace.

PLAN HPT210148

Square Footage: 1,200

Width: 56'-0"
Depth: 36'-0"

This three-bedroom ranch home contains many spacious features. It includes a full-size bath in the master bedroom and a shared bath for the secondary bedrooms. The dining room and living room combine to create a spacious formal or informal gathering area. A two-car garage, a standard deck, decorative louvers and a centrally located fireplace are optional. The blueprints for this home show how to build both the basic version and the enhanced, upgraded version.

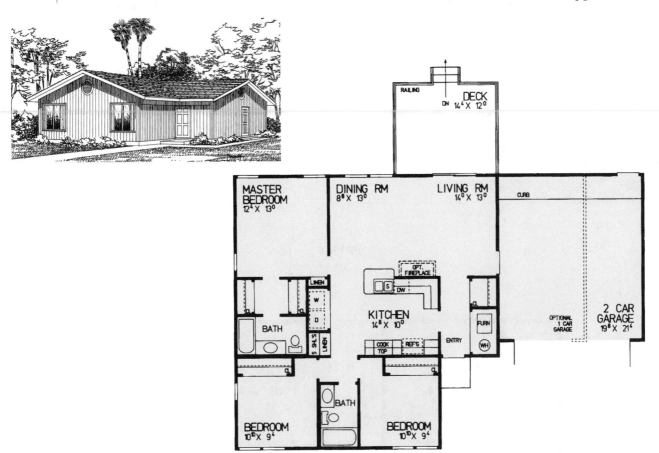

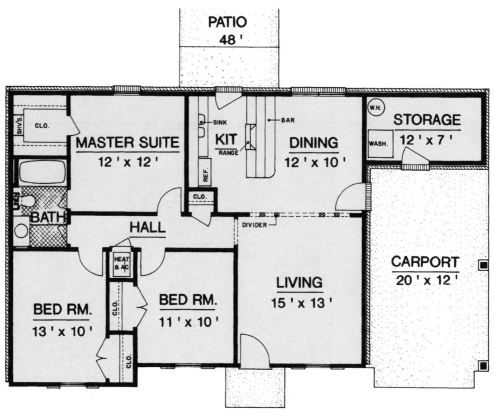

PATIO
48'

CLO.
SHV'S.

MASTER SUITE
12' x 12'

SINK
KIT
RANGE
REF.

BAR

DINING
12' x 10'

W.H.
WASH.

STORAGE
12' x 7'

BATH

HALL

CLO.

DIVIDER

HEAT
& AC

CLO.

BED RM.
13' x 10'

CLO.

BED RM.
11' x 10'

LIVING
15' x 13'

CARPORT
20' x 12'

PLAN HPT210149

Square Footage: 998

Width: 48'-0"

Depth: 29'-0"

Windows allow sunlight to penetrate this home—a perfect cottage for living and enjoying. The open living room extends into the dining room, making a great space for entertaining. The kitchen features a serving bar. Plenty of storage space is located off the carport. Two family bedrooms and a spacious master suite finish this plan. Please specify crawlspace or slab foundation when ordering.

Stucco and stone, shutters and hipped roofs—all are elements of Old-World European architecture. From England come the quaint little garden cottages, while France offers fanciful shutters and elegant details. Other flavors, such as Tudor and Mediterranean, make a showing, giving you a pleasant variety to enjoy. With copper-roofed bay windows, flower boxes and cozy floor plans, these whimsical Old World cottages have a distinctive flair. Featuring wonderful detailing and perfect for weekend getaways or everyday life, these homes range in size from 984 square feet to more than 2,400 square feet.

PLAN HPT210150

First Floor: 1,724 sq. ft.
Second Floor: 700 sq. ft.
Total: 2,424 sq. ft.

Width: 47'-10"
Depth: 63'-6"

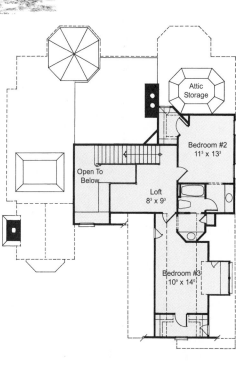

PLAN HPT210151

First Floor: 1,746 sq. ft.
Second Floor: 651 sq. ft.
Total: 2,397 sq. ft.

Width: 50'-0"
Depth: 75'-4"

This elegant home offers a lot in the way of eye candy. The shutters around the windows, flowers in the flower boxes, and the dormers all add beauty. The interior is uniquely designed as the foyer leads into the dining room, which is perfect for formal gatherings. The great room features a grand hearth as a focal point. Cooking is made fun in the octagonal kitchen, which connects with the breakfast room. Access the rear deck through this room. The master suite has its own private fireplace and spacious bath. Plenty of entertainment is located on the second level of this home. A media room and exercise center accompany two family bedrooms. This home is designed with a walkout basement foundation.

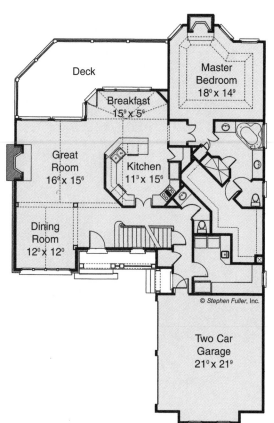

Deck

Breakfast
15⁹ x 5⁶

Master
Bedroom
18⁰ x 14⁹

Great
Room
16⁸ x 15⁶

Kitchen
11³ x 15⁶

Dining
Room
12⁰ x 12⁰

Two Car
Garage
21⁰ x 21⁹

© Stephen Fuller, Inc.

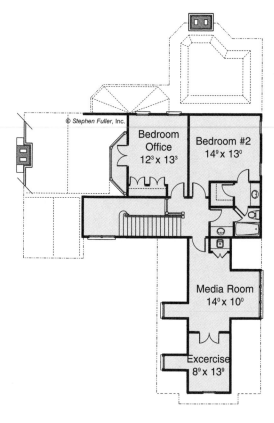

© Stephen Fuller, Inc.

Bedroom
Office
12³ x 13³

Bedroom #2
14⁹ x 13⁰

Media Room
14⁰ x 10⁰

Excercise
8⁹ x 13⁹

© Stephen Fuller, Inc.

Two Car Garage
23⁰ x 23⁰

Deck

Kitchen
11⁰ x 11⁰

Great Room
20⁶ x 21⁶

Master Bedroom
18³ x 14³

Breakfast
15³ x 7⁹

Family Room
15³ x 9⁶

Dining Room
14⁹ x 13³

© Stephen Fuller, Inc.

Bedroom #2
13⁰ x 14³

Unfinished Bedroom
11³ x 15³

Bedroom #3
12⁰ x 15⁶

Study
8⁶ x 9⁹

PLAN HPT210152

First Floor: 1,840 sq. ft.
Second Floor: 840 sq. ft.
Total: 2,680 sq. ft.
Bonus Space: 295 sq. ft.

Width: 66'-0"
Depth: 65'-10"

Multi-pane windows, shutters and shingle accents adorn the stucco facade of this wonderful French country cottage. Inside, the foyer introduces the hearth-warmed great room that features French-door access to the rear deck. The dining room, defined from the foyer and great room by columns, enjoys front-yard views. To the right of the great room, the master bedroom includes two walk-in closets, rear-deck access and a dual vanity bath. The informal living areas have an open plan. The box-bayed breakfast nook joins the cooktop-island kitchen and hearth-warmed family room. The second floor holds two bedrooms with walk-in closets, a study and an unfinished bedroom for future expansion.

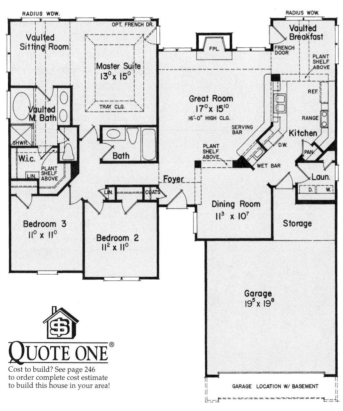

RADIUS WDW.

Vaulted Sitting Room

OPT. FRENCH DR.

Master Suite
13⁰ x 15⁰

TRAY CLG.

Vaulted M. Bath

SHWR

W.i.c.

LIN

PLANT SHELF ABOVE

Bedroom 3
11⁰ x 11⁰

Bedroom 2
11² x 11⁰

LIN.

COATS

Foyer

FPL

Great Room
17⁰ x 15¹⁰
16'-0" HIGH CLG.

SERVING BAR

Bath

PLANT SHELF ABOVE

WET BAR

Dining Room
11³ x 10⁷

Storage

RADIUS WDW.

Vaulted Breakfast

FRENCH DOOR

PLANT SHELF ABOVE

REF

RANGE

Kitchen

D.W.

PAN.

Laun.

D. W.

Garage
19⁵ x 19⁸

GARAGE LOCATION W/ BASEMENT

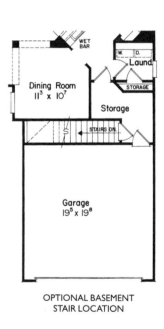

WET BAR

W. D.

Laund.

STORAGE

Dining Room
11³ x 10⁷

Storage

STAIRS DN.

Garage
19⁵ x 19⁸

OPTIONAL BASEMENT
STAIR LOCATION

Quote One®

Cost to build? See page 246
to order complete cost estimate
to build this house in your area!

Plan HPT210153

Square Footage: 1,575

Width: 50'-0"

Depth: 52'-6"

This impressive home will be the envy of the neighborhood during holiday parties. The massive great room, with its fireplace flanked by views to the rear yard, will host many events. A serving bar connects it to the amenity-filled kitchen, which flows to the formal dining room and to the vaulted breakfast nook. The sleeping wing on the left side of the plan features a luxurious master suite with a tray ceiling, separate sitting room (big enough for an office) and vaulted bath with dual sinks and a walk-in closet. Two family bedrooms and a full hall bath complete this stunning plan. Please specify basement or crawlspace foundation when ordering.

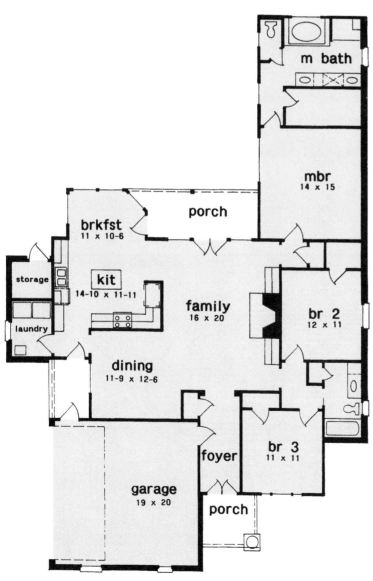

PLAN HPT210154

Square Footage: 1,804

Width: 49'-10"
Depth: 74'-9"

Heavy European influences bring warmth and charm to this lovely cottage home. The family room—with an elaborate fireplace and built-ins—along with the dining room, is the heart of this home. Entertaining will be a snap with the convenience and efficiency of the well-equipped and easily accessible kitchen. An alternate to the formal dining room, the sunny breakfast area allows for more casual dining. A rear porch is accessed via the breakfast area and the family room. An exquisite master suite and two bedrooms with a shared bath complete the living spaces.

PLAN HPT210155

Square Footage: 1,472
Unfinished Basement: 1,169 sq. ft.

Width: 49'-8"
Depth: 45'-0"

This European-style exterior offers plenty of curb appeal, with its combination of stone and stucco, engaging window treatments and paneled front door. The family room boasts a fireplace, while the kitchen has a work island and opens into a breakfast nook. The master suite offers a whirlpool tub, two walk-in closets and easy access to a den, which also opens off the front entry. An optional basement provides two bedrooms, a second family room, a bath and a sizable storage area.

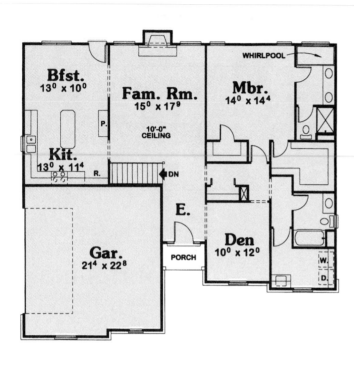

Bfst.
13⁰ x 10⁰

Fam. Rm.
15⁰ x 17⁹

10'-0"
CEILING

Mbr.
14⁰ x 14⁴

WHIRLPOOL

Kit.
13⁰ x 11⁴

R.

P.

DN

E.

Gar.
21⁴ x 22⁸

PORCH

Den
10⁰ x 12⁰

W.
D.

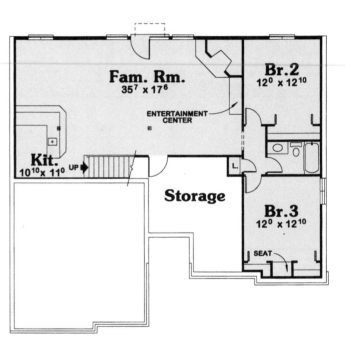

Fam. Rm.
35⁷ x 17⁶

ENTERTAINMENT
CENTER

Br.2
12⁰ x 12¹⁰

Kit.
10¹⁰ x 11⁰

UP

L.

Storage

Br.3
12⁰ x 12¹⁰

SEAT

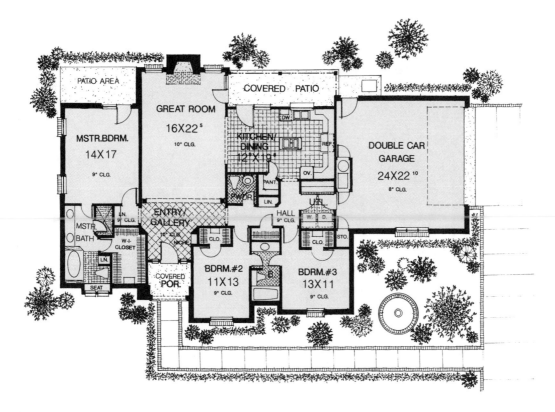

PATIO AREA

GREAT ROOM
16X22⁵
10" CLG.

COVERED PATIO

MSTR.BDRM.
14X17
9" CLG.

KITCHEN/
DINING
12"X19"

DW

REF

DOUBLE CAR
GARAGE
24X22¹⁰
8" CLG.

OV.

PANT.

PWDR.

LIN.

UTIL.
W D

MSTR.
BATH

LN.
9" CLG.

ENTRY
GALLERY
10" CLG.

W-I-
CLOSET

NICHE

CLO.

HALL
9" CLG.

CLO.

STO.

LN.

SEAT

COVERED
POR.

BDRM.#2
11X13
9" CLG.

B

BDRM.#3
13X11
9" CLG.

PLAN HPT210156

Square Footage: 1,807

Width: 74'-0"
Depth: 44'-0"

The striking European facade of this home presents a beautiful stone exterior, complete with stone quoins, a shingled rooftop and French-style shutters on the front windows. Step inside the great room where a ten-foot ceiling and fireplace will greet you. A large island in the kitchen provides plenty of much-needed counter space for the cook of the family. An element of privacy is observed, with the master suite separated from the other two bedrooms, which share a full bath. An oversized two-car garage and a covered patio are just some of the added amenities.

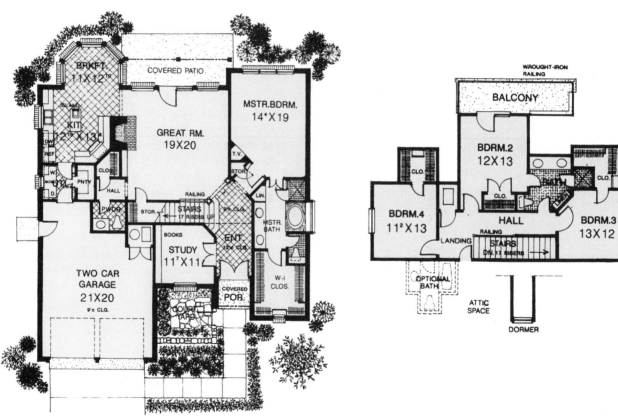

PLAN HPT210157

First Floor: 1,704 sq. ft.
Second Floor: 771 sq. ft.
Total: 2,475 sq. ft.

Width: 50'-0"
Depth: 56'-9"

Detailed for perfection, this home's exterior boasts an eye-lit dormer, a cupola with a weathervane, a charming dormer window and brick and stone accents. A cozy study greets those who enter through double French doors. The first-floor master bedroom boasts a large walk-in closet, garden tub and plenty of windows. The central great room heats the home with a fireplace and accesses the rear covered patio. A bayed breakfast area sits next to the island kitchen. Three family bedrooms reside on the second floor, along with one full bath and a balcony with a wrought-iron railing.

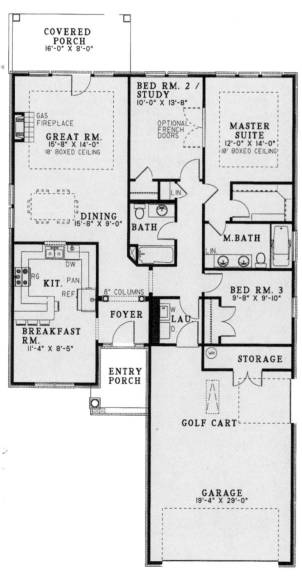

COVERED
PORCH
16'-0" X 8'-0"

GAS
FIREPLACE

GREAT RM.
15'-8" X 14'-0"
10' BOXED CEILING

BED RM. 2 /
STUDY
10'-0" X 13'-8"

OPTIONAL
FRENCH
DOORS

MASTER
SUITE
12'-0" X 14'-0"
10' BOXED CEILING

DINING
15'-8" X 9'-0"

LIN.

BATH

M.BATH

LIN.

KIT.
DW
RG
PAN.
REF.

8" COLUMNS

FOYER

BED RM. 3
9'-8" X 9'-10"

BREAKFAST
RM.
11'-4" X 8'-5"

W
LAU
D.

ENTRY
PORCH

STORAGE

WH

GOLF CART

GARAGE
19'-4" X 29'-0"

PLAN HPT210158

Square Footage: 1,487

Width: 39'-0"
Depth: 73'-10"

A variety of steep rooflines gives an interesting feel to this home. This is a plan that fits comfortably on narrow lots and maintains clean lines. The combined great room, covered porch and dining area can be utilized as one vast space or separated for intimate gatherings. A gas fireplace makes the great room an even more inviting area. The kitchen features a pantry and shares a snack bar with the breakfast room. The sleeping quarters also offer options with a third bedroom that can be a study with French doors. Please specify basement, crawlspace or slab foundation when ordering.

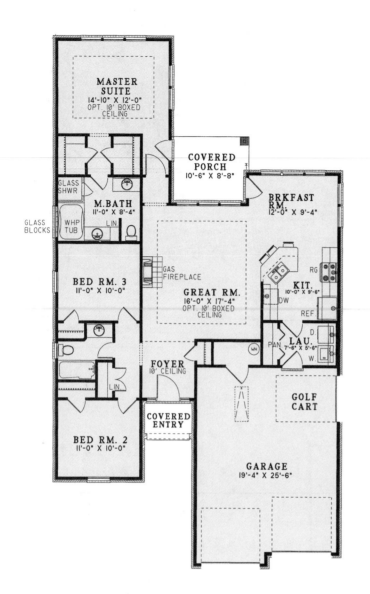

MASTER SUITE
14'-10" X 12'-0"
OPT. 10' BOXED CEILING

COVERED PORCH
10'-6" X 8'-8"

BRKFAST RM.
12'-0" X 9'-4"

GLASS SHWR

M.BATH
11'-0" X 8'-4"

WHP TUB

LIN

GLASS BLOCKS

BED RM. 3
11'-0" X 10'-0"

GAS FIREPLACE

GREAT RM.
16'-0" X 17'-4"
OPT. 10' BOXED CEILING

KIT.
10'-0" X 9'-6"

RG

DW

REF

LAU.
7'-6" X 5'-6"

D

PAN

W

WH

FOYER
10' CEILING

BED RM. 2
11'-0" X 10'-0"

LIN

COVERED ENTRY

GOLF CART

GARAGE
19'-4" X 25'-6"

This house plan offers your choice of a brick or stone facade, either providing an elegant exterior. The fireplace in the great room is the focal point of this home, since it can be seen from the foyer, dining room and kitchen. The dining room and kitchen are also linked by a three-stool snack bar, while views of the covered porch and backyard can be seen from the kitchen sink through the panel of windows that covers the back wall of the house. Two bedrooms are separated from the living areas by a small hallway, where a full-sized bathroom can be found. The master suite also lies apart from the main house and possesses His and Hers walk-in closets, a whirlpool tub, a separate shower and double-sink vanities. Please specify crawlspace or slab foundation when ordering.

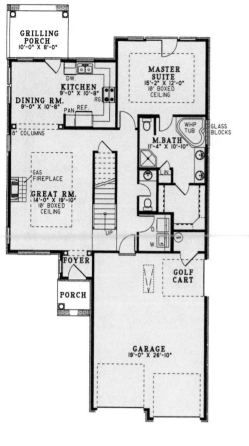

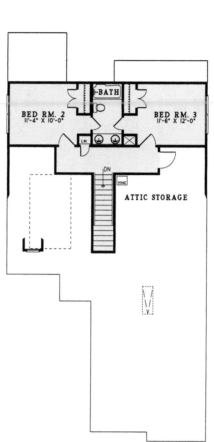

PLAN HPT210160

First Floor: 1,131 sq. ft.
Second Floor: 443 sq. ft.
Total: 1,574 sq. ft.

Width: 34'-0"
Depth: 66'-8"

You'll marvel at the space available in this floor plan. Although total livability is achieved on the first floor for one or two people, the second floor adds two bedrooms and a full bath. The first-floor master suite includes a tray ceiling, outdoor access and a bath with a whirlpool spa and separate shower. The great room with a fireplace is separated from the dining area and adjacent kitchen by decorative columns. Note the grilling porch just beyond. The two-car garage has space for a golf cart, with a private entrance. Please specify crawlspace or slab foundation when ordering.

First Floor plan labels:
- GRILLING PORCH 10'-0" X 8'-0"
- KITCHEN 9'-0" X 10'-8"
- DINING RM. 9'-0" X 10'-8"
- MASTER SUITE 15'-2" X 12'-0" 10' BOXED CEILING
- WHP TUB
- GLASS BLOCKS
- M.BATH 11'-4" X 10'-10"
- LIN.
- GAS FIREPLACE
- GREAT RM. 14'-0" X 19'-10" 10' BOXED CEILING
- UP
- 8" COLUMNS
- FOYER
- GOLF CART
- PORCH
- GARAGE 19'-0" X 26'-10"
- DW
- PAN. REF.
- RG

Second Floor plan labels:
- BATH
- BED RM. 2 11'-4" X 10'-0"
- BED RM. 3 11'-6" X 12'-0"
- LIN.
- DN
- HVAC
- ATTIC STORAGE

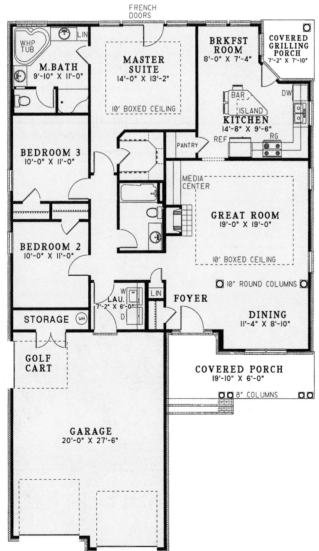

FRENCH DOORS

WHP TUB

M. BATH
9'-10" X 11'-0"

MASTER SUITE
14'-0" X 13'-2"

10' BOXED CEILING

BRKFST ROOM
8'-0" X 7'-4"

COVERED GRILLING PORCH
7'-2" X 7'-10"

BAR ISLAND

KITCHEN
14'-8" X 9'-6"

DW

REF

RG

PANTRY

BEDROOM 3
10'-0" X 11'-0"

MEDIA CENTER

GREAT ROOM
19'-0" X 19'-0"

10' BOXED CEILING

BEDROOM 2
10'-0" X 11'-0"

10" ROUND COLUMNS

LAU.
7'-2" X 6'-0"

W
D

LIN

FOYER

STORAGE

WH

DINING
11'-4" X 8'-10"

GOLF CART

COVERED PORCH
19'-10" X 6'-0"

8" COLUMNS

GARAGE
20'-0" X 27'-6"

PLAN HPT210161

Square Footage: 1,535

Width: 40'-0"
Depth: 67'-4"

With a quaint exterior and action-packed interior, this home will make all your dreams come true. The great room features a boxed ceiling, a fireplace and round columns. The garage has room for your own golf cart, which can be a great toy even if you don't play golf! Marinate your steaks on the giant island in the kitchen and pop out to the grilling porch to cook them to perfection. Then throw a movie in your built-in media center or climb into the whirlpool tub for two. Two family bedrooms are located on the left side of the plan. Please specify crawlspace or slab foundation when ordering.

Optional Outdoor Kitchen

Veranda
48' x 8'

Nook
10' x 8'-4"

Master Bedroom
12' x 15'

Kitchen
9'-6" x 11'

Great Room
15'-6" x 13'-4"

Bedroom 2
12' x 10'-8"

Walk-in Pantry

W.I.C.

W.I.C.

Foyer
7' x 8'

Master Bath
13' x 10'

Bedroom 3
13' x 10'

Dining
12'-2" x 11'-6"

W.I.C.

Util.

Entry
20'-10" x 9'-6"

Garage
21'-4" x 21'-8"

PLAN HPT210162

Square Footage: 1,717

Width: 58'-0"
Depth: 62'-0"

A triplet of keystone arches mimicking recessed fanlight windows hint at the elegance to be found within this charming European-style home. Columns define the dining and great rooms. Both the great room and the master suite boast French doors that open to the expansive veranda with its optional outdoor kitchen. Space is masterfully used in the master suite with its walk-in closet, double-sink vanity, separate shower, tub and compartmented bath. The left side of the plan holds two family bedrooms that share a full bath, a utility room and the two-car garage. Don't miss the sunny nook and the well-equipped kitchen.

PLAN HPT210163

First Floor: 1,276 sq. ft.
Second Floor: 378 sq. ft.
Total: 1,654 sq. ft.

Width: 54'-4"
Depth: 53'-10"

Designed for utmost livability, this English mini-estate is full of charm. A turret entrance leads to the vaulted foyer and the great room beyond. An adjacent kitchen features a 42-inch breakfast bar, a walk-in pantry and a planning desk. The spacious, multi-windowed breakfast room allows access to the octagonal porch—perfect for outdoor dining. Located on the first floor, the master suite includes a relaxing master bath and an enormous walk-in closet. The second floor holds an additional bedroom and a full bath. A large expandable area is available off the balcony and can be used for storage or finished for additional living space. Please specify crawlspace or slab foundation when ordering.

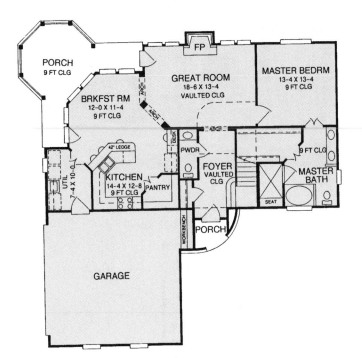

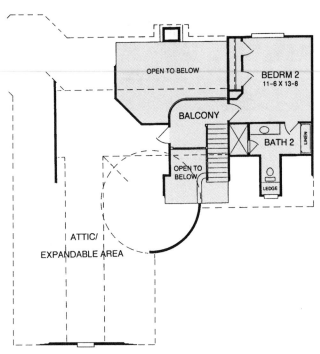

KEEPING ROOM
20'-8" x 14'-0"

PATIO

PATIO

SNACK BAR

GREAT ROOM
14'-4" x 19'-4"

PANTRY

UP

KITCHEN
12'-8" x 11'-0"

REF

MW

RGE

DW

DN

PR

STUDY
13'-0" x 11'-8"

ENTRY

BRM CL

LAUNDRY

W   D

COATS, BOOTS, & HATS

PORCH

GARAGE
20'-8" x 22'-0"

MASTER BEDROOM
12'-0" x 16'-3"

WIC

CEILING

SLOPED

CEILING BEAM

MIRRORS

DRESS

BUILT-IN DRESSERS

DN

MR BATH

(SLOPED FLOOR IN CLOSET)

BEDROOM #3
13'-0" x 11'-8"

B #2

LINEN

CEILING CLIP

BEDROOM #2
11'-4" x 12'-0"

STOR

SLOPE

CEILING CLIP

SLOPE

French Provincial style gives its special touch to this cozy cottage plan. The exterior is resplendent in stucco and features shuttered windows and a cupola with a weathervane over the garage. The main level has an open plan: a great room with fireplace, a keeping room with a snack bar to the kitchen and a tucked-away study. Two patios are accessed through the keeping room and the great room. The second floor holds three bedrooms—two family bedrooms with a shared bath and the master suite with a private bath. A huge walk-in closet and built-in dressers grace the master suite.

PLAN HPT210164

First Floor: 1,278 sq. ft.
Second Floor: 1,027 sq. ft.
Total: 2,305 sq. ft.

Width: 42'-6"
Depth: 61'-2"

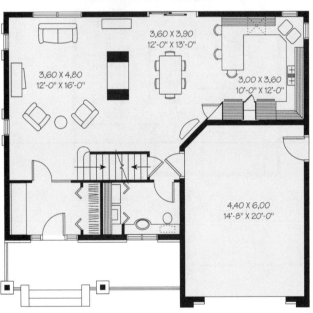

3,60 X 3,90
12'-0" X 13'-0"

3,60 X 4,80
12'-0" X 16'-0"

3,00 X 3,60
10'-0" X 12'-0"

4,40 X 6,00
14'-8" X 20'-0"

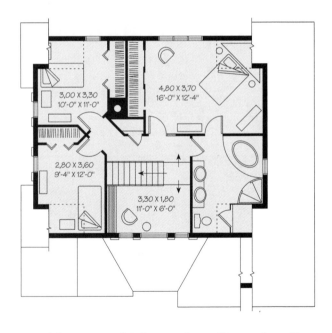

3,00 X 3,30
10'-0" X 11'-0"

4,80 X 3,70
16'-0" X 12'-4"

2,80 X 3,60
9'-4" X 12'-0"

3,30 X 1,80
11'-0" X 6'-0"

PLAN HPT210165

First Floor: 805 sq. ft.
Second Floor: 873 sq. ft.
Total: 1,678 sq. ft.

Width: 37'-4"
Depth: 35'-0"

There are so many grand features on this home—the pedimented rooflines, keystones and lintels, and the large Palladian window on the second level. The grand entry leads into the roomy living room, which is just around the wall divider from the dining room. The open kitchen offers a wraparound snack bar that faces the dining room. Two family bedrooms and a master suite are located on the second level. Dual vanities and a large corner bath make the master bath a treat. This home is designed with a basement foundation.

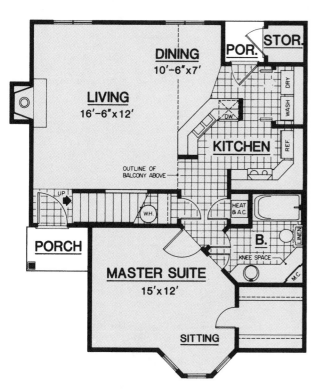

DINING
10'-6"x7'

POR.

STOR.

LIVING
16'-6"x12'

DRY

WASH

DW

KITCHEN

REF

OUTLINE OF
BALCONY ABOVE

UP

W.H.

HEAT
& A.C.

B.

LINEN

PORCH

KNEE SPACE

M.C.

MASTER SUITE
15'x12'

SITTING

PLAN HPT210166

First Floor: 814 sq. ft.
Second Floor: 267 sq. ft.
Total: 1,081 sq. ft.

Width: 28'-0"
Depth: 34'-6"

SLOPED CEILING

FLAT
CEILING

SLOPED
CEILING

HALF WALL

OPEN TO
LIVING BELOW

BALCONY/
BEDROOM
13'x10'

OUTLINE OF
DORMER

HALF WALL

DESK

SHW'R

B.

LINEN

DN

ATTIC

This plan easily fits into established neighborhoods, with a canted bay window, traditional trim and stucco finish. The entry leads into the living room which is complete with a warming hearth. A spacious kitchen offers a snack bar and convenient serving distance to the dining room. A second-floor bedroom with a bath overlooks the vaulted living room over a half-wall that can be finished off for more privacy. The appealing master suite features a sunny sitting area and walk-in closet. Please specify basement, crawlspace or slab foundation when ordering.

PLAN HPT210167

First Floor: 1,078 sq. ft.
Second Floor: 313 sq. ft.
Total: 1,391 sq. ft.

Width: 43'-0"
Depth: 38'-0"

Stucco brings a pure and simple aura to this home. Porch space is plentiful, making outdoor entertaining and relaxing a delight. Family time is enjoyable in the spacious living and dining rooms. The beauty of this house is emphasized by the natural light beaming in through the large windows. Kitchen space is ample and preparing dinner will be a treat. Storage space is conveniently located around the front porch. The master suite sports a large walk-in closet, spacious bath and private access to the rear porch. The second floor is complete with a bedroom, full bath, balcony and access to the attic. Please specify crawlspace or slab foundation when ordering.

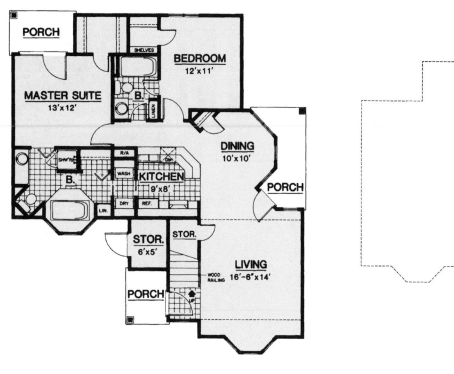

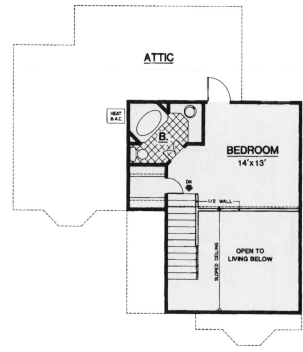

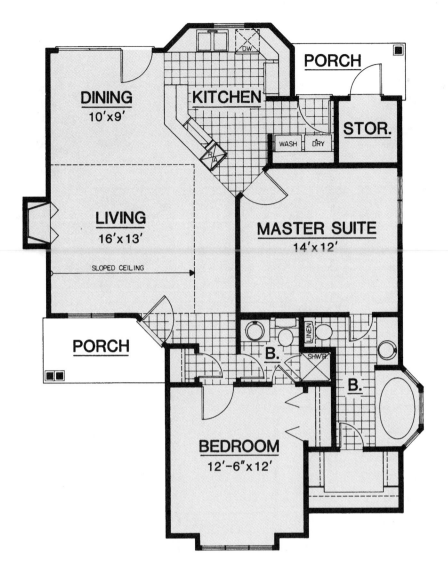

DINING
10'x9'

KITCHEN

DW

PORCH

STOR.

WASH DRY

LIVING
16'x13'

SLOPED CEILING

MASTER SUITE
14'x12'

PORCH

LINEN

B.

SHW'R

B.

BEDROOM
12'-6"x12'

PLAN HPT210168

Square Footage: 984

Width: 33'-9"
Depth: 43'-0"

This snug home uses its square footage efficiently, with no wasted space. Brightened by a clerestory window, the living room features a sloped ceiling and a warming fireplace. The kitchen adjoins the dining room and opens to a back porch with a handy storage closet nearby. A spacious master suite boasts a garden tub set in a bay and a walk-in closet. Wood trim and eye-catching windows make this home charming as well as practical. Please specify crawlspace or slab foundation when ordering.

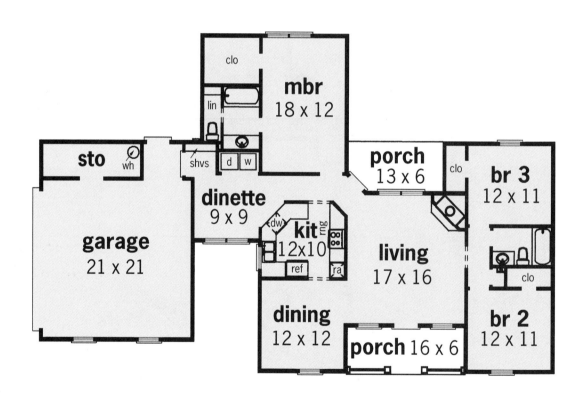

clo

mbr
18 x 12

sto
wh

lin

shvs | d | w

dinette
9 x 9

porch
13 x 6

clo

br 3
12 x 11

garage
21 x 21

dw

kit
12x10

rng

ref | ra

clo

living
17 x 16

dining
12 x 12

porch 16 x 6

br 2
12 x 11

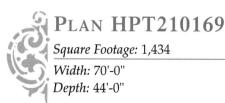

PLAN HPT210169

Square Footage: 1,434

Width: 70'-0"
Depth: 44'-0"

With the facade of a large elegant home, this efficient design creates an exterior that looks much larger than it is. This plan includes formal and informal dining areas, both with direct access to the kitchen. A fireplace can be found in the living room. The isolated and spacious master suite provides a grand bath and a walk-in closet. The secondary bedrooms feature walk-in closets. The living room opens to porches via French doors to the front and back. Please specify crawlspace or slab foundation when ordering.

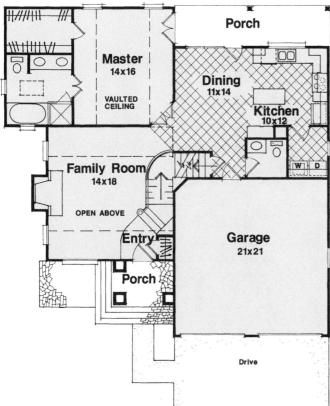

Porch

Master
14x16

VAULTED
CEILING

Dining
11x14

Kitchen
10x12

Family Room
14x18

OPEN ABOVE

W D

Entry

Garage
21x21

Porch

Drive

This stucco treat offers various rooflines and window decor. Three columns introduce an elegant entry that leads to a spacious family room. This room offers a warming fireplace and a curving staircase to the second floor. The L-shaped kitchen is enhanced by a work island and direct access to the dining area as well as a door to the rear porch. The master suite offers a walk-in closet and a private bath with a skylight. Upstairs, a loft is available for studying or reading.

Bedroom #2
13x14

F.M. BELOW

Loft
10x11

Bedroom #3
11x14

Bonus Area
12x10

PLAN HPT210170

First Floor: 1,128 sq. ft.
Second Floor: 631 sq. ft.
Total: 1,759 sq. ft.

Width: 46'-0"
Depth: 46'-0"

PLAN HPT210171

Square Footage: 1,276

Width: 32'-0"
Depth: 40'-0"

This delightful starter home dazzles with a spectacular Palladian window—dressed with a keystone and lintel—in the living room. The entryway is flanked by columns and topped by a dramatic arch. The living and dining areas are a perfect match in this petite home. An elegant covered porch is located off the kitchen/breakfast area. Plenty of counter space wraps around the kitchen. Two family bedrooms sit at the back of the plan for privacy. This home is designed with a basement foundation.

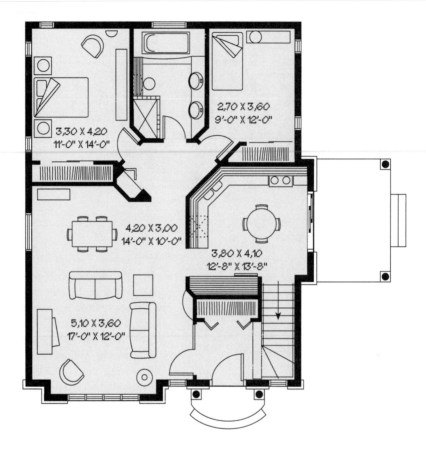

3,30 X 4,20
11'-0" X 14'-0"

2,70 X 3,60
9'-0" X 12'-0"

4,20 X 3,00
14'-0" X 10'-0"

3,80 X 4,10
12'-8" X 13'-8"

5,10 X 3,60
17'-0" X 12'-0"

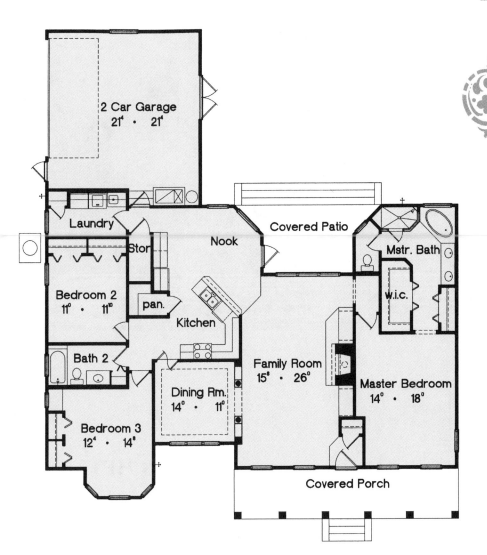

2 Car Garage
21⁴ · 21⁴

Laundry

Stor

Bedroom 2
11⁰ · 11⁰

pan.

Bath 2

Bedroom 3
12⁴ · 14⁸

Nook

Kitchen

Covered Patio

Dining Rm.
14⁰ · 11⁰

Family Room
15⁸ · 26⁰

Covered Porch

Mstr. Bath

w.i.c.

Master Bedroom
14⁰ · 18⁰

PLAN HPT210172

Square Footage: 1,963

Width: 58'-0"

Depth: 66'-8"

Thick columns supporting the porch, plenty of multi-paned windows and a turret create a lovely country retreat. A large family room opens from the covered porch, complete with a warming fireplace. The master suite is tucked to the right of the family room and features a walk-in closet and a sumptuous bath. Columns decorate the entry to the dining room, which views the fireplace in the family room. Conveniently located between the dining room and the garage, the kitchen includes a serving bar, breakfast nook and walk-in pantry. Two family bedrooms share a full bath to the left of the plan. Note the enchanting bay window in Bedroom 3. Please specify crawlspace or slab foundation when ordering.

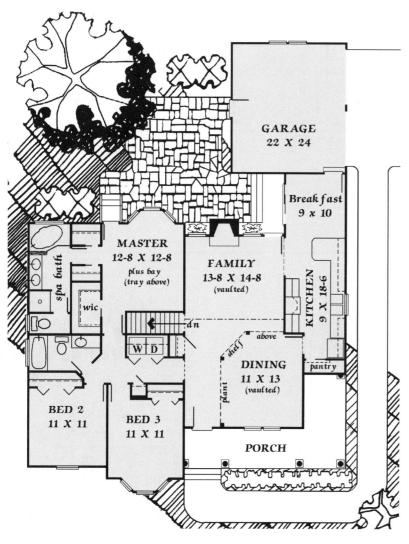

GARAGE
22 X 24

Breakfast
9 x 10

MASTER
12-8 X 12-8
plus bay
(tray above)

spa bath

wic

FAMILY
13-8 X 14-8
(vaulted)

KITCHEN
9 X 18-6

dn

W D

above

shelf

plant

pantry

DINING
11 X 13
(vaulted)

BED 2
11 X 11

BED 3
11 X 11

PORCH

PLAN HPT210173

Square Footage: 1,507

Width: 47'-0"
Depth: 70'-0"

A stucco facade highlights the sophistication offered by this home. The covered porch leads into the dining room, which opens to the family room with a warming hearth. The kitchen and breakfast nook share the right side of the plan. Two family bedrooms share a bath. Down the hall, the master bedroom features a private bath and a walk-in closet.

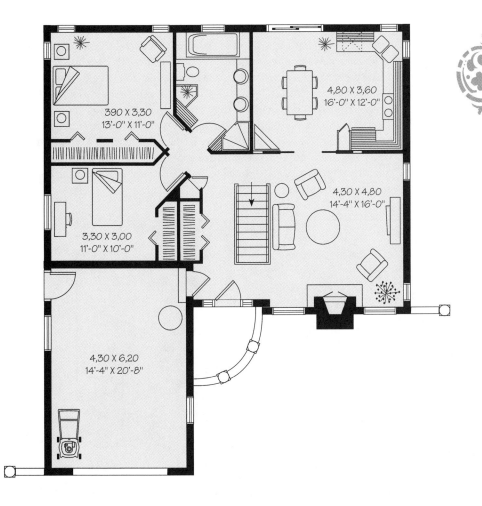

PLAN HPT210174

Square Footage: 1,059

Width: 38'-8"
Depth: 46'-8"

The exterior of this plan is unique and modern with its use of stucco, a front-facing chimney and decorative windows. A triangular stoop leads to an attractive three-part front door. The family room centers on a fireplace framed by soaring, arched windows. The eat-in kitchen includes plenty of room for a table and chairs, as well as a walk-in pantry, a corner sink and sliding doors to the back-yard. Two bedrooms share a bath that includes a corner shower, garden tub and double-sink vanity. This home is designed with a basement foundation.

PLAN HPT210175

Square Footage: 2,137

Width: 44'-0"
Depth: 61'-0"

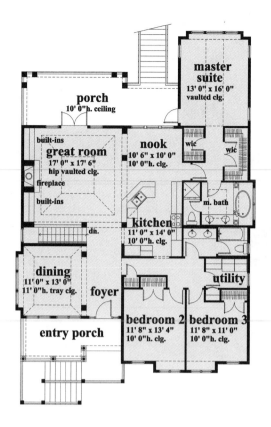

porch
10' 0"h. ceiling

master suite
13' 0" x 16' 0"
vaulted clg.

great room
17' 0" x 17' 6"
hip vaulted clg.

built-ins

fireplace

built-ins

nook
10' 6" x 10' 0"
10' 0"h. clg.

wic

wic

m. bath

kitchen
11' 0" x 14' 0"
10' 0"h. clg.

dn.

dining
11' 0" x 13' 0"
11' 0"h. tray clg.

foyer

utility

entry porch

bedroom 2
11' 8" x 13' 4"
10' 0"h. clg.

bedroom 3
11' 8" x 11' 0"
10' 0"h. clg.

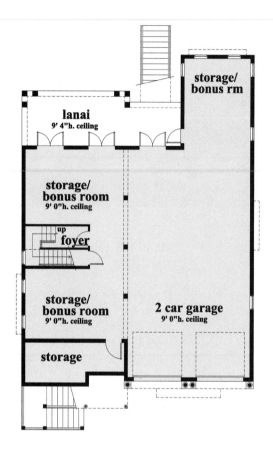

lanai
9' 4"h. ceiling

storage/ bonus rm

storage/ bonus room
9' 0"h. ceiling

up

foyer

storage/ bonus room
9' 0"h. ceiling

2 car garage
9' 0"h. ceiling

storage

The grand balustrade and recessed entry are just the beginning of this truly spectacular home. A hip vaulted ceiling highlights the great room—a perfect place to entertain, made cozy by a massive fireplace and built-in cabinetry. An angled snack counter provides an uninterrupted interior vista of the living area from the gourmet kitchen. On the lower level, separate bonus spaces easily convert to hobby rooms or can be used for additional storage. To the rear of the plan, French doors open to a spacious lanai—a beautiful spot for enjoying the harmonious sounds of the sea. An additional storage area promises room for unused toys and furnishings.

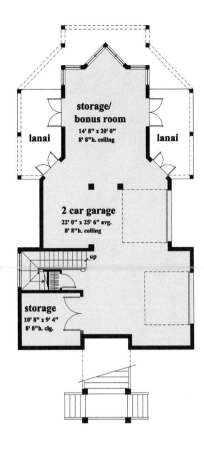

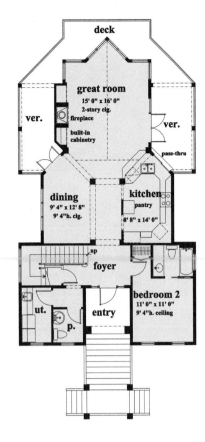

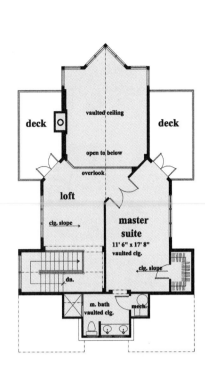

storage/bonus room
14' 8" x 20' 0"
8' 8"h. ceiling

lanai   lanai

2 car garage
22' 0" x 25' 6" avg.
8' 8"h. ceiling

up

storage
10' 8" x 9' 4"
8' 8" clg.

deck

great room
15' 0" x 16' 0"
2-story clg.
fireplace
built-in cabinetry

ver.   ver.

pass-thru

dining
9' 4" x 12' 8"
9' 4"h. clg.

kitchen
pantry
8' 8" x 14' 0"

up

foyer

bedroom 2
11' 0" x 11' 0"
9' 4"h. ceiling

ut.
p.
entry

deck   vaulted ceiling   deck

open to below

overlook

loft

clg. slope

master suite
11' 6" x 17' 8"
vaulted clg.

clg. slope

dn.

m. bath
vaulted clg.

PLAN HPT210176

First Floor: 1,143 sq. ft.
Second Floor: 651 sq. ft.
Total: 1,794 sq. ft.

Width: 32'-0"
Depth: 57'-0"

The traditional stucco facade captures the essence of this distinctly European villa. The covered entryway extends into the foyer, where straight ahead, the two-story great room spaciously enhances the interior. The open dining room extends through double doors to the veranda on the left side on the plan. The adjacent kitchen features efficient pantry space. A family bedroom with a private bath, a powder room and a utility room also reside on this main floor. Upstairs, a vaulted master suite with a vaulted master bath and deck share the floor with a loft area, which overlooks the great room. Downstairs, the basement level bonus room and storage area share space with the two-car garage. Two lanais open on either side of the bonus room for additional outdoor patio space.

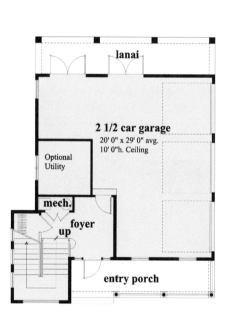

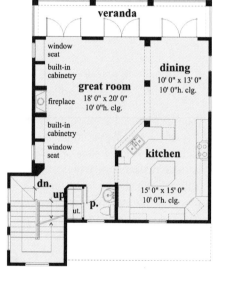

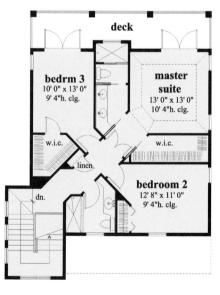

veranda

window seat

built-in cabinetry

great room
18' 0" x 20' 0"
10' 0"h. clg.

fireplace

dining
10' 0" x 13' 0"
10' 0"h. clg.

built-in cabinetry

window seat

dn. up

ut.

p.

kitchen
15' 0" x 15' 0"
10' 0"h. clg.

lanai

2 1/2 car garage
20' 0" x 29' 0" avg.
10' 0"h. Ceiling

Optional Utility

mech.

foyer
up

entry porch

deck

bedrm 3
10' 0" x 13' 0"
9' 4"h. clg.

master suite
13' 0" x 13' 0"
10' 4"h. clg.

w.i.c.

w.i.c.

linen

bedroom 2
12' 8" x 11' 0"
9' 4"h. clg.

dn.

PLAN HPT210177

First Floor: 874 sq. ft.
Second Floor: 880 sq. ft.
Total: 1,996 sq. ft.

Width: 34'-0"
Depth: 43'-0"

A stately tower adds a sense of grandeur to cool, contemporary high-pitched rooflines on this dreamy Mediterranean-style villa. Surrounded by outdoor views, the living space extends to a veranda through three sets of French doors. Decorative columns announce the dining area, which boasts a ten-foot ceiling and views of its own. Tall arch-top windows bathe a winding staircase with sunlight or moonlight. The upper-level sleeping quarters include a master retreat that offers a bedroom with views and access to the observation deck. Secondary bedrooms share a full bath and linen storage. Bedroom 3 features a walk-in closet and French doors to the deck.

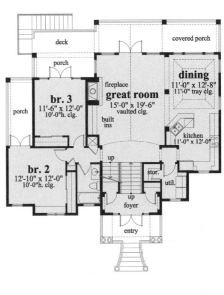

deck

covered porch

porch

fireplace

br. 3
11'-6" x 12'-0"
10'-0"h. clg.

great room
15'-0" x 19'-6"
vaulted clg.

dining
11'-0" x 12'-8"
11'-0" tray clg.

porch

built ins

kitchen
11'-0" x 12'-0"

br. 2
12'-10" x 12'-0"
10'-0"h. clg.

up

stor.

util.

up

foyer

entry

2 car garage

bonus/storage

storage

porch

master suite
12'-8" x 17'-8"
10'-0" tray clg.

open to below

w.i.c.

overlook

dn

master bath

dn

porch

PLAN HPT210178

First Floor: 1,383 sq. ft.
Second Floor: 595 sq. ft.
Total: 1,978 sq. ft.

Width: 48'-0"
Depth: 42'-0"

Those who prefer a spacious master suite set apart from the rest of the home will love this arrangement. The top story is devoted to a private master retreat complete with double doors leading to a private porch and a loft that overlooks the vaulted great room below. On the first floor, each of the two family bedrooms has an adjoining porch. The built-ins and fireplace in the great room give a feeling of casual sophistication. The mixture of grand details with a comfortable layout makes this home a perfect combination of elegance and easy living.

PLAN HPT210179

First Floor: 1,342 sq. ft.
Second Floor: 511 sq. ft.
Total: 1,853 sq. ft.

Width: 44'-0"
Depth: 40'-0"

With a perfect Mediterranean spirit, arch-top windows create curb appeal and allow the beauty and warmth of nature within this home. To the rear of the plan, an elegant dining room easily flexes to serve traditional events as well as impromptu gatherings. An angled island counter accents the gourmet kitchen and permits wide interior vistas. The master retreat features a spacious bedroom that leads outside to a private porch—the best place in the world to count stars. An area framed by the walk-in closet and linen storage leads to a lavish bath with a garden tub and oversized shower. On the upper level, an open deck extends the square footage of one of the secondary bedrooms—an invitation to enjoy sunlight and gentle breezes.

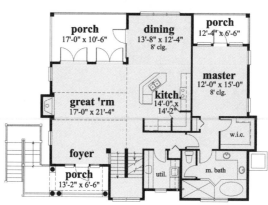

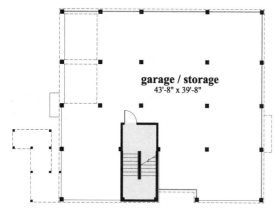

Colonial-style cottages can come in all flavors: salt boxes, Cape Cods, Southern Belles, a touch of Greek Revival and the tried-and-true shotgun houses. With shutters, horizontal siding and covered porches defined by graceful columns, these comfy little cottages offer the ambience of days gone by, when the nation was young and strong and living seemed simpler. Equally attractive on a country lane or just up the street from your child's school, these picturesque little homes feature up-to-date interiors, perfect for either a comfortable getaway or today's families. Sizes run from a petite 767 square feet to just under 2,000 square feet.

PLAN HPT210180

First Floor: 760 sq. ft.
Second Floor: 742 sq. ft.
Total: 1,502 sq. ft.
Bonus Room: 324 sq. ft.

Width: 39'-1"
Depth: 36'-9"

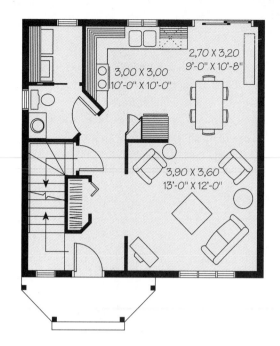

3,00 X 3,00
10'-0" X 10'-0"

2,70 X 3,20
9'-0" X 10'-8"

3,90 X 3,60
13'-0" X 12'-0"

From the memory of early America and Colonial times long past, this simple design emerges as the perfect family home. Enter inside from the petite columned porch. A foyer coat closet resides across from the living room. The nearby family dining area is open to the kitchen with a pantry. The first-floor powder room and laundry facilities are tucked away behind the kitchen. Upstairs, the master bedroom shares a full hall bath with two other family bedrooms. The home is designed with a basement foundation.

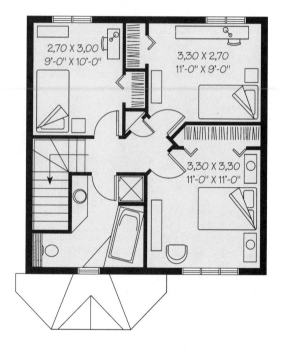

2,70 X 3,00
9'-0" X 10'-0"

3,30 X 2,70
11'-0" X 9'-0"

3,30 X 3,30
11'-0" X 11'-0"

PLAN HPT210181

First Floor: 576 sq. ft.
Second Floor: 576 sq. ft.
Total: 1,152 sq. ft.

Width: 24'-0"
Depth: 24'-0"

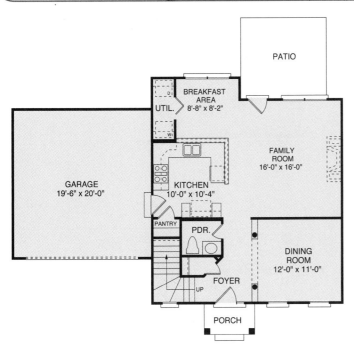

PATIO

BREAKFAST
AREA
8'-8" x 8'-2"

UTIL.

FAMILY
ROOM
16'-0" x 16'-0"

GARAGE
19'-6" x 20'-0"

KITCHEN
10'-0" x 10'-4"

PANTRY

PDR.

DINING
ROOM
12'-0" x 11'-0"

FOYER

UP

PORCH

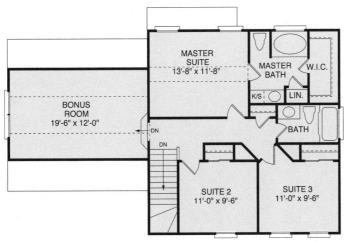

MASTER
SUITE
13'-8" x 11'-8"

MASTER
BATH

W.I.C.

BONUS
ROOM
19'-6" x 12'-0"

DN

DN

K/S

LIN.

BATH

SUITE 2
11'-0" x 9'-6"

SUITE 3
11'-0" x 9'-6"

PLAN HPT210182

First Floor: 774 sq. ft.
Second Floor: 756 sq. ft.
Total: 1,530 sq. ft.
Bonus Room: 251 sq. ft.

Width: 46'-11"
Depth: 35'-1"

This classic Colonial-style home offers a taste of the past with its pedimented rooflines and shuttered windows. Through the entry is the elegantly columned dining room. The spacious family room features an optional warming hearth. The kitchen has plenty of counter space and convenient access to the breakfast area. Two family bedrooms and a master suite are located on the second floor, where a bonus room adds additional space.

PLAN HPT210183

First Floor: 609 sq. ft.
Second Floor: 642 sq. ft.
Total: 1,251 sq. ft.

Width: 27'-0"
Depth: 45'-0"

This double-decker delight allows natural light to illuminate the interior of this home. The spacious great room has an option for a gas fireplace. Columns flank the entrance to the dining room, where the grilling porch is conveniently accessed. The spacious L-shaped kitchen offers pantry space. The master bedroom and two family bedrooms are located upstairs. Please specify basement, crawlspace or slab foundation when ordering.

GRILLING PORCH
10'-0" X 6'-0"

DINING
12'-0" X 9'-0"

KITCHEN
14'-0" X 9'-0"

REF.
PANTRY

DW   RG.

8" COLUMNS

GREAT ROOM.
12'-0" X 17'-0"

D

W.

HVAC

WH

OPTIONAL GAS FIREPLACE

UP

SINGLE GARAGE
10'-4" X 20'-0"

COVERED PORCH
16'-0" X 5'-0"

M.BATH

BEDROOM 2
8'-10" X 10'-4"

DN

MBEDRM.
10'-8" X 15'-0"

BATH

BEDROOM 3
12'-4" X 10'-0"

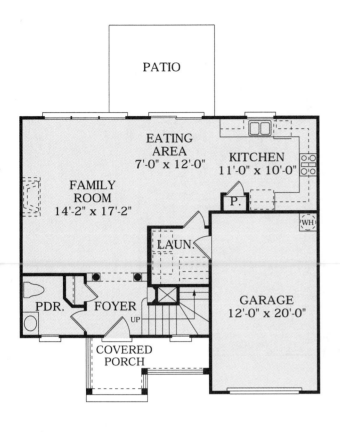

PATIO

EATING AREA
7'-0" x 12'-0"

KITCHEN
11'-0" x 10'-0"

FAMILY ROOM
14'-2" x 17'-2"

P.

LAUN.

WH

PDR.

FOYER

UP

GARAGE
12'-0" x 20'-0"

COVERED PORCH

Shutters, lintels and a pedimented porch lend cheer and eye-appeal to this two-story, three-bedroom home. Decorative columns adorn the entry, which allows access to all living areas including the second floor, the family room and a powder room. The U-shaped kitchen is open to the eating area and family room. The family room has the option of a fireplace. The second level includes two family bedroom suites and a master suite. The master suite features a walk-in closet, oval tub and separate shower.

BATH

SUITE 2
9'-6" x 8'-6"

BATH

SUITE 3
9'-6" x 10'-0"

DN

MASTER SUITE
12'-10" x 13'-0"

W.I.C.

PLAN HPT210184

First Floor: 680 sq. ft.
Second Floor: 674 sq. ft.
Total: 1,354 sq. ft.

Width: 54'-4"
Depth: 31'-2"

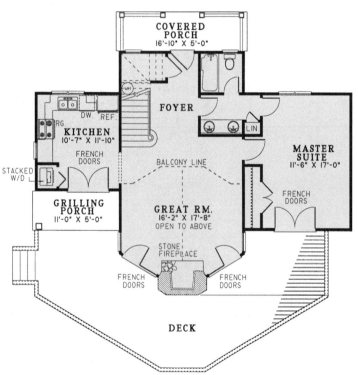

COVERED PORCH
16'-10" X 5'-0"

FOYER

KITCHEN
10'-7" X 11'-10"

DW   REF.

RG

FRENCH DOORS

STACKED W/D

GRILLING PORCH
11'-0" X 5'-0"

BALCONY LINE

MASTER SUITE
11'-6" X 17'-0"

FRENCH DOORS

GREAT RM.
16'-2" X 17'-8"
OPEN TO ABOVE

STONE FIREPLACE

FRENCH DOORS   FRENCH DOORS

DECK

PLAN HPT210185

First Floor: 862 sq. ft.
Second Floor: 332 sq. ft.
Total: 1,194 sq. ft.

Width: 42'-0"
Depth: 36'-2"

The front of this two-bedroom home is sweet and simple, while the rear is dedicated to fun and sun. Inside, the foyer opens to the two-story great room, where sunlight pours into the room not only from the wall of windows but also from four skylights. A large stone fireplace dominates the window wall and offers warmth on cool spring evenings. The L-shaped kitchen features French doors out to the grilling porch, perfect for numerous cookouts. On the opposite side of the home, a large master suite awaits to pamper the homeowner. Here, a second set of French doors leads out to the deck. Upstairs, a loft offers a walk-in closet and a full bath with a skylight. Please specify crawlspace or slab foundation when ordering.

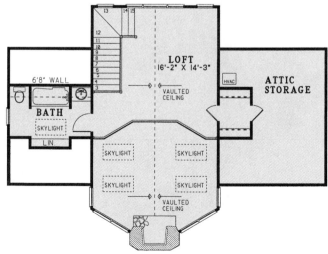

6'8" WALL

BATH

SKYLIGHT

LIN

LOFT
16'-2" X 14'-3"

VAULTED CEILING

SKYLIGHT   SKYLIGHT

HVAC

ATTIC STORAGE

SKYLIGHT   SKYLIGHT

VAULTED CEILING

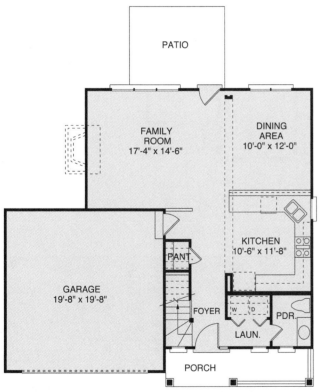

PATIO

FAMILY ROOM
17'-4" x 14'-6"

DINING AREA
10'-0" x 12'-0"

KITCHEN
10'-6" x 11'-8"

PANT.

GARAGE
19'-8" x 19'-8"

FOYER

W D

LAUN.

PDR.

PORCH

Made for a narrow footprint or in-fill lot, this home offers traditional lines with a farmhouse flavor. A welcoming porch ushers family and guests into the foyer. The large U-shaped kitchen is just to the right with a nearby laundry room for convenience. The dining area is found to the rear and enjoys rear views and porch access. The family room is perfect for a fireplace and entertaining guests or spending a quiet night at home. The master suite features a coffered ceiling, walk-in closets and a full bath. Two family suites share a full bath, and a bonus room is found just across the hall.

MASTER SUITE
13'-0" x 14'-6"

MASTER BATH

W.I.C.

LIN.

LIN.

SUITE 2
9'-6" x 10'-0"

DN
DN

BONUS ROOM
16'-0" x 14'-8"

ACCESS

BATH

SUITE 3
9'-6" x 10'-0"

PLAN HPT210186

First Floor: 760 sq. ft.
Second Floor: 742 sq. ft.
Total: 1,502 sq. ft.
Bonus Room: 283 sq. ft.

Width: 39'-1"
Depth: 36'-9"

PLAN HPT210187

First Floor: 945 sq. ft.
Second Floor: 825 sq. ft.
Total: 1,770 sq. ft.

Width: 44'-0"
Depth: 41'-4"

Shutters, window boxes and a square-columned porch add classic finishing touches to this design. The spacious great room, just past the ample foyer, features a fireplace flanked by built-in shelving and an angled border along the casual eating area. Upstairs, you'll find sleeping quarters plus a spacious study with a dormer. The generous master suite includes a walk-in closet and a large bath with separate tub, shower and toilet compartments. This home is designed with a basement foundation.

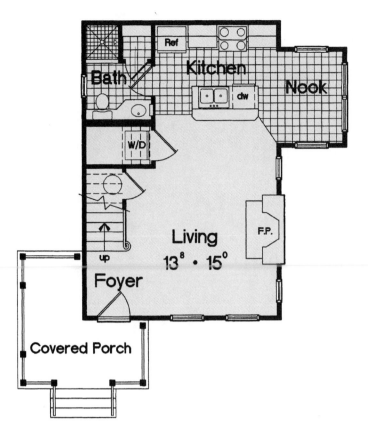

Bath

Kitchen

Ref

dw

Nook

W/D

Living
13⁸ • 15⁰

F.P.

up

Foyer

Covered Porch

PLAN HPT210188

First Floor: 512 sq. ft.
Second Floor: 255 sq. ft.
Total: 767 sq. ft.

Width: 30'-0"
Depth: 32'-0"

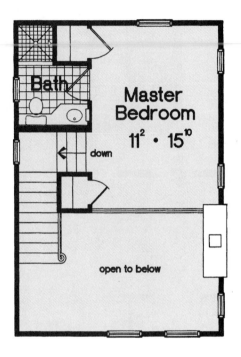

Bath

Master Bedroom
11² • 15¹⁰

down

open to below

Designed for one person or a couple, a vacation retreat or a year-round home, this plan presents simple living with maximum comfort. The corner porch is vast enough for a pair of rocking chairs, and inside, the two-story living room is cozy with a fireplace flanked by windows. The island kitchen boasts a box-bay nook, perfect for every meal of the day. The second floor is dedicated to the master bedroom, which includes a private bath and His and Hers wardrobes.

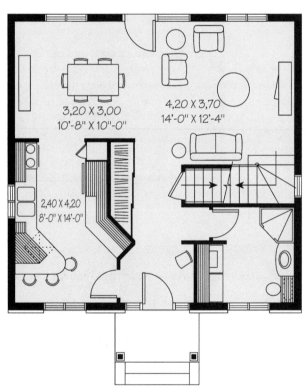

3,20 X 3,00
10'-8" X 10'-0"

4,20 X 3,70
14'-0" X 12'-4"

2,40 X 4,20
8'-0" X 14'-0"

PLAN HPT210189

First Floor: 676 sq. ft.
Second Floor: 676 sq. ft.
Total: 1,352 sq. ft.

Width: 26'-0"
Depth: 26'-0"

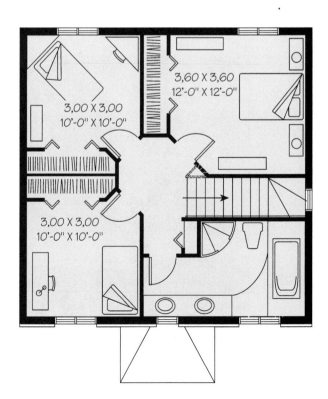

3,00 X 3,00
10'-0" X 10'-0"

3,60 X 3,60
12'-0" X 12'-0"

3,00 X 3,00
10'-0" X 10'-0"

With early American style and colonial quaintness, this dazzling design is a true family favorite. A formal brick facade and a front columned porch define elegance outside, while inside, living areas are impressive. To the left of the entry, a kitchen with a breakfast bar is open to the dining area. A family room and a shower bath flank the stairway. Upstairs, three family bedrooms share a full hall bath. This home is designed with a basement foundation.

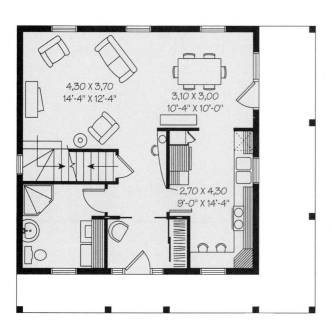

4,30 X 3,70
14'-4" X 12'-4"

3,10 X 3,00
10'-4" X 10'-0"

2,70 X 4,30
9'-0" X 14'-4"

A vision of early American architecture, this Colonial design is the picture of New England family perfection. A relaxing covered front porch encloses an alluring plan. The entry holds a coat closet. A shower bath is located to the left, while the kitchen sits to the right. The formal living and dining rooms are placed to the rear. Upstairs, three family bedrooms share a full hall bath that includes a separate shower and a corner tub. This home is designed with a basement foundation.

PLAN HPT210190

First Floor: 676 sq. ft.
Second Floor: 676 sq. ft.
Total: 1,352 sq. ft.

Width: 26'-0"
Depth: 26'-0"

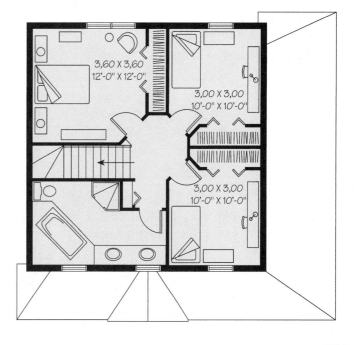

3,60 X 3,60
12'-0" X 12'-0"

3,00 X 3,00
10'-0" X 10'-0"

3,00 X 3,00
10'-0" X 10'-0"

MASTER BEDRM.
13 X 16
VAULTED CEILING
FROM 8'-0" TO 9'-0"

WALK-IN
CLOSET

SHELVES

CLOS.

BEDRM.
TWO
11 X 12
8'-0" CLG. HT.

MSTR.
BATH

LINEN

HALL

BATH TWO

DINETTE
8 X 14
10'-0" CLG. HT.

D.W.

KITCHEN

COVERED
PATIO

LINEN

REF.

PANTRY

LINEN

WASH

BEDRM.
THREE
11 X 12
8'-0" CLG. HT.

UTILITY

DRY

ENTERTAINMENT
CENTER

GREAT
ROOM
21 X 15
10'-0" CLG. HT.

CLOS.

COAT

C/H

H.W.

CLOSET

ENTRY

DOUBLE
GARAGE

COVERED
VERANDA

PORCH

PLAN HPT210191

Square Footage: 1,701

Width: 45'-0"

Depth: 68'-2"

Amazing Colonial details wrap this home in delight and make it a pleasure to view and a joy to inhabit. Double doors open off the covered veranda into the great room where the fireplace awaits. The dinette area is located just off the kitchen. Down the hall from the great room are two family bedrooms and a master bedroom with a spacious walk-in closet and a private bath. Bedrooms 2 and 3 share a bath and each include their own closets.

Patio

Porch

Master
Bedroom

Carport

Living

Bedroom

Dining

Bedroom

Porch

PLAN HPT210192

Square Footage: 1,363

Width: 30'-0"
Depth: 60'-0"

With a master bedroom and living area that open to the rear, this is a home that begs for a terrific backyard. It offers great privacy while creating a sense of spaciousness with its open design. The kitchen includes a breakfast bar that opens to the living room. The living room has a corner fireplace and French doors that lead to the covered rear porch. The master bath has an oversized tub/shower and a double-sink vanity area. In addition to the master suite, this home has two other bedrooms and another full bath.

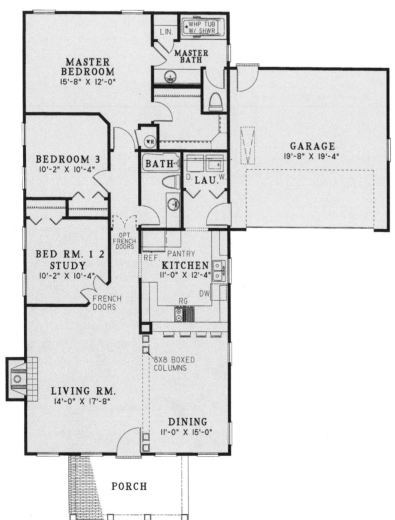

WHP TUB W/ SHWR

LIN.

MASTER BATH

MASTER BEDROOM
15'-8" X 12'-0"

WH

BEDROOM 3
10'-2" X 10'-4"

BATH

D. LAU. W.

GARAGE
19'-8" X 19'-4"

OPT. FRENCH DOORS

BED RM. 1 2 STUDY
10'-2" X 10'-4"

FRENCH DOORS

REF. PANTRY

KITCHEN
11'-0" X 12'-4"

DW

RG

8X8 BOXED COLUMNS

LIVING RM.
14'-0" X 17'-8"

DINING
11'-0" X 15'-0"

PORCH

PLAN HPT210193

Square Footage: 1,404

Width: 48'-4"

Depth: 62'-0"

Graceful columns, reminiscent of fine Greek Revival style, adorn the covered front porch of this compact, yet elegant design. The entry opens directly to the living room and its fireplace. Decorative columns define the boundary between the living and dining rooms. The kitchen has a pass-through counter to the dining room and leads to a service entry with an optional garage. The master suite offers a private bath and a walk-in closet. One of the family bedrooms could be used as a study. Please specify crawlspace or slab foundation when ordering.

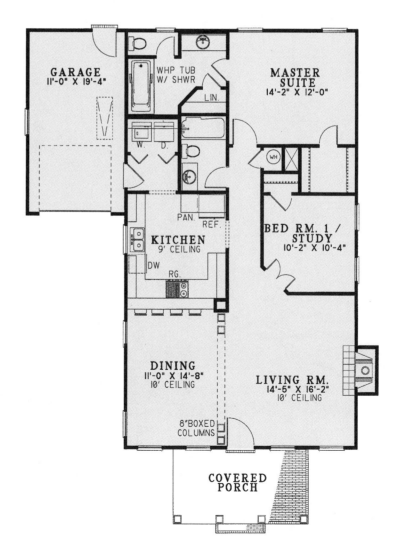

GARAGE
11'-0" X 19'-4"

WHP TUB
W/ SHWR

MASTER
SUITE
14'-2" X 12'-0"

LIN.

W. D.

PAN.   REF.

KITCHEN
9' CEILING

DW

RG.

BED RM. 1 /
STUDY
10'-2" X 10'-4"

WH

DINING
11'-0" X 14'-8"
10' CEILING

LIVING RM.
14'-5" X 16'-2"
10' CEILING

8" BOXED
COLUMNS

COVERED
PORCH

PLAN HPT210194

Square Footage: 1,172

Width: 37'-0"
Depth: 53'-0"

Classic tradition is enhanced in this petite family design. A gracefully columned front porch makes a beautiful first impression. Enter into the living room, which offers a warming fireplace for crisp evenings. The elegant dining room is ideal for formal entertaining. Petite, yet efficient, the kitchen conveniently connects to the garage via the laundry room. The master suite features a walk-in closet and a private bath with a whirlpool tub and a linen closet. An additional bedroom can be converted to a study. Please specify basement, crawlspace or slab foundation when ordering.

PLAN HPT210195

Square Footage: 1,376

Width: 46'-0"
Depth: 38'-2"

L D

This charmingly compact plan is sure to please. The interior plan contains a large living room/dining room combination, a media room, a U-shaped kitchen with a breakfast room, and two bedrooms including a master bedroom with a walk-in closet. If extra space is needed, the media room could serve as a third bedroom. Note the terrace to the rear of the plan off the dining room and the sloped ceilings throughout.

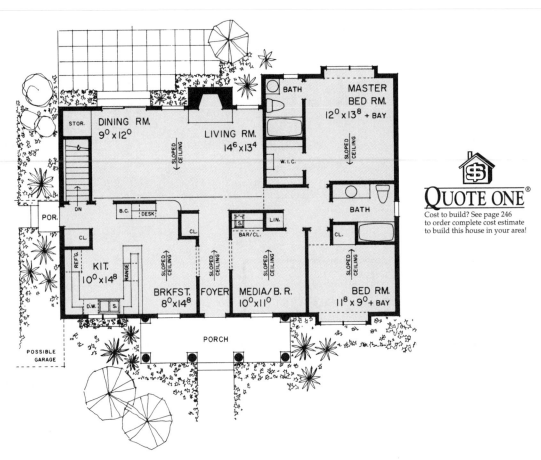

QUOTE ONE®

Cost to build? See page 246 to order complete cost estimate to build this house in your area!

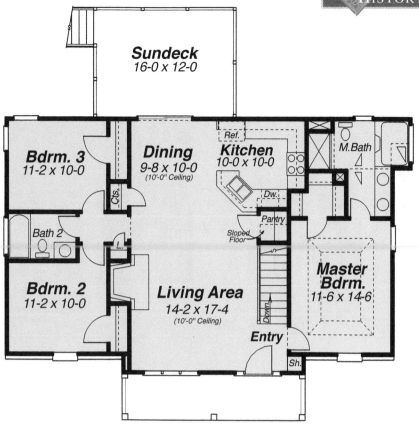

Sundeck
16-0 x 12-0

Bdrm. 3
11-2 x 10-0

Dining
9-8 x 10-0
(10'-0" Ceiling)

Kitchen
10-0 x 10-0

Ref.

M.Bath

Cts.

Dw.

Pantry

Sloped
Floor

Bath 2

Bdrm. 2
11-2 x 10-0

Living Area
14-2 x 17-4
(10'-0" Ceiling)

Down

**Master
Bdrm.**
11-6 x 14-6

Entry

Sh.

PLAN HPT210196

Square Footage: 1,268

Width: 46'-0"
Depth: 33'-0"

As quaint as can be, this wood-sided one-story home offers a covered front porch and a sun deck on the back. In between is a comfortable floor plan. The living area contains a fireplace and is open to the dining room. A modified U-shaped kitchen contains an open counter with double sinks that overlook the living/dining area. Bedrooms 2 and 3 share a full bath and have ample wall closets. The master suite features a private bath with a separate tub and shower and double sinks. A large walk-in closet rounds out the favored master bedroom amenities.

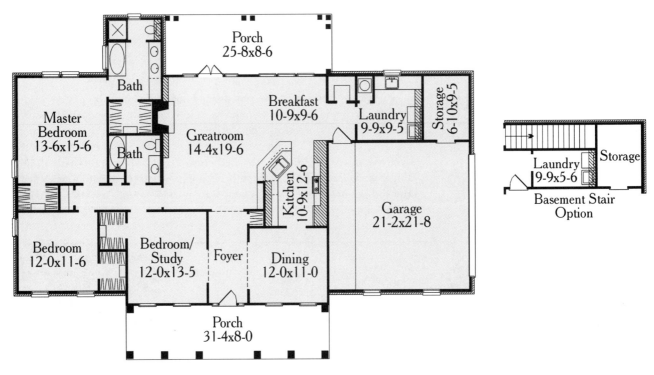

Porch
25-8x8-6

Bath

Master
Bedroom
13-6x15-6

Bath

Greatroom
14-4x19-6

Breakfast
10-9x9-6

Laundry
9-9x9-5

Storage
6-10x9-5

Kitchen
10-9x12-6

Garage
21-2x21-8

Bedroom
12-0x11-6

Bedroom/
Study
12-0x13-5

Foyer

Dining
12-0x11-0

Porch
31-4x8-0

Laundry
9-9x5-6

Storage

Basement Stair
Option

PLAN HPT210197

Square Footage: 1,867

Width: 70'-6"
Depth: 51'-0"

An arched entry is nicely accented by graceful columns on this attractive Southern home. Inside, the foyer is flanked by a formal dining room and a bedroom/study. The spacious great room features a warming fireplace and access to the rear covered porch. An efficient kitchen is complete with an adjacent breakfast area and a nearby pantry. The master suite offers two walk-in closets, a double vanity and a pampering bath with a separate tub and shower. The family bedrooms each have walk-in closets and share a hall bath. Note the plentiful storage in the two-car garage. Please specify basement, crawlspace or slab foundation when ordering.

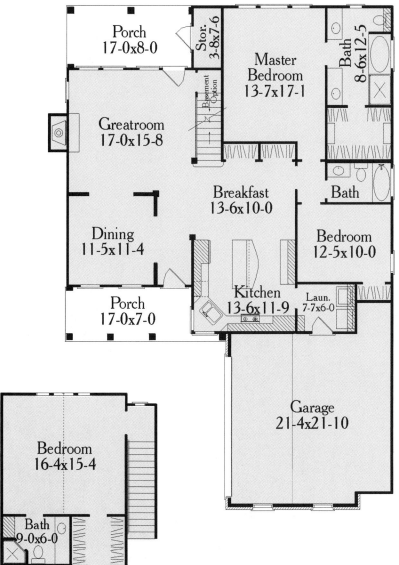

Porch
17-0x8-0

Stor.
3-8x7-6

Master
Bedroom
13-7x17-1

Bath
8-6x12-5

Greatroom
17-0x15-8

Basement
Option

Breakfast
13-6x10-0

Bath

Dining
11-5x11-4

Bedroom
12-5x10-0

Porch
17-0x7-0

Kitchen
13-6x11-9

Laun.
7-7x6-0

Garage
21-4x21-10

Bedroom
16-4x15-4

Bath
9-0x6-0

PLAN HPT210198

First Floor: 1,596 sq. ft.
Second Floor: 387 sq. ft.
Total: 1,983 sq. ft.

Width: 46'-6"
Depth: 65'-0"

Front and rear covered porches add comfortable outdoor space to this fine three-bedroom home. A formal dining room is located near the entry. Nearby, a wall of windows and a warming fireplace characterize the comfortable great room. Just off the great room is a covered porch, perfect for quiet reflection. The island work area in the kitchen will make food preparation a breeze. A luxurious master suite contains a private dual-vanity bath with a garden tub and separate shower. The other two bedrooms each have a full bath. Note the extra storage space available off the rear porch. Please specify basement, crawlspace or slab foundation when ordering.

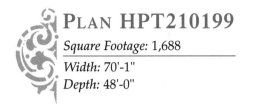

PLAN HPT210199

Square Footage: 1,688

Width: 70'-1"
Depth: 48'-0"

Dormers and columns decorate the exterior of this three-bedroom country home. Inside, the foyer immediately accesses one family bedroom and the formal dining area. Ahead is the great room with a warming fireplace and ribbon windows for natural lighting. The galley kitchen adjoins a breakfast area with a lovely bay window. The master suite, set to the back of the plan, features a lavish bath with a garden tub, separate shower and two vanities. Storage is not a problem in this comfortable home, with walk-in closets in each bedroom and an additional storage room off the two-car garage. Please specify basement, crawlspace or slab foundation when ordering.

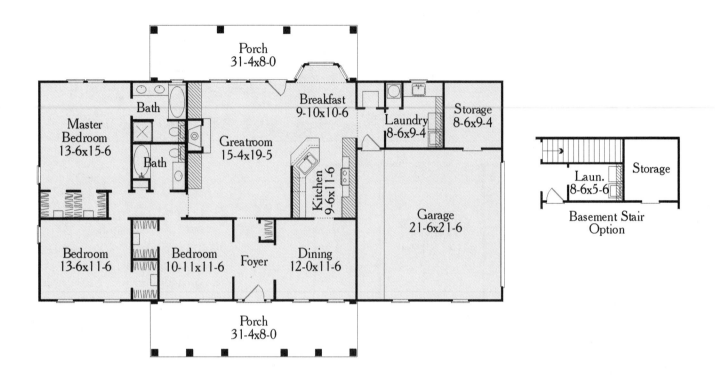

Porch
31-4x8-0

Bath

Master Bedroom
13-6x15-6

Bath

Breakfast
9-10x10-6

Greatroom
15-4x19-5

Laundry
8-6x9-4

Storage
8-6x9-4

Kitchen
9-6x11-6

Garage
21-6x21-6

Bedroom
13-6x11-6

Bedroom
10-11x11-6

Foyer

Dining
12-0x11-6

Porch
31-4x8-0

Laun.
8-6x5-6

Storage

Basement Stair
Option

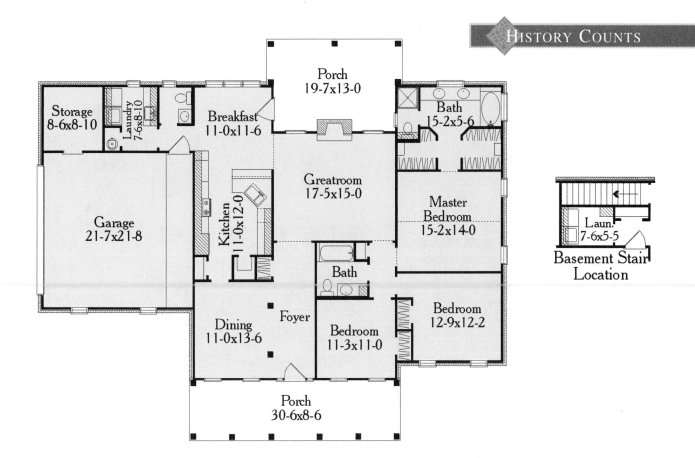

Porch
19-7x13-0

Storage
8-6x8-10

Laundry
7-6x8-10

Breakfast
11-0x11-6

Bath
15-2x5-6

Garage
21-7x21-8

Greatroom
17-5x15-0

Kitchen
11-0x12-0

Master
Bedroom
15-2x14-0

Bath

Dining
11-0x13-6

Foyer

Bedroom
11-3x11-0

Bedroom
12-9x12-2

Porch
30-6x8-6

Laun.
7-6x5-5

Basement Stair
Location

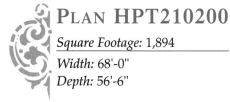

PLAN HPT210200

Square Footage: 1,894

Width: 68'-0"
Depth: 56'-6"

Multiple windows offer insight into this beautiful home and accent this brilliant design. To avoid disarray, the storage room is located in the garage. Entering from the garage, a laundry room is on the left, while to the right await a powder room and breakfast room. The kitchen provides plenty of counter space and is adjacent to the dining room. A vast great room includes a fireplace framed by windows. The master suite is to the far right of the home and boasts two walk-in closets, dual sinks, a separate shower and a tub. Directly across from Bedrooms 2 and 3, a full bath is available. Please specify basement, crawlspace or slab foundation when ordering.

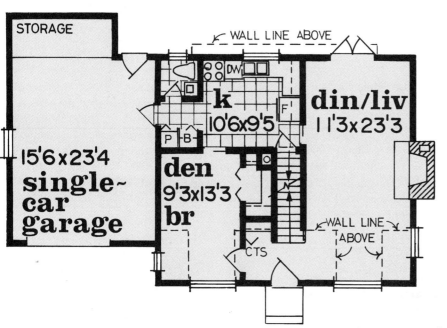

STORAGE

k
10'6x9'5

din/liv
11'3x23'3

15'6 x 23'4
single~
car
garage

den
9'3x13'3
br

WALL LINE ABOVE

DW

F

P   B

WALL LINE
ABOVE

CTS

PLAN HPT210201

First Floor: 672 sq. ft.
Second Floor: 571 sq. ft.
Total: 1,243 sq. ft.

Width: 44'-0"
Depth: 28'-4"

This charming and affordable starter or retirement home presents an exterior finished in beveled siding and shutters. The combination living room/dining room sits on the right of the foyer and offers a fireplace and double-door access to the rear yard. A cozy yet adorable kitchen includes a window sink and direct access to a den or bedroom. On the second story, the master bedroom and Bedroom 2 each furnish built-in shelves. A full hall bath and a linen closet are shared between the bedrooms. Note the single-car garage with storage space and a second backyard door.

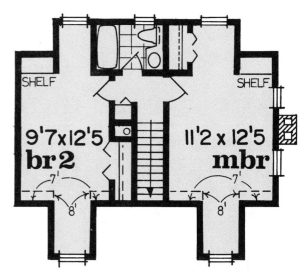

SHELF

SHELF

9'7x12'5
br2

11'2 x 12'5
mbr

7'

7'

8'

8'

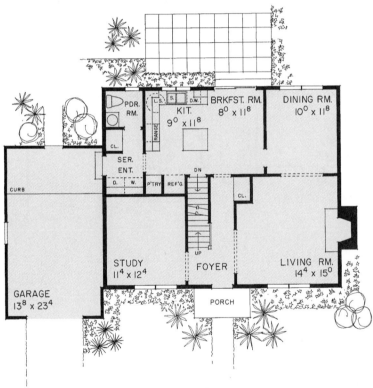

QUOTE ONE®
Cost to build? See page 246
to order complete cost estimate
to build this house in your area!

PLAN HPT210202

First Floor: 964 sq. ft.
Second Floor: 783 sq. ft.
Total: 1,747 sq. ft.

Width: 48'-0"
Depth: 32'-0"

L D

For those interested in both traditional charm and modern convenience, this Cape Cod home fits the bill. Enter the foyer and find a quiet study to the left and a living room with a fireplace to the right. Straight ahead lies the kitchen and breakfast room. The island countertop affords lots of room for meal preparation. The service entry introduces a laundry and powder room. Look for three bedrooms upstairs, including a pampering master suite with a whirlpool tub, separate shower, double vanity and walk-in closet.

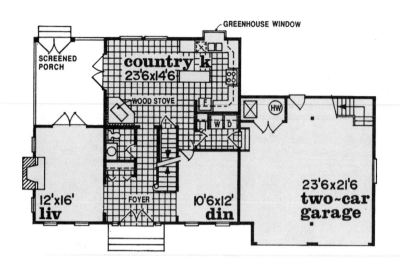

A richly gabled roofline defines this fine three-bedroom home. Double doors open to a wide foyer flanked by the formal living and dining rooms. The living room features a fireplace and double-door access to a screened porch. The country kitchen also accesses the screened porch and boasts a center work island, wood stove, greenhouse window and space for a breakfast table. The two-car garage is reached via the service entrance through the laundry alcove. Three bedrooms on the second floor include a master suite with a walk-in closet and private, skylit bath. Bedroom 3 also has a walk-in closet. Both family bedrooms share the use of a full hall bath that includes a skylight.

PLAN HPT210203

First Floor: 996 sq. ft.
Second Floor: 831 sq. ft.
Total: 1,827 sq. ft.
Bonus Room: 342 sq. ft.

Width: 61'-0"
Depth: 35'-6"

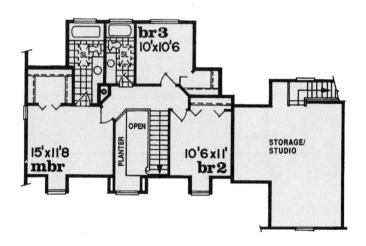

Porch
25'-0" x 7'-0"

Kitchen
19'-4" x 12'-4"

Utility

Pantry

Living Room
13'-2" x 17'-4"

Foyer
10'-0" x 8'-6"

Master Bedroom
13'-2" x 14'-10"

Bedroom
11'-0" x 14'-0"

Bedroom
11'-0" x 14'-0"

Balcony

PLAN HPT210204

First Floor: 778 sq. ft.
Second Floor: 571 sq. ft.
Total: 1,349 sq. ft.

Width: 38'-0"
Depth: 45'-6"

Double columns along with transoms and a sunburst create an enticing entrance to this lovely home. The living room with a fireplace is accessible to the island kitchen. Double doors in the kitchen lead to the covered porch in the backyard. The utility room and pantry are strategically placed near the powder room. The master bedroom is sumptuous; it includes its own fireplace and a private bath with dual vanities. Two family bedrooms can be found upstairs, both with two closets. A full hall bath is also provided on the second floor. Please specify basement or crawlspace foundation when ordering.

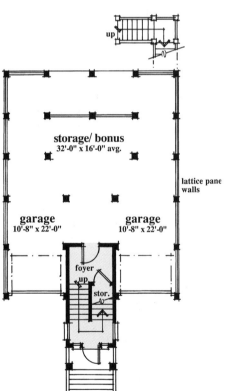

storage/ bonus
32'-0" x 16'-0" avg.

lattice pane
walls

garage
10'-8" x 22'-0"

garage
10'-8" x 22'-0"

foyer
up

stor.

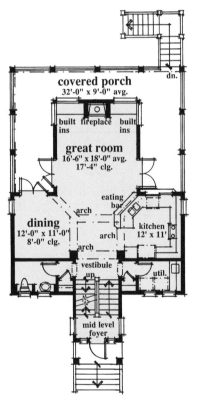

covered porch
32'-0" x 9'-0" avg.

built ins   fireplace   built ins

great room
16'-6" x 18'-0" avg.
17'-4" clg.

eating bar

dining
12'-0" x 11'-0"
8'-0" clg.

arch

kitchen
12' x 11'

arch

arch

vestibule

up

util.

mid level foyer

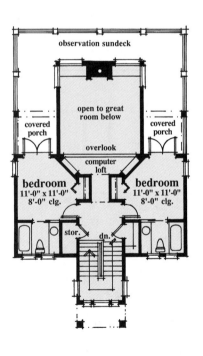

observation sundeck

open to great room below

covered porch

covered porch

overlook

computer loft

bedroom
11'-0" x 11'-0"
8'-0" clg.

bedroom
11'-0" x 11'-0"
8'-0" clg.

stor.

dn.

PLAN HPT210205

First Floor: 942 sq. ft.
Second Floor: 571 sq. ft.
Total: 1,513 sq. ft.
Bonus Space: 167 sq. ft.

Width: 32'-0"
Depth: 53'-0"

The modest detailing of Greek Revival style gave rise to this grand home. A mid-level foyer eases the trip from ground level to the raised living area, while an arched vestibule announces the great room. The formal dining room offers French door access to the covered porch. Built-ins, a fireplace and two ways to access the porch make the great room truly great. A well-appointed kitchen serves a casual eating bar as well as the dining room. Upstairs, each of two private suites has a windowed tub, a vanity and wardrobe space. A pair of French doors opens each of the bedrooms to an observation sun deck through covered porches. This home is designed with a pier foundation.

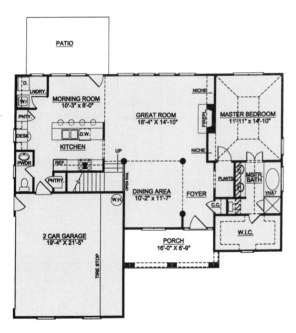

PATIO

LNDRY.

MORNING ROOM
10'-3" x 8'-0"

PNTY

DESK

KITCHEN

D.W.

PWDR

REF.

PNTRY.

2 CAR GARAGE
19'-4" X 21'-5"

GREAT ROOM
18'-4" X 14'-10"

NICHE

FIREPL

MASTER BEDROOM
11'-11" x 14'-10"

NICHE

UP

PLANTS

MSTR. BATH

VAULT

DINING AREA
10'-2" x 11'-7"

FOYER

C.C.

W.H.

PORCH
16'-0" X 6'-9"

W.I.C.

With New England charm, this early American Cape Cod home is a quaint haven for any family. Enter from the porch to the foyer, which opens to the dining area and great room. The great room is illuminated by a wall of windows, and features a fireplace with two built-in niches on either side. An efficient kitchen is brightened by the morning room, which accesses an outdoor porch. The opposite side of the home is dedicated to the master suite, which includes a vaulted master bath and a spacious walk-in closet. A two-car garage completes this level. Two secondary bedrooms reside upstairs and share a full hall bath. An optional bonus room can be used as a fourth bedroom, a playroom or a home office.

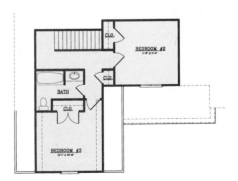

CLO.

BEDROOM #2
11'-4" X 11'-4"

CLO.

BATH

CLO.

BEDROOM #3
12'-1" X 10'-6"

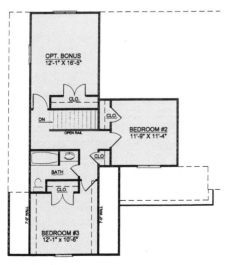

OPT. BONUS
12'-1" X 16'-5"

CLO.

DN

CLO.

BEDROOM #2
11'-9" X 11'-4"

OPEN RAIL

CLO.

BATH

CLO.

BEDROOM #3
12'-1" X 10'-6"

OPTIONAL LAYOUT

PLAN HPT210206

First Floor: 1,234 sq. ft.
Second Floor: 458 sq. ft.
Total: 1,692 sq. ft.
Bonus Space: 236 sq. ft.

Width: 48'-6"
Depth: 42'-4"

PLAN HPT210207

First Floor: 844 sq. ft.
Second Floor: 690 sq. ft.
Total: 1,534 sq. ft.

Width: 37'-0"
Depth: 34'-6"

Fitting well on a narrow lot, this traditional two-story home features spacious living areas and many gracious details. The living and dining area is open and contains a fireplace and a bay window overlooking the front. A U-shaped kitchen with a pass-through counter separates this area from the more casual living space. The combination breakfast room/family room is also warmed by a fireplace and has sliding glass doors to a patio in the rear. A single-car garage may be expanded to a two-car version, if you choose. Bedrooms on the second level include two family bedrooms and a master bedroom. All three share a full compartmented bath that has three sinks.

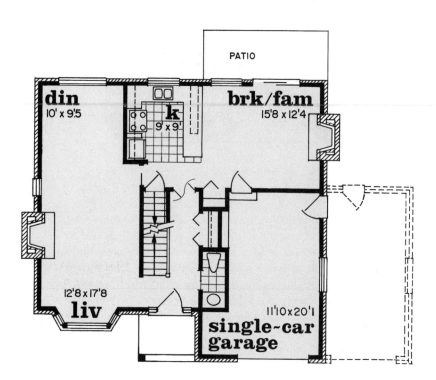

PATIO

din 10' x 9'5

k 9' x 9'

brk/fam 15'8 x 12'4

liv 12'8 x 17'8

single-car garage 11'10 x 20'1

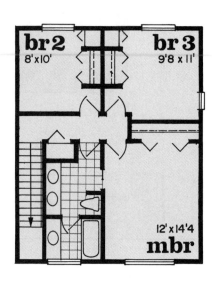

br 2 8' x 10'

br 3 9'8 x 11'

mbr 12' x 14'4

Typically one- to one-and-a-half stories, with a long sloping roofline, the Bungalow is a comfortable cottage that encourages hours of outdoor enjoyment. Wide covered porches and plenty of windows combine to bring nature up to the doorstep and into the home. Craftsman influences are displayed via the use of natural materials such as stone and wood, as well as efficient interior layouts. Rough-looking, usually with a fireplace or two, these cottages can do well on a mountain, in the woods or just about anywhere. Ranging from just over 1,000 square feet to 2,430 square feet, these cozy cottages offer something for everyone.

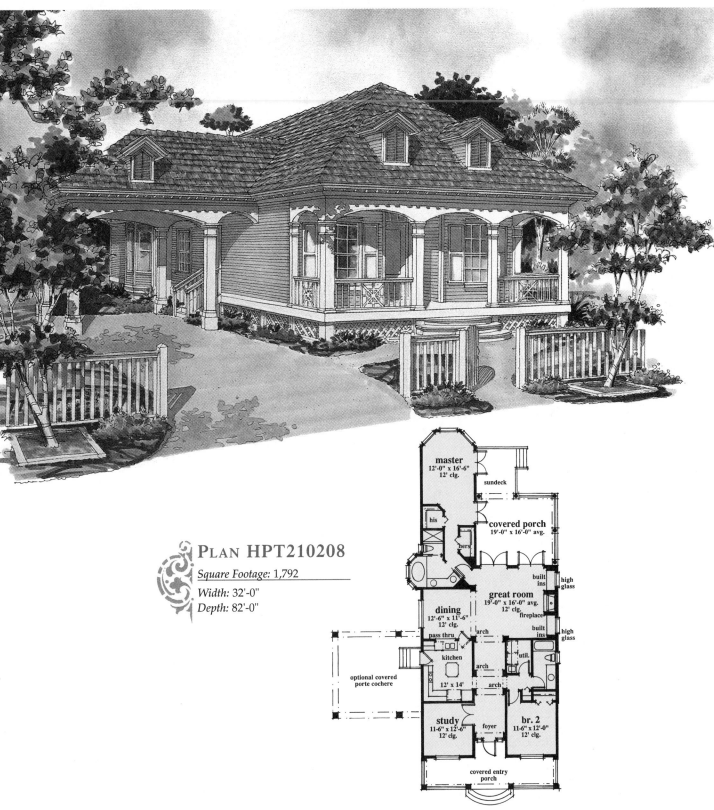

PLAN HPT210208

Square Footage: 1,792

Width: 32'-0"
Depth: 82'-0"

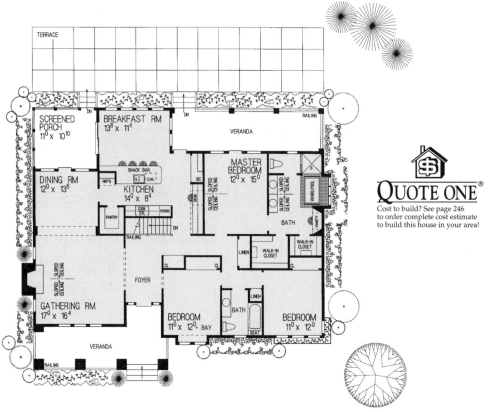

PLAN HPT210209

Square Footage: 1,959

Width: 56'-0"
Depth: 48'-8"

L

Formal living areas in this plan are joined by a three-bedroom sleeping wing. One bedroom, with foyer access, could function as a study. Two verandas and a screened porch enlarge the plan and enhance indoor/outdoor livability. Notice the added extras: the abundant storage space, walk-in pantry, built-in planning desk, whirlpool tub and pass-through snack bar. The sloped ceiling in the gathering room gives this area an open, airy quality. The breakfast room, with its wealth of windows, will be a cheerful and bright space to enjoy a cup of morning coffee.

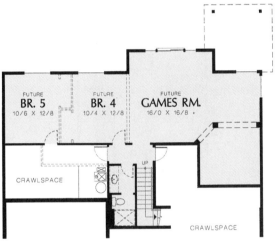

FUTURE
BR. 5
10/6 X 12/8

FUTURE
BR. 4
10/4 X 12/8

FUTURE
GAMES RM.
16/0 X 16/8

CRAWLSPACE

UP

CRAWLSPACE

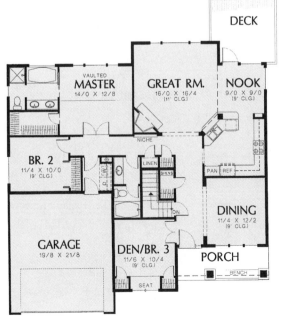

DECK

VAULTED
MASTER
14/0 X 12/8

GREAT RM.
16/0 X 16/4
(11' CLG.)

NOOK
9/0 X 9/0
(9' CLG.)

NICHE

BR. 2
11/4 X 10/0
(9' CLG.)

LINEN

SHLVS

PAN REF

GARAGE
19/8 X 21/8

DINING
11/4 X 12/2
(9' CLG.)

DEN/BR. 3
11/6 X 10/4
(9' CLG.)

PORCH

SEAT

BENCH

PLAN HPT210210

Square Footage: 1,632
Finished Basement: 1,043 sq. ft.

Width: 50'-0"
Depth: 50'-0"

Lower-level space adds to the compact floor plan of this home and gives it future possibilities. The main level opens off a covered porch to a dining room on the right and a den or bedroom on the left. The great room with an attached nook opens to the rear deck. Note the amount of counter and cabinet space in the L-shaped kitchen. Two bedrooms—a master suite and a family bedroom—are on the left, as is a laundry alcove. The lower level has space for a game room, two additional bedrooms and a full bath. Develop this area as needed or finish it along with the main level for immediate use.

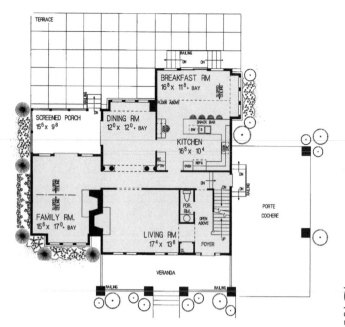

TERRACE

BREAKFAST RM
16⁸ x 11⁸ BAY

SCREENED PORCH
15⁶ x 9⁸

DINING RM
12⁰ x 12⁰ BAY

KITCHEN
16⁸ x 10⁴

SNACK BAR

FLOOR ABOVE

FAMILY RM.
15⁶ x 17⁰ BAY

LIVING RM
17⁴ x 13⁸

POR. RM.

FOYER

OPEN ABOVE

PORTE COCHERE

VERANDA

RAILING

Cozy living abounds in this comfortable two-story bungalow. Enter the foyer and find a spacious living room with a fireplace to the left. Straight ahead is a U-shaped kitchen with a snack bar, a planning desk and easy access to the formal dining room. The box-bay family room features a fireplace and entry to a screened porch. Upstairs, secondary bedrooms offer ample closet space and direct access to a shared bath. The master suite contains a large walk-in closet, double-bowl vanity and compartmented shower and toilet.

QUOTE ONE®

Cost to build? See page 246 to order complete cost estimate to build this house in your area!

PLAN HPT210211

First Floor: 1,482 sq. ft.
Second Floor: 885 sq. ft.
Total: 2,367 sq. ft.

Width: 64'-0"
Depth: 50'-0"

L

ROOF

UPPER BREAKFAST RM.

BEDROOM
12⁰ x 10⁰

BATH

BEDROOM
11⁴ x 12⁸

LINEN

ROOF

ROOF

BATH

OPEN BELOW

WALK-IN CLOSET

MASTER BEDROOM
12⁴ x 16⁰

RAILING

ROOF

WINDOW WELL

ROOF

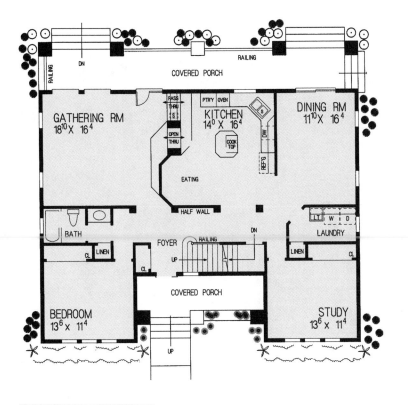

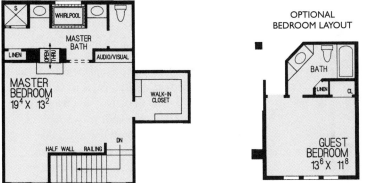

PLAN HPT210212

First Floor: 1,557 sq. ft.
Second Floor: 540 sq. ft.
Total: 2,097 sq. ft.

Width: 48'-0"
Depth: 43'-8"

L D

Details make the difference in this darling two-bedroom—or make it a three-bedroom—bungalow. From the front covered porch to the rear porch with decorative railings and stairs, this home offers a sense of comfortable elegance. A gathering room with a through-fireplace offers wide views to the outdoors, while the formal dining room has its own door to the rear porch. To the front of the plan, a family bedroom has its own full bath, while a secluded study—or guest bedroom—offers space for reading or quiet conversation. Upstairs, the master suite offers a through-fireplace that it shares with a private bath, space for an audio/visual center and a roomy walk-in closet.

QUOTE ONE®

Cost to build? See page 246
to order complete cost estimate
to build this house in your area!

OPTIONAL
BEDROOM LAYOUT

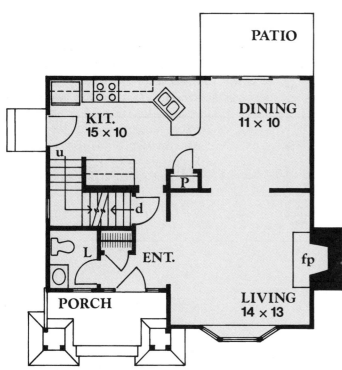

PATIO

KIT.
15 × 10

DINING
11 × 10

u

P

d

L

ENT.

fp

PORCH

LIVING
14 × 13

A shed-dormered roof with rolled eaves, a great stone chimney and a shingled exterior lend rusticity to this Craftsman-inspired retreat. Multi-wooden posts are anchored by stone piers, framing the welcoming front entry. Inside, a stone fireplace warms the living room, providing an ideal setting to curl up with a good book and enjoy the window seat that graces the bay window overlooking the front yard. A countertop separates the kitchen from the dining area, where sliding glass doors lead onto a rear patio. The second floor contains two bedrooms and a full bath. One of the bedrooms features a trio of period-style windows set into a centered dormer.

PLAN HPT210213

First Floor: 605 sq. ft.
Second Floor: 432 sq. ft.
Total: 1,037 sq. ft.

Width: 33'-9"
Depth: 27'-6"

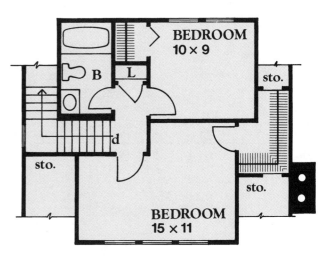

B

L

BEDROOM
10 × 9

sto.

d

sto.

sto.

BEDROOM
15 × 11

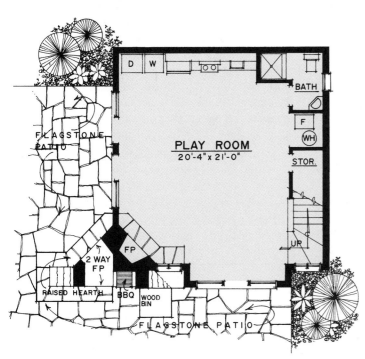

FLAGSTONE PATIO

D W

BATH

F

WH

PLAY ROOM
20'-4" x 21'-0"

STOR.

2 WAY FP

FP

UR

RAISED HEARTH BBQ WOOD BIN

FLAGSTONE PATIO

With woodsy charm and cozy livability, this cottage plan offers comfortable living space in a smaller footprint. The exterior is geared for outdoor fun, with two flagstone patios connected by a two-way fireplace and graced by a built-in barbecue. French doors on two sides lead into the large play room, which features a kitchen area, washer and dryer space and a bath with a corner sink and a shower. Take the stairway to the bunk room upstairs, where there's space for sleeping and relaxing.

PLAN HPT210214

First Floor: 665 sq. ft.
Second Floor: 395 sq. ft.
Total: 1,060 sq. ft.

Width: 34'-3"
Depth: 32'-5"

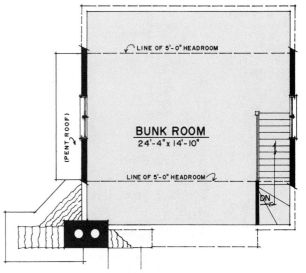

LINE OF 5'-0" HEADROOM

(PENT ROOF)

BUNK ROOM
24'-4" x 14'-10"

LINE OF 5'-0" HEADROOM

DN

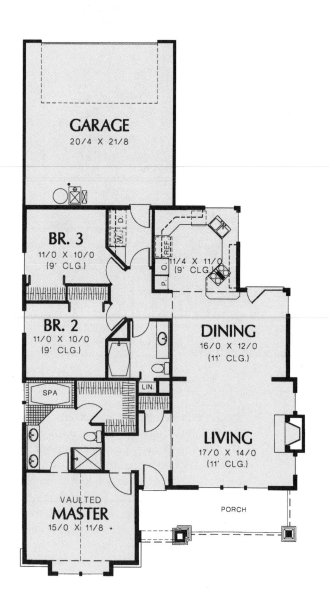

GARAGE
20/4 X 21/8

BR. 3
11/0 X 10/0
(9' CLG.)

BR. 2
11/0 X 10/0
(9' CLG.)

W. D.

P. O.

REF

11/4 X 11/0
(9' CLG.)

DINING
16/0 X 12/0
(11' CLG.)

LIN.

SPA

LIVING
17/0 X 14/0
(11' CLG.)

VAULTED
MASTER
15/0 X 11/8 +

PORCH

PLAN HPT210215

Square Footage: 1,520

Width: 38'-0"

Depth: 72'-0"

Gables and a welcoming covered porch introduce this fine three-bedroom home and give it plenty of curb appeal. Inside, this charming cottage-style home offers a spacious living room with a focal-point fireplace and window transoms to let in the light. The dining room is served by a C-shaped kitchen with an angled double sink—directly under a corner window. A secluded master suite features a vaulted ceiling, a box-bay window, a lavish bath with a spa-style tub, and a walk-in closet. Two secondary bedrooms reside in the back of the plan. The two-car garage has rear-entry access—perfect for narrow lots.

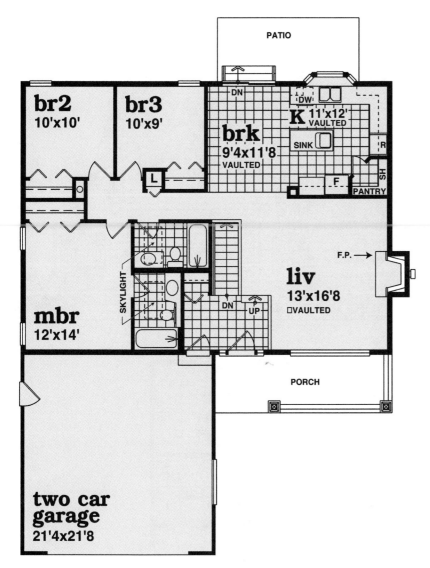

br2 10'x10'

br3 10'x9'

PATIO

DN

DW

K 11'x12' VAULTED

brk 9'4x11'8 VAULTED

SINK

R

F

PANTRY

SH

SKYLIGHT

mbr 12'x14'

DN

UP

liv 13'x16'8 VAULTED

F.P. →

PORCH

two car garage 21'4x21'8

PLAN HPT210216

Square Footage: 1,260

Width: 42'-0"

Depth: 52'-0"

This economical-to-build bungalow works well as a small family home or a retirement cottage. The covered porch leads to a vaulted living room with a fireplace. Behind this living space is the L-shaped kitchen with a walk-in pantry and an island with a utility sink. An attached breakfast nook has sliding glass doors to a rear patio. There are three bedrooms, each with a roomy wall closet. The master bedroom has a private full bath, while the family bedrooms share a main bath. Both baths have bright skylights. A two-car garage sits to the front of the plan to protect the bedrooms from street noise.

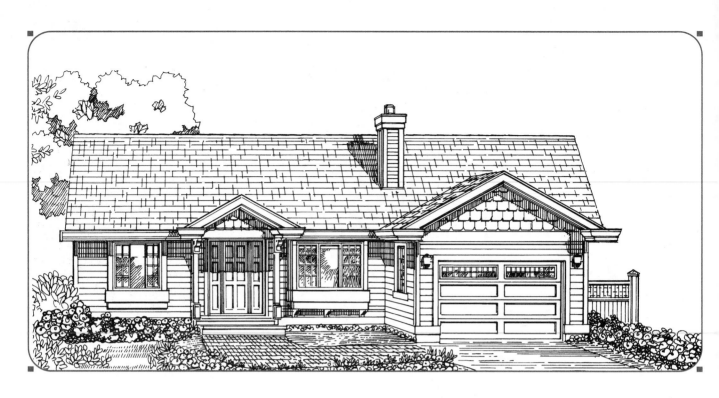

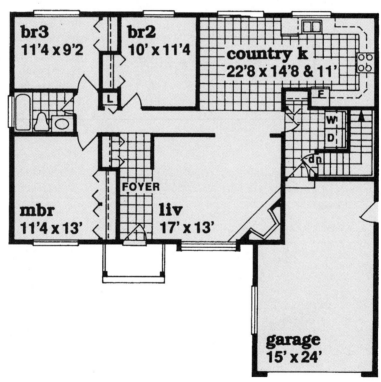

br3
11'4 x 9'2

br2
10' x 11'4

country k
22'8 x 14'8 & 11'

L

FOYER

mbr
11'4 x 13'

liv
17' x 13'

W
D

F

dn

garage
15' x 24'

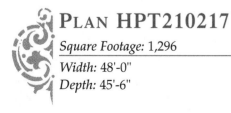

PLAN HPT210217

Square Footage: 1,296

Width: 48'-0"

Depth: 45'-6"

Perfect for a starter or empty-nester home, this economical-to-build one-story plan is as delightful on the inside as it is appealing on the outside. Fish-scale siding, a covered porch and window boxes adorn the exterior. Inside, the foyer spills over to a spacious living room with a corner fireplace. The country kitchen across the hall offers a unique U-shaped counter and ample space for a large dining table. Sliding glass doors lead to the rear yard and a handy service entrance leads past the laundry alcove to the single-car garage. The three bedrooms (or make it two and a den) revolve around the central bath with a soaking tub. The master bedroom has His and Hers entries to the wall closet.

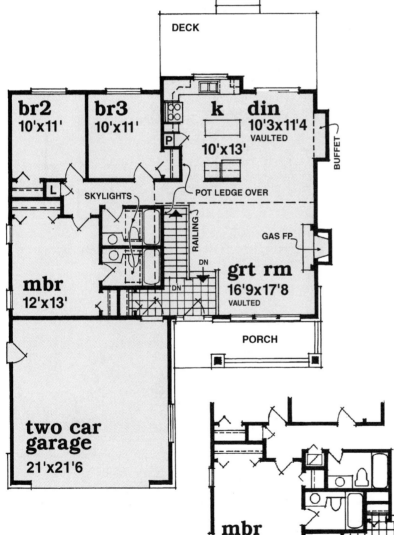

DECK

br2
10'x11'

br3
10'x11'

k
10'x13'

din
10'3x11'4
VAULTED

BUFFET

L

SKYLIGHTS

POT LEDGE OVER

RAILING

GAS FP.

mbr
12'x13'

DN

DN

grt rm
16'9x17'8
VAULTED

PORCH

two car garage
21'x21'6

mbr
12'x13'

grt rm
16'9x17'8

OPTIONAL CRAWLSPACE LAYOUT

PLAN HPT210218

Square Footage: 1,293

Width: 42'-0"
Depth: 54'-4"

Meeting the needs of first-time home-builders, this design is economical to build. Craftsman detailing and a quaint covered porch go a long way to create the charming exterior. Open planning adds to this design's livability. The foyer opens to a hearth-warmed great room. Vaulted ceilings and a half-wall separating the stairs to the basement and the foyer add to the spaciousness. An open island kitchen has an adjoining dining room with sliding glass doors to the deck and box-bay buffet space. The master suite is adjacent to two family bedrooms. It boasts His and Hers wall closets and a full bath with a soaking tub. Two family bedrooms—or make one a den—share a full bath.

233

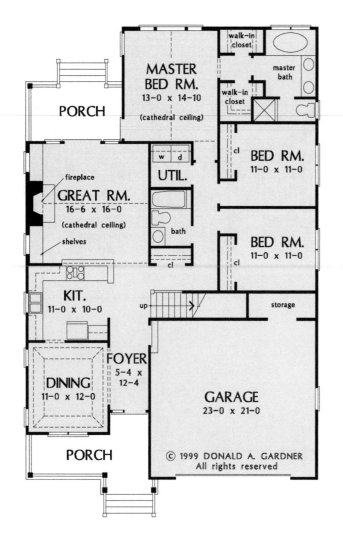

MASTER BED RM.
13-0 x 14-10
(cathedral ceiling)

PORCH

walk-in closet

master bath

walk-in closet

fireplace

GREAT RM.
16-6 x 16-0
(cathedral ceiling)

shelves

w   d

UTIL.

bath

cl

BED RM.
11-0 x 11-0

cl

BED RM.
11-0 x 11-0

KIT.
11-0 x 10-0

cl

up

storage

FOYER
5-4 x 12-4

DINING
11-0 x 12-0

GARAGE
23-0 x 21-0

PORCH

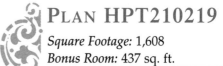

PLAN HPT210219

Square Footage: 1,608
Bonus Room: 437 sq. ft.

Width: 40'-8"
Depth: 62'-8"

This rustic beauty provides a practical floor plan. The great room is warmed by a fireplace and enhanced by a cathedral ceiling. Another cathedral ceiling adds a spacious feel to the master bedroom. Additional luxuries in the master suite include a private bath, two walk-in closets and access to a covered porch (also accessible from the great room). Two additional bedrooms share a hall bath, with the utility room conveniently nearby. A bonus room is available for extra storage.

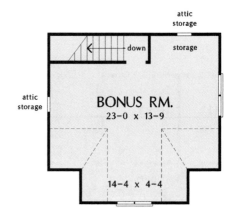

attic storage

down

storage

attic storage

BONUS RM.
23-0 x 13-9

14-4 x 4-4

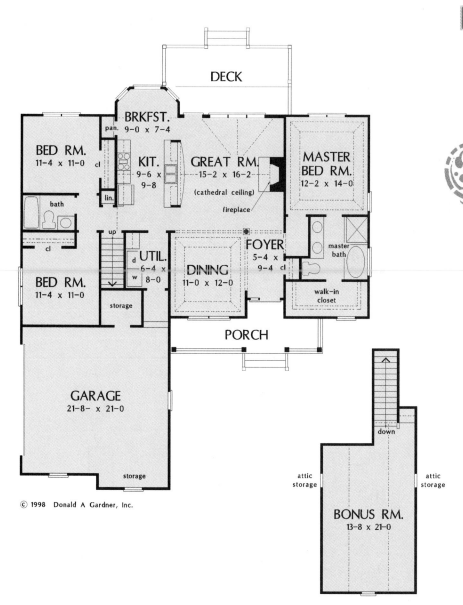

DECK

BRKFST.
pan. 9-0 x 7-4

BED RM.
11-4 x 11-0

cl

KIT.
9-6 x
9-8

lin.

GREAT RM.
15-2 x 16-2
(cathedral ceiling)

fireplace

MASTER
BED RM.
12-2 x 14-0

bath

cl

up

UTIL.
6-4 x
8-0

d

w

FOYER
5-4 x
9-4 cl

master
bath

BED RM.
11-4 x 11-0

storage

DINING
11-0 x 12-0

walk-in
closet

PORCH

GARAGE
21-8- x 21-0

storage

© 1998 Donald A Gardner, Inc.

down

attic
storage

attic
storage

BONUS RM.
13-8 x 21-0

PLAN HPT210220

Square Footage: 1,488
Bonus Room: 375 sq. ft.

Width: 51'-10"
Depth: 58'-0"

Rustic on the exterior, this appealing one-story home is a paragon of fine floor planning inside. Tray ceilings decorate both the dining room and the master bedroom. The great room features a cathedral ceiling and a large fireplace. To pamper the homeowner, the master retreat offers a huge walk-in closet and a bath with a shower, spa tub and dual sinks. The breakfast room is set in a bay-window area for sunny, casual meals.

©1998 Donald A. Gardner, Inc.

B. NATHAN

© 1999 Donald A. Gardner, Inc

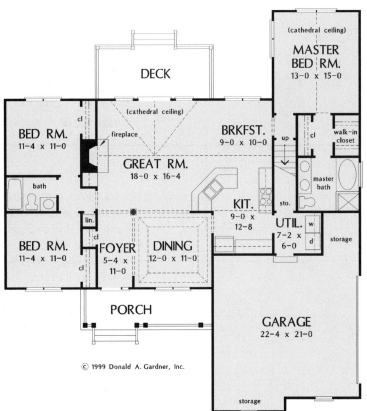

DECK

(cathedral ceiling)
MASTER
BED RM.
13-0 x 15-0

BED RM.
11-4 x 11-0

cl

fireplace

(cathedral ceiling)

BRKFST.
9-0 x 10-0

up

cl

walk-in
closet

GREAT RM.
18-0 x 16-4

master
bath

KIT.
9-0 x
12-8

sto.

bath

UTIL.
7-2 x
6-0

w
d

storage

lin.

cl

BED RM.
11-4 x 11-0

cl

FOYER
5-4 x
11-0

DINING
12-0 x 11-0

PORCH

GARAGE
22-4 x 21-0

storage

© 1999 Donald A. Gardner, Inc.

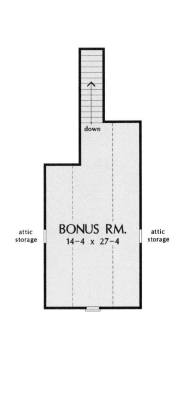

down

attic
storage

BONUS RM.
14-4 x 27-4

attic
storage

PLAN HPT210221

Square Footage: 1,590
Bonus Room: 425 sq. ft.

Width: 55'-0"
Depth: 59'-10"

A cozy front porch and gables create warmth and style for this economical home with an open floor plan and a sizable bonus room. The openness of the great room, dining room, kitchen and breakfast room increases spaciousness. Additional volume is created by the cathedral ceiling that tops the great room and breakfast area, while a tray ceiling adds distinction and elegance to the formal dining room. Living space is extended to the outdoors by way of a rear deck. The master suite is separated from family bedrooms for parental privacy and features a luxurious bath with plenty of closet space for him and her. Two family bedrooms share a hall bath on the opposite side of the home.

© 1999 Donald A. Gardner, Inc.

B. NATHAN

© 1999 Donald A. Gardner, Inc.

BED RM.
11-0 x 12-0
(cathedral ceiling)

bath

walk-in closet | lin.

BED RM.
11-0 x 12-0

walk-in closet

storage

KIT.
11-0 x 12-0

BRKFST.
9-4 x 11-4

PORCH

GREAT RM.
17-8 x 19-4
(cathedral ceiling)

fireplace

MASTER BED RM.
13-0 x 18-0

walk-in closet

walk-in closet

up

UTIL.
6-0 x 5-8

d w

DINING
11-4 x 13-0

FOYER
6-0 x 9-2

cl

master bath

PORCH

GARAGE
22-4 x 21-0

storage

BONUS RM.
15-6 x 21-0

down

attic storage

attic storage

PLAN HPT210222

Square Footage: 1,821
Bonus Room: 409 sq. ft.

Width: 54'-4"
Depth: 61'-6"

This design features exterior Craftsman character and interior interest. The covered front porch opens to the foyer and dining room on the left. Columns separate the dining room from the great room, which includes a fireplace, cathedral ceiling, back-porch access and a see-through counter to the kitchen. The breakfast nook contains a bay window overlooking the backyard and porch. The master bedroom is highlighted by a tray ceiling and two walk-in closets. Upstairs, a bonus room provides space for future expansion.

PLAN HPT210223

Square Footage: 1,410

Width: 66'-7"
Depth: 55'-0"

L

Horizontal siding with brick accents and multi-pane windows enhance the exterior of this home. A large living/dining room provides plenty of space for formal and informal activities. A fireplace makes a delightful focal point. Located for efficiency, the kitchen easily serves this area. The centrally located main bath has twin lavatories and a nearby linen closet. One of the two family bedrooms has direct access to the veranda. The master bedroom is flanked by the master bath and its own covered porch.

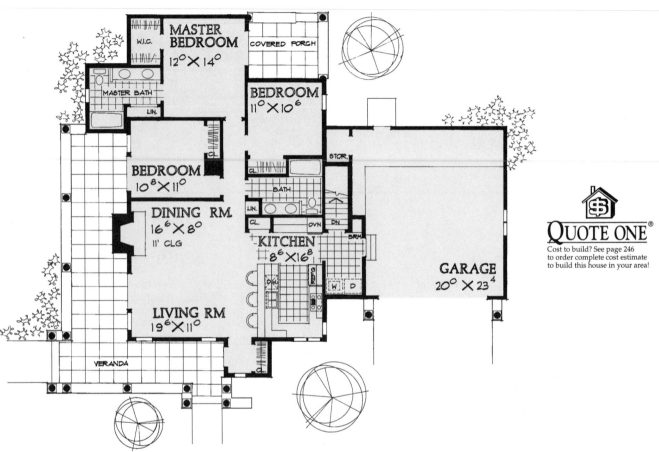

MASTER BEDROOM 12⁰ X 14⁰
W.I.C.
MASTER BATH
LIN.
COVERED PORCH
BEDROOM 11⁰ X 10⁶
STOR.
BEDROOM 10⁸ X 11⁰
CL.
DINING RM. 16⁶ X 8⁰
11' CLG
BATH
LIN.
CL.
OVN
DN
B/RM
KITCHEN 8⁶ X 16⁸
GARAGE 20⁰ X 23⁴
LIVING RM 19⁶ X 11⁰
W D
REF'S
VERANDA

QUOTE ONE®

Cost to build? See page 246 to order complete cost estimate to build this house in your area!

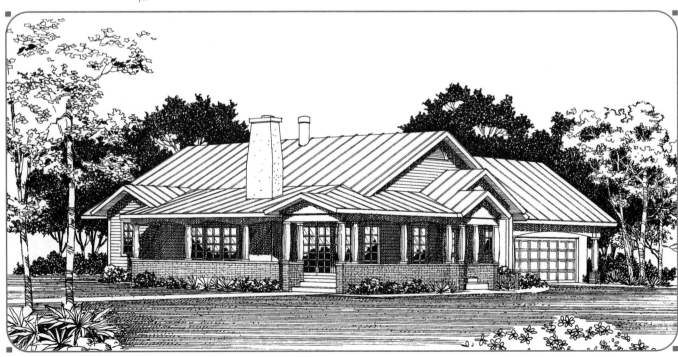

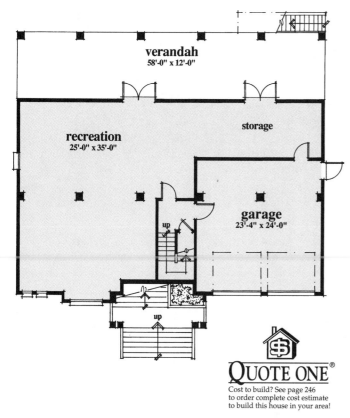

verandah
58'-0" x 12'-0"

recreation
25'-0" x 35'-0"

storage

up

garage
23'-4" x 24'-0"

up

PLAN HPT210224

Square Footage: 2,190

Width: 58'-0"
Depth: 54'-0"

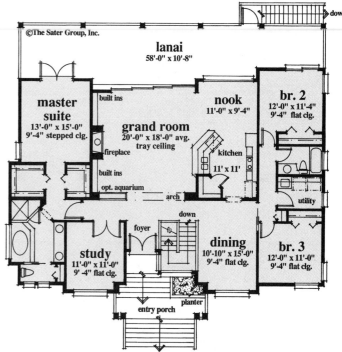

©The Sater Group, Inc.

lanai
58'-0" x 10'-8"

dow

master suite
13'-0" x 15'-0"
9'-4" stepped clg.

built ins

nook
11'-0" x 9'-4"

br. 2
12'-0" x 11'-4"
9'-4" flat clg.

grand room
20'-0" x 18'-0" avg.
tray ceiling

fireplace

kitchen
11' x 11'

built ins

opt. aquarium

arch

utility

down

foyer

study
11'-0" x 11'-0"
9'-4" flat clg.

dining
10'-10" x 15'-0"
9'-4" flat clg.

br. 3
12'-0" x 11'-0"
9'-4" flat clg.

planter

entry porch

Quote One®
Cost to build? See page 246
to order complete cost estimate
to build this house in your area!

A dramatic set of stairs leads to the entry of this home. The foyer opens to an expansive grand room with a fireplace and built-in bookshelves. For formal meals, a front-facing dining room offers plenty of space and a bumped-out bay. The kitchen serves this area easily as well as the breakfast nook. A study and three bedrooms make up the rest of the floor plan. Two secondary bedrooms share a full bath. The master suite contains two walk-in closets and a full bath.

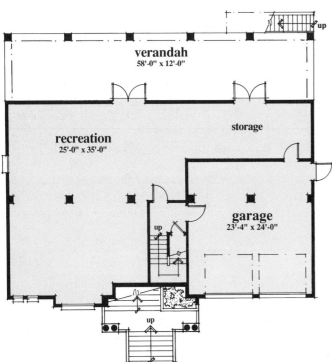

verandah
58'-0" x 12'-0"

storage

recreation
25'-0" x 35'-0"

up

garage
23'-4" x 24'-0"

up

up

PLAN HPT210225

Square Footage: 2,190

Width: 58'-0"
Depth: 54'-0"

The dramatic arched entry of this Southampton-style cottage borrows freely from its Southern coastal past. The foyer and central hall open to the grand room. The kitchen is flanked by the dining room and the morning nook, which opens to the lanai. On the left side of the plan, the master suite also accesses the lanai. Two walk-in closets and a compartmented bath with a separate tub and shower and a double-bowl vanity complete this opulent retreat. The right side of the plan includes two secondary bedrooms and a full bath.

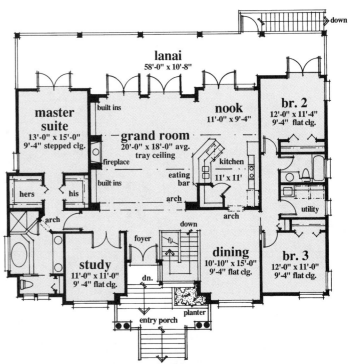

down

lanai
58'-0" x 10'-8"

nook
11'-0" x 9'-4"

br. 2
12'-0" x 11'-4"
9'-4" flat clg.

master suite
13'-0" x 15'-0"
9'-4" stepped clg.

built ins

grand room
20'-0" x 18'-0" avg.
tray ceiling

kitchen
11' x 11'

fireplace

built ins

eating bar

arch

arch

utility

hers

his

arch

arch

study
11'-0" x 11'-0"
9'-4" flat clg.

foyer

down

dn.

dining
10'-10" x 15'-0"
9'-4" flat clg.

br. 3
12'-0" x 11'-0"
9'-4" flat clg.

planter

entry porch

With a rugged blend of stone and siding, an inviting mix of details creates the kind of comfortable beauty that every homeowner craves. Massive stone columns support a striking pediment entry. A spacious formal dining room complements a gourmet kitchen designed to serve any occasion and equipped with a walk-in pantry and a nearby powder room. The morning nook boasts a wall of glass that allows casual diners to kick back and be at one with nature. Separate sleeping quarters thoughtfully place the master suite to the right of the plan, in a wing of the home that includes a private porch. Guest suites on the opposite side of the plan share a hall and a staircase that leads to a lower-level mudroom, porch and ski storage.

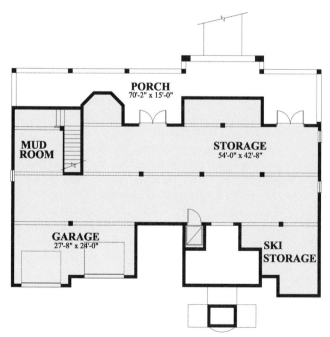

PLAN HPT210226

Square Footage: 2,430

Width: 70'-2"
Depth: 53'-0"

*A new Web site, **www.eplans.com**, provides a way for you to*

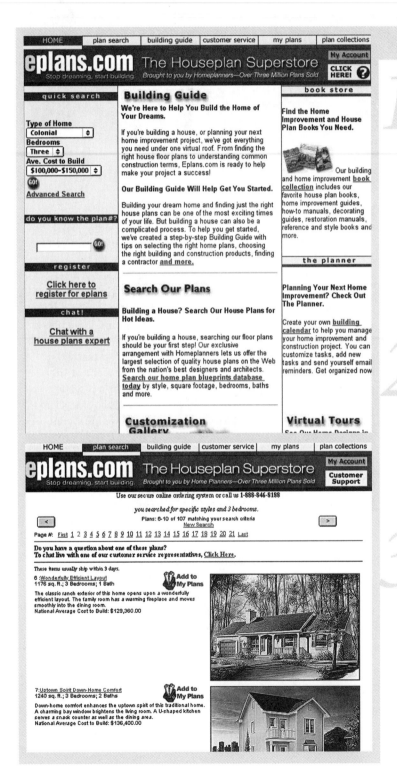

THE EPLANS SITE

SEARCH FOR PLANS

The heart of the site is the Plan Search feature that offers an extensive database of plans for your consideration. Do a simplified search by style, number of bedrooms and approximate cost to build in order to find appropriate homes in your range. Or, choose a more advanced search that includes choices for square footage, number of floors, number of bedrooms and baths, width and depth, style, amenities, garage size and, if you prefer, a specified designer.

Either way, you gain access to a selection of homes that meets your specifications, allowing you to easily make comparisons. The site shows front perspectives as well as detailed floor plans for each of your choices. You can even look at enlarged versions of the drawings to make more serious analyses.

SAVE FAVORITE PLANS

As you're doing your searches, you can save favorite plans to a personal portfolio called My Plans so that you can easily recall them for future reference and review. This feature stores summary information for each of the plans you select and allows you to review details of the plan quickly without having to re-search or re-browse. You can even compare plans, deleting those that don't measure up and keeping those that appeal, so you can narrow down your search more quickly.

PURCHASE PLANS

Once you've made your final choice, you can proceed to purchase your plan, either by checking out through our secure online ordering process or by calling the toll-free number offered in the site. If you choose to check out online, you'll receive information about foundation options for your chosen plan, plus other helpful products such as a building cost estimator to help you gauge costs to build the plan in your zip code area, a materials list specific to your plan, color and line renderings of the plan, and mirror and full reverses. Information relating to all of these products can also be reviewed with a customer service representative if you choose to order by phone.

search for home plans that is as simple as pointing and clicking.

also on the EPLANS site...

VIRTUAL TOURS

In order to help you more completely visualize the homes as built, eplans offers virtual tours of a select group of homes. Showing both interior and exterior features of the homes, the virtual tour gives you a complete vision of how the floor plans for the home will look when completed. All you have to do is choose a home in the Virtual Tour gallery, then click on an exterior or interior view. The view pops up and immediately begins a slow 360° rotation to give you the complete picture. Special buttons allow you to stop the rotation anywhere you like, reverse the action, or move it up or down, and zoom in on a particular element. There's even a large-screen version to allow you to review the home in greater detail.

CUSTOMIZATION GALLERY

For a special group of plans, a customization option allows you to try out building product selections to see which looks the best and to compare styles, colors, and textures. You'll start with an eplans design rendering and then be given options for such elements as roofing, columns, siding, and trim, among others. A diverse grouping of materials and color options is available in each product category. As you choose each option, it will appear on the rendering, allowing you to mix and match options and try out various design ideas. When you're satisfied with your choices, you can enlarge the view, print it out or save it in your personalized Home Project Folder for future reference.

The eplans site is convenient and contains not only the best home plans in the business, but also a host of other features and services. Like Home Planners handy books and magazines, it speaks your language in user-friendly fashion.

In fact, if you want or need more help, there is a Live Person, real-time chat opportunity available with one of our customer service representatives right on the site to answer questions and help you make plans selections.

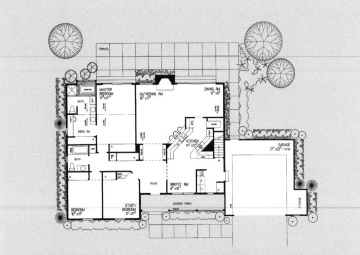

also on the EPLANS site...

BUILDING GUIDE AND TASK PLANNER

Because building a home is a complicated process, eplans gets you started with a step-by-step Building Guide. Covering everything from choosing a lot to settling into your new home, the Building Guide gives tips and valuable information to help you understand the entire process of constructing your new home. Learn about the steps in framing your home, different foundation types and which might work best for your building situation, financing your project, home products such as appliances, and much, much more. A handy glossary is available in each section that helps define terms that relate to the information in that section.

Within the Building Guide is a unique Task Planner outlining each of the various tasks involved in residential construction over the entire 16-week (average) life of the project. Simply tell Task Planner when you plan to start construction or when you plan to move into the finished home, and it will create a calendar that shows each of the many steps involved in building your home. You can customize tasks, add new tasks, and send yourself email reminders that help you manage the building project. In addition, each task in the calendar is linked to a tip or information piece in the Building Guide to help make the process easier to follow and understand. Choose the Calendar View, which shows a month-by-month progression of construction, or the Task View, which lists each task by category and shows its due date.

Customize your plan—without spending a penny or hammering a nail! The Customization Gallery lets you "try on" various material colors and styles before you make decisions.

The **eplans.com** Advantage

While there are hundreds of home plans sites on the Web, only eplans.com offers the variety, quality, and ease of use you want when doing a search for the perfect home. From expert advice to online ordering of plans, eplans gives you a full complement of services, information, home plans, and planning tools to make your building experience easy and enjoyable. Log on to www.eplans.com to begin your search for the home you've always wanted.

LET US SHOW YOU OUR HOME BLUEPRINT PACKAGE.

BUILDING A HOME? PLANNING A HOME?

OUR BLUEPRINT PACKAGE HAS NEARLY EVERYTHING YOU NEED TO GET THE JOB DONE RIGHT,

whether you're working on your own or with help from an architect, designer, builder or subcontractors. Each Blueprint Package is the result of many hours of work by licensed architects or professional designers.

QUALITY

Hundreds of hours of painstaking effort have gone into the development of your blueprint plan. Each home has been quality-checked by professionals to insure accuracy and buildability.

VALUE

Because we sell in volume, you can buy professional quality blueprints at a fraction of their development cost. With our plans, your dream home design costs substantially less than the fees charged by architects.

SERVICE

Once you've chosen your favorite home plan, you'll receive fast, efficient service whether you choose to mail or fax your order to us or call us toll free at 1-800-521-6797. After you have received your order, call for customer service toll free 1-888-690-1116.

SATISFACTION

Over 50 years of service to satisfied home plan buyers provide us unparalleled experience and knowledge in producing quality blueprints.

ORDER TOLL FREE 1-800-521-6797

After you've looked over our Blueprint Package and Important Extras, call toll free on our Blueprint Hotline: 1-800-521-6797, for current pricing and availability prior to mailing the order form on page 253. We're ready and eager to serve you. After you have received your order, call for customer service toll free 1-888-690-1116.

Each set of blueprints is an interrelated collection of detail sheets which includes components such as floor plans, interior and exterior elevations, dimensions, cross-sections, diagrams and notations. These sheets show exactly how your house is to be built.

SETS MAY INCLUDE:

FRONTAL SHEET
This artist's sketch of the exterior of the house gives you an idea of how the house will look when built and landscaped. Large floor plans show all levels of the house and provide an overview of your new home's livability, as well as a handy reference for deciding on furniture placement.

FOUNDATION PLANS
This sheet shows the foundation layout including support walls, excavated and unexcavated areas, if any, and foundation notes. If slab construction rather than basement, the plan shows footings and details for a monolithic slab. This page, or another in the set, may include a sample plot plan for locating your house on a building site.

DETAILED FLOOR PLANS
These plans show the layout of each floor of the house. Rooms and interior spaces are carefully dimensioned and keys are given for cross-section details provided later in the plans. The positions of electrical outlets and switches are shown.

HOUSE CROSS-SECTIONS
Large-scale views show sections or cut-aways of the foundation, interior walls, exterior walls, floors, stairways and roof details. Additional cross-sections may show important changes in floor, ceiling or roof heights or the relationship of one level to another. Extremely valuable for construction, these sections show exactly how the various parts of the house fit together.

INTERIOR ELEVATIONS
Many of our drawings show the design and placement of kitchen and bathroom cabinets, laundry areas, fireplaces, bookcases and other built-ins. Little "extras," such as mantelpiece and wainscoting drawings, plus molding sections, provide details that give your home that custom touch.

EXTERIOR ELEVATIONS
These drawings show the front, rear and sides of your house and give necessary notes on exterior materials and finishes. Particular attention is given to cornice detail, brick and stone accents or other finish items that make your home unique.

IMPORTANT EXTRAS TO DO THE JOB RIGHT!

INTRODUCING IMPORTANT PLANNING AND CONSTRUCTION AIDS DEVELOPED BY OUR PROFESSIONALS TO HELP YOU SUCCEED IN YOUR HOME-BUILDING PROJECT

MATERIALS LIST

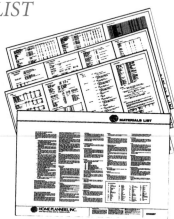

(Note: Because of the diversity of local building codes, our Materials List does not include mechanical materials.)

For many of the designs in our portfolio, we offer a customized materials take-off that is invaluable in planning and estimating the cost of your new home. This Materials List outlines the quantity, type and size of materials needed to build your house (with the exception of mechanical system items). Included are framing lumber, windows and doors, kitchen and bath cabinetry, rough and finish hardware, and much more. This handy list helps you or your builder cost out materials and serves as a reference sheet when you're compiling bids. Some Materials Lists may be ordered before blueprints are ordered, call for information.

SPECIFICATION OUTLINE

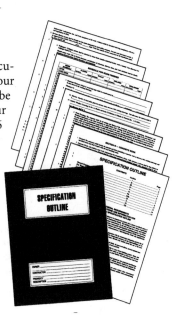

This valuable 16-page document is critical to building your house correctly. Designed to be filled in by you or your builder, this book lists 166 stages or items crucial to the building process. It provides a comprehensive review of the construction process and helps in choosing materials. When combined with the blueprints, a signed contract, and a schedule, it becomes a legal document and record for the building of your home.

QUOTE ONE®

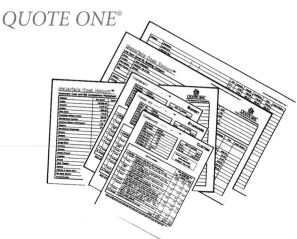

SUMMARY COST REPORT   **MATERIAL COST REPORT**

A product for estimating the cost of building select designs, the Quote One® system is available in two separate stages: The Summary Cost Report and the Material Cost Report.

The **Summary Cost Report** is the first stage in the package and shows the total cost per square foot for your chosen home in your zip-code area and then breaks that cost down into various categories showing the costs for building materials, labor and installation. The report includes three grades: Budget, Standard and Custom. These reports allow you to evaluate your building budget and compare the costs of building a variety of homes in your area.

Make even more informed decisions about your home-building project with the second phase of our package, our **Material Cost Report.** This tool is invaluable in planning and estimating the cost of your new home. The material and installation (labor and equipment) cost is shown for each of over 1,000 line items provided in the Materials List (Standard grade), which is included when you purchase this estimating tool. It allows you to determine building costs for your specific zip-code area and for your chosen home design. Space is allowed for additional estimates from contractors and subcontractors, such as for mechanical materials, which are not included in our packages. This invaluable tool includes a Materials List. A Material Cost Report cannot be ordered before blueprints are ordered. Call for details. In addition, ask about our Home Planners Estimating Package.

If you are interested in a plan that is not indicated as Quote One®, please call and ask our sales reps. They will be happy to verify the status for you. To order these invaluable reports, use the order form.

CONSTRUCTION INFORMATION

If you want to know more about techniques—and deal more confidently with subcontractors — we offer these useful sheets. Each set is an excellent tool that will add to your understanding of these technical subjects. These helpful details provide general construction information and are not specific to any single plan.

PLUMBING

The Blueprint Package includes locations for all the plumbing fixtures, including sinks, lavatories, tubs, showers, toilets, laundry trays and water heaters. However, if you want to know more about the complete plumbing system, these Plumbing Details will prove very useful. Prepared to meet requirements of the National Plumbing Code, these fact-filled sheets give general information on pipe schedules, fittings, sump-pump details, water-softener hookups, septic system details and much more. Sheets also include a glossary of terms.

ELECTRICAL

The locations for every electrical switch, plug and outlet are shown in your Blueprint Package. However, these Electrical Details go further to take the mystery out of household electrical systems. Prepared to meet requirements of the National Electrical Code, these comprehensive drawings come packed with helpful information, including wire sizing, switch-installation schematics, cable-routing details, appliance wattage, doorbell hook-ups, typical service panel circuitry and much more. A glossary of terms is also included.

CONSTRUCTION

The Blueprint Package contains information an experienced builder needs to construct a particular house. However, it doesn't show all the ways that houses can be built, nor does it explain alternate construction methods. To help you understand how your house will be built—and offer additional techniques—this set of Construction Details depicts the materials and methods used to build foundations, fireplaces, walls, floors and roofs. Where appropriate, the drawings show acceptable alternatives.

MECHANICAL

These Mechanical Details contain fundamental principles and useful data that will help you make informed decisions and communicate with subcontractors about heating and cooling systems. Drawings contain instructions and samples that allow you to make simple load calculations, and preliminary sizing and costing analysis. Covered are the most commonly used systems from heat pumps to solar fuel systems. The package is filled with illustrations and diagrams to help you visualize components and how they relate to one another.

THE HANDS-ON HOME FURNITURE PLANNER

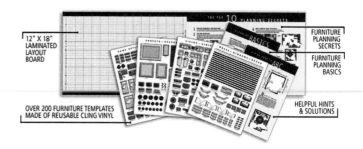

Effectively plan the space in your home using The **Hands-On Home Furniture Planner**. It's fun and easy—no more moving heavy pieces of furniture to see how the room will go together. And you can try different layouts, moving furniture at a whim.

The kit includes reusable peel and stick furniture templates that fit onto a 12" x 18" laminated layout board—space enough to layout every room in your home.

Also included in the package are a number of helpful planning tools. You'll receive:

✓ Helpful hints and solutions for difficult situations.
✓ Furniture planning basics to get you started.
✓ Furniture planning secrets that let you in on some of the tricks of professional designers.

The **Hands-On Home Furniture Planner** is the one tool that no new homeowner or home remodeler should be without. It's also a perfect housewarming gift!

To Order, Call Toll Free
1-800-521-6797

After you've looked over our Blueprint Package and Important Extras on these pages, call for current pricing and availability prior to mailing the order form. We're ready and eager to serve you. After you have received your order, call for customer service toll free 1-888-690-1116.

THE FINISHING TOUCHES...

THE DECK BLUEPRINT PACKAGE

Many of the homes in this book can be enhanced with a professionally designed Home Planners Deck Plan. Those homes marked with a **D** have a complementary Deck Plan, sold separately, which includes a Deck Plan Frontal Sheet, Deck Framing and Floor Plans, Deck Elevations and a Deck Materials List. A Standard Deck Details Package, also available, provides all the how-to information necessary for building *any* deck. Our Complete Deck Building Package contains one set of Custom Deck Plans of your choice, plus one set of Standard Deck Building Details, all for one low price. Our plans and details are carefully prepared in an easy-to-understand format that will guide you through every stage of your deck-building project. This page shows a sample Deck layout to match your favorite house. See Blueprint Price Schedule for ordering information.

THE LANDSCAPE BLUEPRINT PACKAGE

For the homes marked with an **L** in this book, Home Planners has created a front-yard Landscape Plan that is complementary in design to the house plan. These comprehensive blueprint packages include a Frontal Sheet, Plan View, Regionalized Plant & Materials List, a sheet on Planting and Maintaining Your Landscape, Zone Maps and Plant Size and Description Guide. These plans will help you achieve professional results, adding value and enjoyment to your property for years to come. Each set of blueprints is a full 18" x 24" in size with clear, complete instructions and easy-to-read type. A sample Landscape Plan is shown below. See Blueprint Price Schedule for ordering information.

CONTEMPORARY LEISURE DECK
Deck ODA021

CAPE COD COTTAGE
Landscape OLA003

REGIONAL ORDER MAP

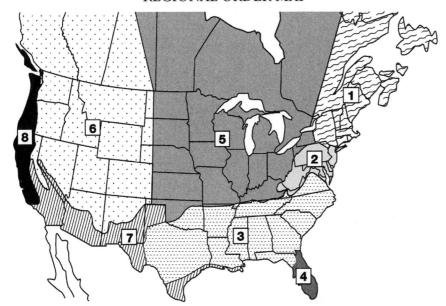

Most Landscape Plans are available with a Plant & Materials List adapted by horticultural experts to 8 different regions of the country. Please specify the Geographic Region when ordering your plan. See Blueprint Price Schedule for ordering information and regional availability.

Region	1	Northeast
Region	2	Mid-Atlantic
Region	3	Deep South
Region	4	Florida & Gulf Coast
Region	5	Midwest
Region	6	Rocky Mountains
Region	7	Southern California & Desert Southwest
Region	8	Northern California & Pacific Northwest

BLUEPRINT PRICE SCHEDULE

Prices guaranteed through December 31, 2002

TIERS	1-SET STUDY PACKAGE	4-SET BUILDING PACKAGE	8-SET BUILDING PACKAGE	1-SET REPRODUCIBLE*
P1	$20	$50	$90	$140
P2	$40	$70	$110	$160
P3	$70	$100	$140	$190
P4	$100	$130	$170	$220
P5	$140	$170	$210	$270
P6	$180	$210	$250	$310
A1	$440	$480	$520	$660
A2	$480	$520	$560	$720
A3	$520	$560	$600	$780
A4	$565	$605	$645	$850
C1	$610	$655	$700	$915
C2	$655	$700	$745	$980
C3	$700	$745	$790	$1050
C4	$750	$795	$840	$1125
L1	$825	$875	$925	$1240
L2	$900	$950	$1000	$1350
L3	$1000	$1050	$1100	$1500
L4	$1100	$1150	$1200	$1650

* Requires a fax number

OPTIONS FOR PLANS IN TIERS A1–L4

Additional Identical Blueprints
in same order for "A1–L4" price plans ....$50 per set
Reverse Blueprints (mirror image)
with 4- or 8-set order for "A1–L4" plans..$50 fee per order
Specification Outlines...$10 each
Materials Lists for "A1–C3" plans ....$60 each
Materials Lists for "C4–L4" plans..$70 each

OPTIONS FOR PLANS IN TIERS P1–P6

Additional Identical Blueprints
in same order for "P1–P6" price plans..$10 per set
Reverse Blueprints (mirror image) for "P1–P6" price plans ....$10 fee per order
1 Set of Deck Construction Details ....$14.95 each
Deck Construction Package ....**add $10 to Building Package price**
(includes 1 set of "P1–P6" plans, plus 1 set Standard Deck Construction Details)

IMPORTANT NOTES

• The 1-set study package is marked "not for construction."
• Prices for 4- or 8-set Building Packages honored only at time of original order.
• Some foundations carry a $225 surcharge.
• Right-reading reverse blueprints, if available, will incur a $165 surcharge.
• Additional identical blueprints may be purchased within 60 days of original order.

TO USE THE INDEX, refer to the design number listed in numerical order (a helpful page reference is also given). Note the price tier and refer to the House Blueprint Price Schedule above for the cost of one, four or eight sets of blueprints or the cost of a reproducible drawing. Additional prices are shown for identical and reverse blueprint sets, as well as a very useful Materials List for some of the plans. Also note in the Plan Index those plans that have Deck Plans or Landscape Plans. Refer to the schedules above for prices of these plans. The letter "Y" identifies plans that are part of our Quote One® estimating service and those that offer Materials Lists.

TO ORDER, Call toll free 1-800-521-6797 for current pricing and availability prior to mailing the order form. FAX: 1-800-224-6699 or 520-544-3086.

PLAN INDEX

DESIGN	PRICE	PAGE	MATERIALS LIST	QUOTE ONE®	DECK	DECK PRICE	LANDSCAPE	LANDSCAPE PRICE	REGIONS
HPT210001	A3	10							
HPT210002	A3	14	Y	Y			OLA003	P3	123568
HPT210003	A4	16	Y	Y	ODA016	P2	OLA093	P3	12345678
HPT210004	A4	19	Y	Y	ODA003	P2			
HPT210005	A1	20		Y					
HPT210006	A4	21					OLA024	P4	123568
HPT210007	A3	22	Y	Y			OLA001	P3	123568
HPT210008	A2	23							
HPT210009	A3	24	Y						
HPT210010	A4	25	Y						
HPT210011	A2	26							
HPT210012	A3	27	Y						
HPT210013	A4	28	Y						
HPT210014	C2	29	Y	Y					
HPT210015	A4	30	Y	Y					
HPT210016	A3	31	Y						
HPT210017	A3	32							
HPT210018	A4	33	Y	Y					
HPT210019	A3	34	Y	Y					
HPT210020	A4	35	Y	Y	ODA012	P3	OLA083	P3	12345678
HPT210021	A4	36							
HPT210022	A3	37							
HPT210023	A2	38	Y						
HPT210024	A4	39	Y				OLA003	P3	123568
HPT210025	A4	40	Y	Y	ODA012	P3	OLA083	P3	12345678
HPT210026	A4	41	Y	Y					
HPT210027	A4	42	Y	Y	ODA012	P3	OLA083	P3	12345678
HPT210028	A4	43	Y	Y					
HPT210029	A3	44	Y						
HPT210030	A3	45	Y						
HPT210031	A4	46	Y	Y	ODA012	P3	OLA083	P3	12345678
HPT210032	A3	47							
HPT210033	A3	48							
HPT210034	A2	49							
HPT210035	A4	50	Y						
HPT210036	A3	51	Y	Y					
HPT210037	A4	52							
HPT210038	A3	53	Y						
HPT210039	A3	54							
HPT210040	A4	55							
HPT210041	A3	56	Y						
HPT210042	A3	57	Y						
HPT210043	A3	58							
HPT210044	A3	59	Y	Y			OLA091	P3	12345678
HPT210045	A3	60							
HPT210046	A3	61	Y	Y	ODA016	P2			

BEFORE FILLING OUT THE ORDER FORM, PLEASE CALL US ON OUR TOLL-FREE BLUEPRINT HOTLINE 1-800-521-6797. YOU MAY WANT TO LEARN MORE ABOUT OUR SERVICES AND PRODUCTS. HERE'S SOME INFORMATION YOU WILL FIND HELPFUL.

OUR EXCHANGE POLICY

With the exception of reproducible plan orders, we will exchange your entire first order for an equal or greater number of blueprints within our plan collection within 90 days of the original order. The entire content of your original order must be returned before an exchange will be processed. Please call our customer service department for your return authorization number and shipping instructions. If the returned blueprints look used, redlined or copied, we will not honor your exchange. Fees for exchanging your blueprints are as follows: 20% of the amount of the original order...plus the difference in cost if exchanging for a design in a higher price bracket or less the difference in cost if exchanging for a design in a lower price bracket. **(Reproducible blueprints are not exchangeable or refundable.)** Please call for current postage and handling prices. Shipping and handling charges are not refundable.

ABOUT REPRODUCIBLES

When purchasing a reproducible you may be required to furnish a fax number. The designer will fax documents that you must sign and return to them before shipping will take place.

ABOUT REVERSE BLUEPRINTS

Although lettering and dimensions will appear backward, reverses will be a useful aid if you decide to flop the plan. See Price Schedule and Plans Index for pricing.

REVISING, MODIFYING AND CUSTOMIZING PLANS

Like many homeowners who buy these plans, you and your builder, architect or engineer may want to make changes to them. We recommend purchase of a reproducible plan for any changes made by your builder, licensed architect or engineer. As set forth below, we cannot assume any responsibility for blueprints which have been changed, whether by you, your builder or by professionals selected by you or referred to you by us, because such individuals are outside our supervision and control.

ARCHITECTURAL AND ENGINEERING SEALS

Some cities and states are now requiring that a licensed architect or engineer review and "seal" a blueprint, or officially approve it, prior to construction due to concerns over energy costs, safety and other factors. Prior to application for a building permit or the start of actual construction, we strongly advise that you consult your local building official who can tell you if such a review is required.

ABOUT THE DESIGNS

The architects and designers whose work appears in this publication are among America's leading residential designers. Each plan was designed to meet the requirements of a nationally recognized model building code in effect at the time and place the plan was drawn. Because national building codes change from time to time, plans may not comply with any such code at the time they are sold to a customer. In addition, building officials may not accept these plans as final construction documents of record as the plans may need to be modified and additional drawings and details added to suit local conditions and requirements. We strongly advise that purchasers consult a licensed architect or engineer, and their local building official, before starting any construction related to these plans.

LOCAL BUILDING CODES AND ZONING REQUIREMENTS

At the time of creation, our plans are drawn to specifications published by the Building Officials and Code Administrators (BOCA) International, Inc.; the Southern Building Code Congress (SBCCI) International, Inc.; the International Conference of Building Officials (ICBO); or the Council of American Building Officials (CABO). Our plans are designed to meet or exceed national building standards. Because of the great differences in geography and climate throughout the United States and Canada, each state, county and municipality has its own building codes, zone requirements, ordinances and building regulations. Your plan may need to be modified to comply with local requirements regarding snow loads, energy codes, soil and seismic conditions and a wide range of other matters. In addition, you may need to obtain permits or inspections from local governments before and in the course of construction. Prior to using blueprints ordered from us, we strongly advise that you consult a licensed architect or engineer—and speak with your local building official—before applying for any permit or beginning construction. We authorize the use of our blueprints on the express condition that you strictly comply with all local building codes, zoning requirements and other applicable laws, regulations, ordinances and requirements. Notice: Plans for homes to be built in Nevada must be re-drawn by a Nevada-registered professional. Consult your building official for more information on this subject.

TOLL FREE
1-800-521-6797

REGULAR OFFICE HOURS:
8:00 a.m.-10:00 p.m. EST, Monday-Friday,
10:00 a.m.-7:00 p.m. EST Sat & Sun.

If we receive your order by 3:00 p.m. EST, Monday-Friday, we'll process it and ship within **two business days**. When ordering by phone, please have your credit card or check information ready. We'll also ask you for the Order Form Key Number at the bottom of the order form.

By FAX: Copy the Order Form on the next page and send it on our FAX line: 1-800-224-6699 or 520-544-3086.

Canadian Customers
Order Toll Free 1-877-223-6389

DISCLAIMER

The designers we work with have put substantial care and effort into the creation of their blueprints. However, because they cannot provide on-site consultation, supervision and control over actual construction, and because of the great variance in local building requirements, building practices and soil, seismic, weather and other conditions, WE CANNOT MAKE ANY WARRANTY, EXPRESS OR IMPLIED, WITH RESPECT TO THE CONTENT OR USE OF THE BLUEPRINTS, INCLUDING BUT NOT LIMITED TO ANY WARRANTY OF MERCHANTABILITY OR OF FITNESS FOR A PARTICULAR PURPOSE. **ITEMS, PRICES, TERMS AND CONDITIONS ARE SUBJECT TO CHANGE WITHOUT NOTICE. REPRODUCIBLE PLAN ORDERS MAY REQUIRE A CUSTOMER'S SIGNED RELEASE BEFORE SHIPPING.**

TERMS AND CONDITIONS

These designs are protected under the terms of United States Copyright Law and may not be copied or reproduced in any way, by any means, unless you have purchased Reproducibles which clearly indicate your right to copy or reproduce. We authorize the use of your chosen design as an aid in the construction of one single family home only. You may not use this design to build a second or multiple dwellings without purchasing another blueprint or blueprints or paying additional design fees.

HOW MANY BLUEPRINTS DO YOU NEED?

Although a standard building package may satisfy many states, cities and counties, some plans may require certain changes. For your convenience, we have developed a Reproducible plan which allows a local professional to modify and make up to 10 copies of your revised plan. As our plans are all copyright protected, with your purchase of the Reproducible, we will supply you with a Copyright release letter. The number of copies you may need: 1 for owner; 3 for builder; 2 for local building department and 1-3 sets for your mortgage lender.

ORDER TOLL FREE!

**For information about
any of our services
or to order call
1-800-521-6797**

**Browse our website:
www.eplans.com**

**BLUEPRINTS ARE
NOT REFUNDABLE
EXCHANGES ONLY**

**For Customer Service,
call toll free
1-888-690-1116.**

HOME PLANNERS, LLC wholly owned by Hanley-Wood, LLC
3275 WEST INA ROAD, SUITE 110 • TUCSON, ARIZONA • 85741

THE BASIC BLUEPRINT PACKAGE
Rush me the following (please refer to the Plans Index and Price Schedule in this section):
___Set(s) of reproducibles*, plan number(s) _____ $_____
    indicate foundation type _____ surcharge (if applicable): $_____
___Set(s) of blueprints, plan number(s) _____ $_____
    indicate foundation type _____ surcharge (if applicable): $_____
___Additional identical blueprints (standard or reverse) in same order @ $50 per set $_____
___Reverse blueprints @ $50 fee per order. Right-reading reverse @ $165 surcharge $_____

IMPORTANT EXTRAS
Rush me the following:
___Materials List: $60 (Must be purchased with Blueprint set.) Add $10 for Schedule C4–L4 plans $_____
___**Quote One®** Summary Cost Report @ $29.95 for one, $14.95 for each additional,
    for plans _____ $_____
    Building location: City _____ Zip Code _____
___**Quote One®** Material Cost Report @ $120 Schedules P1–C3; $130 Schedules C4–L4,
    for plan _____(Must be purchased with Blueprints set.) $_____
    Building location: City _____ Zip Code _____
___Specification Outlines @ $10 each $_____
___Detail Sets @ $14.95 each; any two $22.95; any three $29.95; all four for $39.95 (save $19.85) $_____
___❑ Plumbing ❑ Electrical ❑ Construction ❑ Mechanical
___Home Furniture Planner @ $15.95 each $_____

DECK BLUEPRINTS
(Please refer to the Plans Index and Price Schedule in this section)
___Set(s) of Deck Plan _____ $_____
___Additional identical blueprints in same order @ $10 per set. $_____
___Reverse blueprints @ $10 fee per order. $_____
___Set of Standard Deck Details @ $14.95 per set. $_____
___Set of Complete Deck Construction Package (Best Buy!) Add $10 to Building Package.
    Includes Custom Deck Plan _____ Plus Standard Deck Details

LANDSCAPE BLUEPRINTS
(Please refer to the Plans Index and Price Schedule in this section.)
___Set(s) of Landscape Plan _____ $_____
___Additional identical blueprints in same order @ $10 per set $_____
___Reverse blueprints @ $10 fee per order $_____
Please indicate appropriate region of the country for Plant & Material List. Region _____

POSTAGE AND HANDLING *SIGNATURE IS REQUIRED FOR ALL DELIVERIES.*	1–3 sets	4+ sets
DELIVERY No CODs (Requires street address—No P.O. Boxes)		
•Regular Service (Allow 7–10 business days delivery)	❑ $20.00	❑ $25.00
•Priority (Allow 4–5 business days delivery)	❑ $25.00	❑ $35.00
•Express (Allow 3 business days delivery)	❑ $35.00	❑ $45.00
OVERSEAS DELIVERY	fax, phone or mail for quote	

Note: All delivery times are from date Blueprint Package is shipped.

POSTAGE (From box above) $_____
SUBTOTAL $_____
SALES TAX (AZ & MI residents, please add appropriate state and local sales tax.) $_____
TOTAL (Subtotal and tax) $_____

YOUR ADDRESS (please print legibly)

Name _____

Street _____

City _____ State _____ Zip _____

Daytime telephone number (required) (_____) _____

* Fax number (required for reproducible orders) _____
TeleCheck® Checks By Phone℠ available
FOR CREDIT CARD ORDERS ONLY

Credit card number _____ Exp. Date: (M/Y) _____

Check one ❑ Visa ❑ MasterCard ❑ Discover Card ❑ American Express

Order Form Key

HPT212

Signature (required) _____
Please check appropriate box: ❑ Licensed Builder-Contractor ❑ Homeowner

ORDER TOLL FREE!
1-800-521-6797

BY FAX: Copy the order form above and send it on
our FAXLINE: 1-800-224-6699 OR 520-544-3086

1 BIGGEST & BEST

1001 of our best-selling plans in one volume. 1,074 to 7,275 square feet. 704 pgs $12.95 1K1

2 ONE-STORY

450 designs for all lifestyles. 800 to 4,900 square feet. 384 pgs $9.95 OS

3 MORE ONE-STORY

475 superb one-level plans from 800 to 5,000 square feet. 448 pgs $9.95 MO2

4 TWO-STORY

443 designs for one-and-a-half and two stories. 1,500 to 6,000 square feet. 448 pgs $9.95 TS

5 VACATION

430 designs for recreation, retirement and leisure. 448 pgs $9.95 VS3

6 HILLSIDE

208 designs for split-levels, bi-levels, multi-levels and walkouts. 224 pgs $9.95 HH

7 FARMHOUSE

300 Fresh Designs from Classic to Modern. 320 pgs. $10.95 FCP

8 COUNTRY HOUSES

208 unique home plans that combine traditional style and modern livability. 224 pgs $9.95 CN

9 BUDGET-SMART

200 efficient plans from 7 top designers, that you can really afford to build! 224 pgs $8.95 BS

10 BARRIER-FREE

Over 1,700 products and 51 plans for accessible living. 128 pgs $15.95 UH

11 ENCYCLOPEDIA

500 exceptional plans for all styles and budgets—the best book of its kind! 528 pgs $9.95 ENC

12 ENCYCLOPEDIA II

500 completely new plans. Spacious and stylish designs for every budget and taste. 352 pgs $9.95 E2

13 AFFORDABLE

300 Modest plans for savvy homebuyers.256 pgs. $9.95 AH2

14 VICTORIAN

210 striking Victorian and Farmhouse designs from today's top designers. 224 pgs $15.95 VDH2

15 ESTATE

Dream big! Eighteen designers showcase their biggest and best plans. 224 pgs $16.95 EDH3

16 LUXURY

170 lavish designs, over 50% brand-new plans added to a most elegant collection. 192 pgs $12.95 LD3

17 EUROPEAN STYLES

200 homes with a unique flair of the Old World. 224 pgs $15.95 EURO

18 COUNTRY CLASSICS

Donald Gardner's 101 best Country and Traditional home plans. 192 pgs $17.95 DAG

19 COUNTRY

85 Charming Designs from American Home Gallery. 160 pgs. $17.95 CTY

20 TRADITIONAL

85 timeless designs from the Design Traditions Library. 160 pgs. $17.95 TRA

21 COTTAGES

245 Delightful retreats from 825 to 3,500 square feet. 256 pgs. $10.95 COOL

22 CABINS TO VILLAS

Enchanting Homes for Mountain Sea or Sun, from the Sater collection. 144 pgs $19.95 CCV

23 CONTEMPORARY

The most complete and imaginative collection of contemporary designs available anywhere. 256 pgs. $10.95 CM2

24 FRENCH COUNTRY

Live every day in the French countryside using these plans, landscapes and interiors. 192 pgs. $14.95 PN

25 SOUTHERN

207 homes rich in Southern styling and comfort. 240 pgs $8.95 SH

26 SOUTHWESTERN

138 designs that capture the spirit of the Southwest. 144 pgs $10.95 SW

27 SHINGLE-STYLE

155 Home plans from Classic Colonials to Breezy Bungalows. 192 pgs. $12.95 SNG

28 NEIGHBORHOOD

170 designs with the feel of main street America. 192 pgs $12.95 TND

29 CRAFTSMAN

170 Home plans in the Craftsman and Bungalow style. 192 pgs $12.95 CC

30 GRAND VISTAS

200 Homes with a View. 224 pgs. $10.95 GV

31 DUPLEX & TOWNHOMES

115 Duplex, Multiplex &
Townhome Designs. 128 pgs.
$17.95 MFH

32 WATERFRONT

200 designs perfect for your
waterside wonderland.
208 pgs $10.95 WF

33 NATURAL LIGHT

223 Sunny home plans for all
regions. 240 pgs. $8.95 NA

34 NOSTALGIA

100 Time-Honored designs
updated with today's features.
224 pgs. $14.95 NOS

35 STREET OF DREAMS

Over 300 photos showcase
54 prestigious homes.
256 pgs $19.95 SOD

36 NARROW-LOT

250 Designs for houses
17' to 50' wide. 256 pgs.
$9.95 NL2

37 SMALL HOUSES

Innovative plans for
sensible lifestyles.
224 pgs. $8.95 SM2

38 GARDENS & MORE

225 gardens, landscapes,
decks and more to
enhance every home.
320 pgs. $19.95 GLP

39 EASY-CARE

41 special landscapes
designed for beauty and
low maintenance.
160 pgs $14.95 ECL

40 BACKYARDS

40 designs focused solely on
creating your own specially
themed backyard oasis. 160
pgs $14.95 BYL

41 BEDS & BORDERS

40 Professional designs
for do-it-yourselfers
160 pgs. $14.95 BB

42 BUYER'S GUIDE

A comprehensive look at 2700
products for all aspects of
landscaping & gardening.
128 pgs $19.95 LPBG

LANDSCAPE DESIGNS

43 OUTDOOR

74 easy-to-build designs,
lets you create and build
your own backyard oasis.
128 pgs $9.95 YG2

44 GARAGES

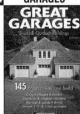

145 exciting projects from
64 to 1,900 square feet.
160 pgs. $9.95 GG2

45 DECKS

A brand new collection
of 120 beautiful and
practical decks. 144 pgs.
$9.95 DP2

46 HOME BUILDING

Everything you need to know
to work with contractors and
subcontractors. 212 pgs
$14.95 HBP

47 RURAL BUILDING

Everything you need to know
to build your home in the
country. 232 pgs.
$14.95 BYC

48 VACATION HOMES

Your complete guide to
building your vacation
home. 224 pgs.
$14.95 BYV

PROJECT GUIDES

Book Order Form

To order your books, just check the box of the book numbered below and complete the coupon. We will process your order and ship it from our office within two business days. Send coupon and check (in U.S. funds).

YES! Please send me the books I've indicated:

❑ **1:1K1** $12.95	❑ **17:EURO** ...$15.95	❑ **33:NA** $8.95
❑ **2:OS** $9.95	❑ **18:DAG** $17.95	❑ **34:NOS** $14.95
❑ **3:MO2** $9.95	❑ **19:CTY** $17.95	❑ **35:SOD** $19.95
❑ **4:TS** $9.95	❑ **20:TRA** $17.95	❑ **36:NL2** $9.95
❑ **5:VS3** $9.95	❑ **21:COOL** ...$10.95	❑ **37:SM2** $8.95
❑ **6:HH** $9.95	❑ **22:CCV** $19.95	❑ **38:GLP** $19.95
❑ **7:FCP** $10.95	❑ **23:CM2** $10.95	❑ **39:ECL** $14.95
❑ **8:CN** $9.95	❑ **24:PN** $14.95	❑ **40:BYL** $14.95
❑ **9:BS** $8.95	❑ **25:SH** $8.95	❑ **41:BB** $14.95
❑ **10:UH** $15.95	❑ **26:SW** $10.95	❑ **42:LPBG** ...$19.95
❑ **11:ENC** $9.95	❑ **27:SNG** $12.95	❑ **43:YG2** $9.95
❑ **12:E2** $9.95	❑ **28:TND** $12.95	❑ **44:GG2** $9.95
❑ **13:AH2** $9.95	❑ **29:CC** $12.95	❑ **45:DP2** $9.95
❑ **14:VDH2** ...$15.95	❑ **30:GV** $10.95	❑ **46:HBP** $14.95
❑ **15:EDH3** ...$16.95	❑ **31:MFH** $17.95	❑ **47:BYC** $14.95
❑ **16:LD3** $12.95	❑ **32:WF** $10.95	❑ **48:BYV** $14.95

Canadian Customers Order Toll Free 1-877-223-6389

Books Subtotal $ _____
ADD Postage and Handling (allow 4–6 weeks for delivery) $ _4.00_
Sales Tax: (AZ & MI residents, add state and local sales tax.) $ _____
YOUR TOTAL (Subtotal, Postage/Handling, Tax) $ _____

YOUR ADDRESS (PLEASE PRINT)

Name _____

Street _____

City _____ State _____ Zip _____

Phone (_____) _____ — _____

YOUR PAYMENT

TeleCheck® Checks By Phone℠ available

Check one: ❑ Check ❑ Visa ❑ MasterCard ❑ Discover ❑ American Express

Required credit card information:

Credit Card Number _____

Expiration Date (Month/Year)_____ / _____

Signature Required _____

Home Planners, LLC
3275 W. Ina Road, Suite 110, Dept. BK, Tucson, AZ 85741

| HPT212 |

HEAT-N-GLO
1-888-427-3973
WWW.HEATNGLO.COM

No one builds a better fire

Heat-N-Glo offers quality gas, woodburning and electric fireplaces, including gas log sets, stoves, and inserts for preexisting fireplaces. Now available gas grills and outdoor fireplaces. Send for a free brochure.

Ideas for your next project. Beautiful, durable, elegant low-maintenance millwork, mouldings, balustrade systems and much more. For your free catalog please call us at 1-800-446-3040 or visit www.stylesolutionsinc.com.

ARISTOKRAFT
ONE MASTERBRAND CABINETS DRIVE
JASPER, IN 47546
(812) 482-2527
WWW.ARISTOKRAFT.COM

Cabinetry

Great Ideas
Made Easy

Aristokraft offers you superb value, outstanding quality and great style that fit your budget. Transform your great ideas into reality with popular styles and features that reflect your taste and lifestyle. $5.00

THERMA-TRU DOORS
1687 WOODLANDS DRIVE
MAUMEE, OH 43537
1-800-THERMA-TRU
WWW.THERMATRU.COM

THERMA TRU® DOORS

THE DOOR SYSTEM YOU CAN BELIEVE IN

The undisputed brand leader, Therma-Tru specializes in fiberglass and steel entry doors for every budget. Excellent craftsmanship, energy efficiency and variety make Therma-Tru the perfect choice for all your entry door needs.

225 GARDEN, LANDSCAPE
AND PROJECT PLANS
TO ORDER, CALL
1-800-322-6797

225 Do-It-Yourself designs that help transform boring yards into exciting outdoor entertainment spaces. Gorgeous gardens, luxurious landscapes, dazzling decks and other outdoor amenities. Complete construction blueprints available for every project. Only $19.95 (plus $4 shipping/handling).

HAVE WE GOT PLANS FOR YOU!

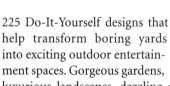

eplans.com
Stop dreaming. Start building.

Your online source for home designs and ideas. Find thousands of plans from the nation's top designers...all in one place. Plus, links to the best known names in building supplies and services.